The Fly Tyers
Nymph Manual

Books by Randall Kaufmann:

American Nymph Fly Tying Manual
Lake Fishing With A Fly
Fly Tyers Nymph Manual
Tying Dry Flies
Bonefishing With A Fly

THE FLY TYERS
NYMPH MANUAL

*The Complete Nymph Instruction
and Pattern Manual*

By Randall Kaufmann

Illustrations by Mike Stidham

Foreword by Charles E. Brooks

Western Fisherman's Press

*This book is dedicated to:
The fly tying anglers of today,
whose ideas and innovations have
made this work possible, and to
the fly tying anglers of tomorrow,
with the hope that they will be able
to continue today's unending
enlightenment and enjoyment of the
magical world of trout.*

Published by
Western Fisherman's Press
P.O. Box 23943
Portland, Oregon 97281-3943
503-639-4848

Printed in the United States of America
10 9 8 7 6 5

Library of Congress Catalog Card Number: 86-050380
International Standard Book Number 0-9617059-0-6

Edited by Marc Bale
Designed by Randall Kaufmann

Contents

Contents
(continued)

Acknowledgments

First, thanks to all those who purchased my first book, the *American Nymph Fly Tying Manual*, making this book possible, and to the hundreds of tying students who, with their many questions and observations, greatly helped me organize and assemble this book.

Thanks to the many sport shop operators along the east slope of the High Sierra, who gave me, as a youngster, the opportunity to tie flies on a commercial basis, especially Ken and Louise Willingham of June Lake, who provided a home away from home, Doug Kittredge of Mammoth Lakes, and the many others who encouraged my early fly tying, fishing and backpacking activities.

Thanks to George Anderson, Fred Arbona, Gene Armstrong, Gary Borger, Charlie Brooks, Gary LaFontaine, Mike Lawson and Al Troth, who provided pattern information. Thanks to all the preceding angler-tyer-authors who have shared their knowledge in a wealth of literature.

Special thanks go to Mary Erickson for encouragement in this project and for proofreading the original manuscript, Bob Rector and Pat Cooper for proofreading, Jean Kincaid and Pamela Ford for proofreading and typesetting, Marc Bale for editing, Sue Smith for typing, Chris Marrs and Alicia Cash for format advice, Ron McCowan for pasteup, Tony Capone for getting my photography room organized and for the many hours of darkroom work, David Berg for darkroom work, Charlie Brooks for writing the foreword, Mike Stidham for the illustrations and cover design, and Dennis Black, who became my friend, and more than anyone else, got me into the business.

Introduction

Nymph is a general term used to describe a particular stage of immature underwater insects. Stoneflies, dragonflies, damselflies, mayflies and caddisflies spend most of their lives in this subaquatic stage, but, depending on the insects, underwater life cycles can also include an egg, larva and pupa stage.

The term nymph, as broadly applied to this book, is the subaquatic stage of any aquatic insect, plus Crustaceans (scud, crayfish, etc.), Hemiptera (waterboatmen) and Hirudinea (leech).

It is the explicit intent of this book to instruct, explain and simplify the techniques necessary to construct nymph imitations.

The information presented here has been accumulated, refined and simplified during the past 20 years and will save you many, many years of struggling and frustration. Some short cuts and tricks I learned by trial and error, but most were gathered from numerous other tyers.

All major food sources of trout and all pertinent nymph tying techniques are represented by the 30 detailed patterns. Techniques and patterns follow a logical sequence. For ease in understanding and tying you should progress from start to finish, tying all 30 patterns in the order they are presented. When finished you will have the necessary skills to construct most nymph patterns.

The pattern directory contains 200 patterns. This list is by no means complete. I have tried to select only widely known and universal patterns in use today. Many are cataloged by mail order houses, are readily available in specialty shops, or have been published in books and magazines. Others have been garnered on my travels about the fishing world and still others are favorites of professional tyers and guides.

I believe that an angler needs one, or perhaps two patterns to represent the *various stages* of particular food sources. However, particular food source representations should be carried in a broad selection of colors and sizes. As an example, about the only stonefly nymph imitation I carry is the Kaufmann Stone, but I have five colors in six sizes. This selection allows me to represent most stonefly species I happen upon. After all, most stonefly nymphs are shaped about the same. There are exceptions, but, *generally,* to anglers, different species mean different sizes and colors. This type of blanket coverage is far superior to carrying ten patterns in hit and miss colors and sizes. It is fun to experiment with different patterns and ideas. Indeed, creativity is a compelling reason for tying in the first place. Experiment on your own and tie a broad range of patterns, but when you are *seriously* stocking your fly box, don't get carried away with hundreds of "patterns."

Foreword

Randall Kaufmann is perhaps the best tyer of nymph patterns that also catch fish of any professional tyer that I know. I have been a fly tyer for over 55 years and have read every book on fly tying that I know of. There are dozens of them, and one would think the subject had been so extensively covered that there would be nothing new to write about. This book proves that not to be so.

There are hundreds of tiny but important details in this book that have never been mentioned in any others I have read. They are details most experienced professional tyers know so well that they assume everybody does, and so, they have gone unmentioned until now.

For instance, this manual is the only one I've seen that tells you not only to mash down the barbs of your hooks, but how and *when* to do it, and with *what*. It took me over 30 years to discover that the *what* was very important. You'll find that and many other answers here. The book also tells you that both practice *and* reading are essential to becoming a finished tyer.

It delineates the joys of fly tying, and of collecting materials — which Arnold Gingrich labeled a separate mania — as well as any book ever has. It is so loaded with information that one will never outgrow it. The large close-up pictures — over 500 of them — will make understanding of both technique and design so much easier than instructions alone could ever do.

The book serves the dual purpose of a nymph tying manual *and* a nymph pattern dictionary. Since Randall is a devout top level fly fisherman who associates with hundreds of others in the same category, the patterns herein are among the best in the country for catching fish. That, after all, is the ultimate aim, and the reader will find this book right on target in all respects.

Charlie Brooks
West Yellowstone, Montana

Part One

Getting Started – Basic Techniques

Part I will explain tools and materials and will allow for a general overview of nymph construction. Basic techniques necessary to begin actual fly construction are discussed and demonstrated. It is suggested that you practice the techniques and thoroughly understand the ideas discussed before progressing to Part II.

One of the many beautiful riffles on Oregon's Deschutes River. A unique fishery, it offers superb trout *and* steelhead fishing.

1

Should You Tie Your Own Flies

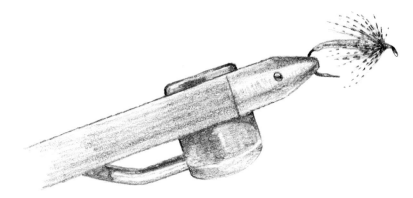

Absolutely! Few pastimes offer so much for so little. Many anglers begin tying with the justification that they can tie their own for 10-15 cents, rather than buying them for $1.50 or more.

While the financial side of tying is attractive, there are other, more compelling reasons. For me, tying is as much fun as fishing. Cluttered thoughts become non-existent and soon your mind is drifting effortlessly with your favorite stream or riffling along the surface of a pristine lake, and it is not long before several trout have been fooled into accepting your half finished imitation. There is little doubt that more fish are hooked at the tying bench than in the water.

When I tied commercially, the instant I sat down at the tying bench I was on "automatic tie," which meant my mind was free to wander and dream in any direction I chose.

I recently spent a week bonefishing in the South Pacific and purposely arrived without any flies, but I did bring a bag stuffed full of colorful materials. Evenings were spent tying flies in preparation for the next day's fishing. Much experimenting was possible and it was great fun tying with others, sharing ideas and discussing the day's angling over cocktails. Not only did I have a tremendous angling advantage over those who did not tie, but my pleasure probably exceeded theirs.

Another strong reason for tying your own is that you cannot always buy what you really need. Tying gets you into entomology, broadens your scope and automatically makes you a better angler. Just offhand, I cannot think of any *exceptional* anglers who do not tie their own flies. Tying is such a tremendous advantage that you will need and want to tie your own, and besides, there is a great deal of satisfaction in releasing a fish on a fly you tied yourself!

2

Getting Started

Fly fishermen, and especially fly tyers, are, for the most part, an opinionated group of eccentrics, any two of whom agree on little more than that the sun *might* rise tomorrow! Such diverse ideas are partly the reason fly tying has progressed so rapidly during the past 20 years.

I didn't realize it at the time, but as a youngster I became hooked on two pioneering sports, backpacking and fly fishing-tying. Both sports were centuries old, but only practiced and enjoyed by a few. If I located a broken down rack of chenille and tinsel in a dusty corner of an old time tackle shop I was a happy boy. Two decades ago fly tying was difficult at best and it was no secret why so few anglers were involved in the sport. In the interim, fly tying has progressed nicely out of dark times and today it is easy to become a competent angler-tyer. Still, there are only a relatively few state-of-the-art tyers around, but there are many *very good* tyers. My advice to all tyers is to search out the absolutely best individuals in the sport and become acquainted and watch them tie. Why struggle along on your own when someone can show you a lifetime of information? This book is the next best thing to standing over the shoulder of a master, but if a picture is worth a thousand words, a "you are there" experience is priceless.

I can empathize with tyers at all levels of expertise and it was for this reason that I began our streamside fly tying schools. Small groups of tyers gather along the banks of Oregon's Deschutes River for three days of intensive feather bending and fishing. Such a crash course will save you a decade of learning.

It would be in your best interest to at least take advantage of a local tying class. They are usually available at sport shops and sometimes at colleges.

Get into the habit of hanging around fly shops. Attend local classes, seminars, lectures, sport shows and tie and fish all you can. There are several very good videos available on both fly tying and fishing and, of course, many books. Books are an essential asset to all anglers. Without them it would be very difficult to obtain the knowledge currently available to followers of the sport. I have several hundred titles in my library and it is certainly far from complete. I find myself walking to its colorful shelves several times a week both for research and pleasure. Some of the better books currently in print which are highly recommended include:

Aquatic Entomology – Patrick McCafferty
Caddisflies – Gary LaFontaine
Complete Book of Western Hatches – Rick Hafele and Dave Hughes
Fly Fishing Strategy – Doug Swisher and Carl Richards
Guide to Aquatic Trout Foods – Dave Whitlock
Lake Fishing With A Fly – Ron Cordes and Randall Kaufmann
Larger Trout for the Western Fisherman – Charles Brooks
Masters on the Nymph – J. Michael Migel and Leonard M. Wright, Jr.
Mayflies, the Angler and the Trout – Fred Arbona, Jr.
Nymphs – Ernest Schwiebert
Nymph Fishing for Larger Trout – Charles Brooks
Selective Trout – Doug Swisher and Carl Richards
The Trout and the Stream – Charles Brooks
The Trout and the Fly – Brian Clarke and John Goddard
Trout – Ernest Schwiebert

As with fly fishing, there is no one magical answer to fly tying success, but rather a series of subtle techniques which come together to provide success and pleasure. Remember, many clever minds have made fly fishing a profession or obsession and have already done much groundwork. Take advantage of this windfall. Watch, listen, read, question, tie, and fish!

3

Tools

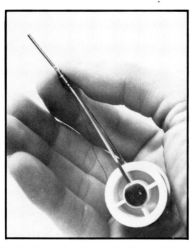

Hold the plastic pad of the bobbin between your thumb and first finger, allowing the thread spool to rest in the palm of your hand.

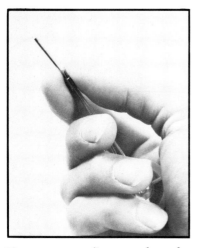

Close your fingers loosely around the thread spool. This is the standard tying position. Tighten up on the tension and thread will not feed out. To become familiar with thread breaking strength, stretch it to its breaking point several times.

Good tools are to a fly tyer what balanced tackle is to an angler. While it is possible to tie a fly with little more aid than one's hands, why do it? There is no reason for making such an enjoyable hobby difficult. Do not skimp on the quality of tools. If you buy them right the first time you will not have to buy them again. Whenever possible stick with American products.

Vise:

A vise is supposed to hold a hook *securely*. If it does not, get one that does. The Price Jr. is an excellent buy and offers a lifetime guarantee. The Regal will hold a hook so securely that you will break the hook before it slips from the jaws. The Regal will hold the largest and smallest hook without adjustment. The Thompson "A" is the old standby and the best inexpensive buy. I do not recommend foreign vises, if for no other reason than that you cannot get parts. You should adjust the height of your vise so that you have 8-10 inches clearance between the table surface and the jaws.

Bobbin:

A good bobbin is like having a third hand at the vise. When I began tying flies there were no decent bobbins on the market so I tied without one. Since then, Frank Matarelli has developed a bobbin that is the current standard of excellence. There are many copies but his is still the best. It is lightweight, durable, made of stainless steel, finely polished and easily adjustable for tension simply by spreading out or squeezing the arms together. Tension is properly adjusted when you can quickly pull size 6/0 thread without it breaking. If tension is too loose thread will unspool as it hangs from the hook. The bobbin should rest in the palm of your hand and you should grip the plastic pad with your thumb and first finger. Do not hold onto the round shaft as it will roll between your fingers and you will have less control. Do not hold onto the thread. By squeezing the spool in your palm the thread will not feed out. By easing off the tension and winding a bit harder, thread will feed out as you wrap it onto the hook. The top of the bobbin shaft should be close to the hook shank, that is, you should be wrapping a small (one-inch diameter) circle around the hook shank, not a large one. This will allow you to place thread *exactly* where you want it and wrapping a small circle is much more time efficient than a large one. It is nice to have a half dozen bobbins so it is not necessary to re-thread them when you change thread colors or break the thread while tying. A short shaft is nice for short shank and smaller flies while a long shaft is nice for tying on long shank hooks.

Scissors:

It is important to have scissors with a *fine* point and large enough finger holes so you can carry them on your hand. When the scissors is carried on your hand you always have them ready to cut without wasting time looking for them, picking them up and putting them down. All cuts should be made with the tip of your scissors.

Fur Blender:

A must for the nymph tyer. Texture and color combinations are instantly available. More blending ideas are mentioned in the material section.

Bodkin:

A needle point used for picking out dubbing, lacquering heads and, if it has a hole in the end, for tying half hitches. Select one with a hexagonal shaft as these will not roll off the table.

Material Clip:

This mind saver slips onto the vise and holds hackles, tinsels, and other miscellaneous materials out of your way until you are ready for them.

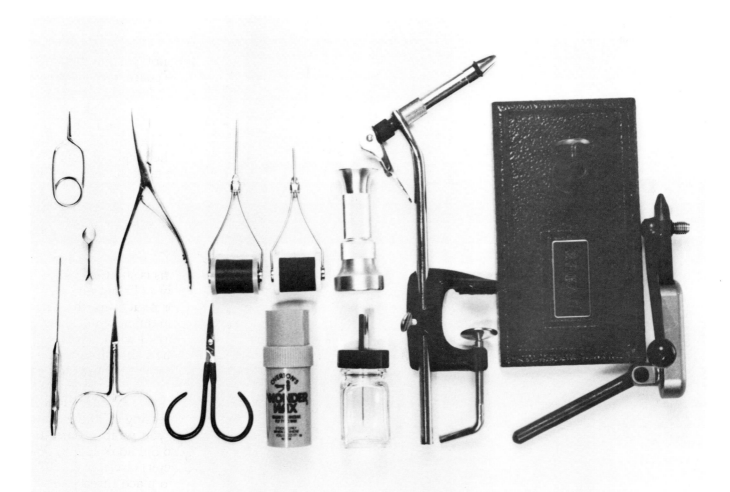

Stacker:

Indispensable for evening hair tails and wings. It is nice to have both a large and small diameter stacker but if you are just purchasing one, get a large diameter. The material to be stacked is placed with the natural tips pointing down into the bottom of the stacker. Place one finger over the open end and tap it onto a hard surface. Hold the stacker level and slowly pull off the end. I like the Gausdal but other open end styles are also okay.

Application Jar:

A neat way to keep lacquer from evaporating and scenting the air. Attach the jar to the shaft of your vise with rubber bands and it is always handy. When applying lacquer pick up a small drop on the *tip* of the bodkin and apply to entire head. If lacquer does not soak in or penetrate the thread head it is too thick and should be thinned.

Hackle Pliers:

If possible, tie without pliers. It is another tool to look for, pick up and set down. Pliers often grip so tight they break the feather or they do not grip tight enough and the feather slips. Also, it is difficult to wrap two hackles at once. Tyers of small dry flies will find pliers very handy and if you must use them I suggest the metal to metal style.

Threader-Cleaner:

A simple tool used to unclog wax from the bobbin shaft and pull thread through. Thread the bobbin by inserting the loop wire end of the threader-cleaner into the bobbin. Trim off the thread end and insert it through the wire loop. Pull the wire loop and thread through the bobbin shaft.

Smooth Nose Pliers:

Should be kept on the bench for flattening lead and smashing barbs. In case of hook breakage, barbs should be smashed before you tie the fly.

Waste Trol:

This is a basket that attaches to your vise under the table top and catches dropped tools, materials, spilled lacquer and material wastes, keeping your tying bench neat and the floor clean.

Lamp:

I suggest a Luxo Pro Tyers high intensity light. These have a weighted base, throw a concentrated light beam and are always cool. They are compact, easy to pack and have adjustable arms.

Wonder Wax:

Very tacky wax in an easy to apply container that helps prepare dubbing. Highly recommended.

Cements:

Head lacquer should be fast drying and of relatively high gloss. There are many such products available. Vinyl cement, marketed under the name Flexament is useful for reinforcing or stiffening feather material such as turkey wing quills. I apply cement with a small brush as, unlike spray cans, the brush always works. Head epoxy, packaged under the name Crystal Clear Epoxy, is perfect for those wishing a superior high gloss and smooth professional finish on their heads.

Opposite page: a tough afternoon of "nymphing" from hot springs adjacent to the Middle Fork of the Salmon River, Idaho.

4

Materials

Collecting Materials

When I think back to my early days of tying I am amazed I kept at it. Tools were barbaric at best and materials were nearly non-existent. There were no specialty fly tying establishments close by and only a handful of mail order houses were in business. Today a tremendous variety of tools, hooks, materials and assorted accouterments are readily available. Even with all this "choice" material, it is still easy to purchase junk. In other words, not all deer hair or hackle is the same. Buy from a knowledgeable dealer who specializes in materials and who keeps a good supply available. If such an establishment is not available, buy mail order. Most mail order houses offer a wide selection of goods and fast service. Stay away from those who do not. Tying supplies found in chain stores and general sporting goods stores are seldom of top quality. There are many fly tying kits available. They offer good, bad and ugly (most often the last) and are best avoided.

The art of fly tying, and it *is* an art as practiced by many innovative followers of the sport, can be as consuming as fly fishing itself. The devotee ponders over a collection of genetically bred feathers, a rainbow of synthetics and fur mixes. Collecting these various materials is like collecting anything rare and beautiful. One should seldom pass up the chance to obtain high quality items. Pick them up and you will find yourself deriving more and more pleasure at the vise as your hoard of paraphernalia grows. The more and varied your goodies the less time you will be frustrated at the midnight tying bench.

It is not a good idea to skimp or make do with a material or color when clearly another would be more productive and self satisfying, especially in the hands of a discriminating admirer or when in view of fish. Time spent tying and fishing is precious and you should not limit your chances of pleasure. It is not possible to measure your success in fly tying with dollars spent or saved. Collecting is part of the enjoyment so drift with the game and fill up the boxes.

If you are interested enough to read this far you are probably "hooked." The material list at the end of this chapter contains everything you will need to tie all 30 demonstration patterns and most of the other 200 listed in the pattern directory. If you want to start on a smaller scale, merely select the materials for as many patterns as you like and expand as you are ready.

Thread:

A strong, prewax, fine diameter nylon thread will allow you to secure materials onto the hook with a minimum amount of bulk. Size 6/0, commonly sold under the name Danville, is currently the best and it is available in a wide range of colors. As a matter of aesthetics, tying thread should match the overall color of the fly. Size 6/0 will allow you to construct a small, neatly tapered head, which is necessary if you are to secure your leader properly. If a tyer has constructed a neat head the balance of the fly is usually nicely tied as well. Larger diameter threads can be useful for special effects or ribbing but are not needed for tying nymphs. Thread sizing is denoted by both numbers and letters, with size E (commonly used for rod building) being larger than A, 1/0, 3/0, 6/0 and finally the smallest available, 15/0. Applying Wonder Wax to thread, even prewaxed thread, adds strength, allows you to more easily dub a fur body and keeps thread from unwinding easily.

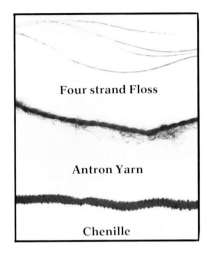

Four strand Floss

Antron Yarn

Chenille

Yarn, Chenille, Floss:

Most yarn and chenille bodied nymphs have been replaced by natural or synthetic fur, or dubbing. Some notable exceptions are the Montana Stone, Carey Special, Woolly Worm and Woolly Bugger but I will usually tie these patterns with a blend of rabbit and goat. A few flies might also call for a floss body, such as Soft Hackles, but fur can easily be substituted. Mohlon is no longer available and patterns that once specified Mohlon are either tied with Antron or other fuzzy yarn. However, you will still need a skeleton selection of chenille and floss in black, browns and olives.

Hair:

Nymph tyers will find very little use for hair, but some elk, deer, moose and squirrel should be on hand.

Fur:

Muskrat, beaver, otter and a *complete* color selection of dyed hare's ears-mask, rabbit and goat is a *must*. Goat fur, actually referred to as goat hair, or angora goat, has replaced seal, which is no longer available. Antron, a soft four-ply yarn interwoven with silver sparkle fibers, can be blended into a fine dubbing and it also blends well with natural fur. The following products are available pre-packaged and a wide selection of colors should be obtained: Antron dubbing, Antron blend and Hairtron. When you have the chance to procure an odd shade of dyed fur, pick it up. The broader your selection the better. I have a pound bag of tiny dyed fur pieces and find that I am constantly rummaging through it. With a broad selection of furs you will be able to mix and match most color schemes in nature. The other advantage in blending dubbing is creating lifelike textures. As an example, I often blend a smooth fur (rabbit or Hairtron) with a coarse fur (goat). I can blend similar colors (Timberline Emerger), throw in a contrasting color (olive-gray *Gammarus-Hyalella* Scud), or blend a combination of bright and dark colors (Kaufmann Stone). The smooth fur allows you to more easily dub the mixture while the coarser goat protrudes slightly from the body, creating translucent light patterns and animation. Hold some blended goat and rabbit up to the light and you will quickly understand the advantages. Such subtleties ultimately allow for greater encounters with fish.

Note: The terms "hare's ear," "hare's mask" and "hare's ears-mask" all refer to the same material. Hare's ear is actually a European hare that is commonly purchased on-the-skin and includes the entire face, or mask.

Hare's Ear - Mask

All fur, except a small patch in the center that is useful for tying tails, should be trimmed off and blended in a fur blender. Be certain to trim the actual ears very close and avoid any white fur on the mask. A complete mask will tie a few hundred flies.

Tinsel:

A selection of fine wire, flat mylar and oval tinsels in gold, silver and copper is mandatory. Fine wire is used for ribbing small flies and to reinforce fragile bodies, such as peacock and palmered hackle. Besides lending a slight amount of flash to flies, tinsel and wire help depict segmentation. Tinsel ribbing should be subtle and not overpowering.

Hackle:

A selection of hackle colors will be needed and these will be discussed later in the book.

Miscellaneous Materials:

Numerous other materials are needed to represent legs, wings, wingcases, bodies and tails. Strip goose is invaluable for tying tails and antennae. Mallard, partridge and ringneck pheasant tail will have numerous uses as will turkey and peacock. Swannundaze has replaced flat monofilament. Swannundaze is an oval plastic that is primarily used for stonefly bodies. Marabou and filoplume will be invaluable and ostrich is useful for heads, gills, wings and special effect. Rubber strips are like rubber band material and are required on some special stonefly style patterns, such as the Rubber Legs and Rubber Legs Brown Stone.

Dying Materials:

Most fly fishing specialty establishments offer such a wide array of materials as to make dying unnecessary. If you feel you must obtain a particular color, blend the needed color or attempt to use Pantone waterfast marking pens. If you are still unable to satisfy your needs, pick up a quality dye notably Veniard or other pre-packaged dyes available through your local fly shop or from a mail order house. Directions are usually included, but I might add that you should not immerse the total neck or bunch of feathers without first testing the mixture, being certain the color is what you desire.

The following list of materials is very comprehensive and will allow you to construct nearly all the patterns listed in this book and most others you may happen upon or wish to devise yourself. Those tyers who wish to tie dry flies or forage fish imitations (streamers) will need very few additional materials.

Recommended Material List for Tying Nymphs:

_____ brown neck (Metz)
_____ grizzly hen neck (Metz or Hoffman)
_____ Indian saddle hackle – brown (furnace), black, olive, blue dun
_____ grizzly saddle patch (Hoffman)
_____ grizzly neck, optional (Metz or Hoffman)
_____ 6/0 prewax thread – black, brown, olive, gray, orange, yellow
_____ chenille – black, olive, yellow; size fine, small, medium
_____ floss – olive, yellow, greens, browns
_____ rubber strips – black, white
_____ hare's mask – natural, olive, brown, black, golden olive
_____ muskrat
_____ otter

_____ rabbit – black, browns, olives, yellows
_____ moose body – dark
_____ Hairtron – 20 colors
_____ Swannundaze – clear, brown, black, medium and fine
purple, orange, yellow, red
_____ Antron fibers – clear
_____ Antron dubbing – 20 assorted colors
_____ turkey, white tip, select tail feathers
_____ marabou – black, olive, brown, gray
_____ ostrich – black, gray, olive, tan
_____ guinea body feathers
_____ partridge – brown, gray
_____ peacock – eyed tails, sword
_____ ringneck tails – natural, green
_____ ringneck skin – natural, black, olive, brown (filoplumes)
_____ mallard – natural and dyed woodduck
_____ goose quills – natural, black, olive
_____ stripped goose – black, brown, olive, gray
_____ flat tinsel – small, fine
_____ wire – silver, gold, copper
_____ oval tinsel – fine gold, silver
_____ lead wire – size 1, 2, 3, 4 fine – large
_____ Tiemco 101 – sizes 12-20
_____ Tiemco 200 – sizes 8-20
_____ Tiemco 300 – sizes 4-12
_____ Tiemco 5262 – sizes 8-18
_____ Tiemco 5263 – sizes 8-18
_____ domestic hen saddle patch – mottled dark brown
_____ vise
_____ lamp
_____ bobbins – short, long
_____ scissors
_____ hackle pliers
_____ bodkin (dubbing needle – half hitch)
_____ material clip
_____ Waste Trol
_____ hair stacker
_____ smooth nose pliers
_____ threader-cleaner
_____ applicator jar
_____ lacquer, thinner
_____ Wonder Wax
_____ Flexament
_____ blender

Left: Hen neck feather
Right: Partridge body feather

Strung India Saddle feathers

Left: Select white tip turkey tail feather
Middle: White tip turkey tail feather
Right: Turkey wing quill feather

Stripped goose

5

Hooks

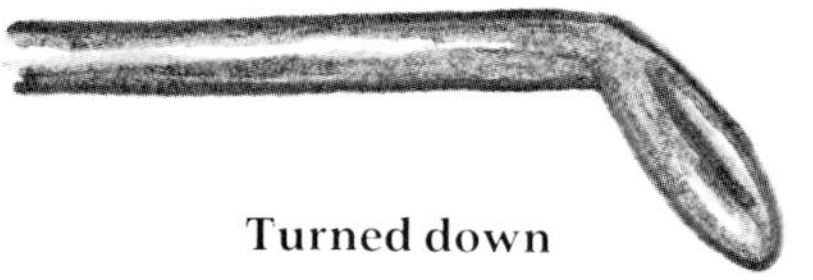

Turned down

Turned up

Straight

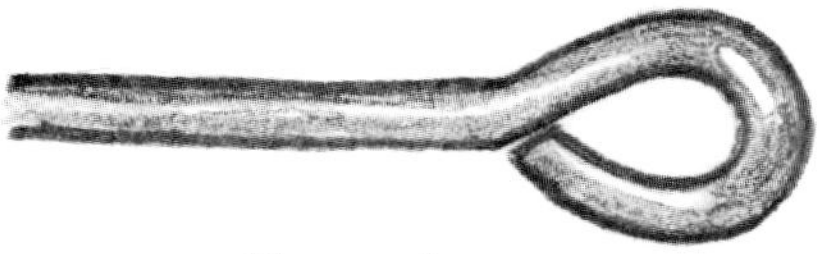

Tapered

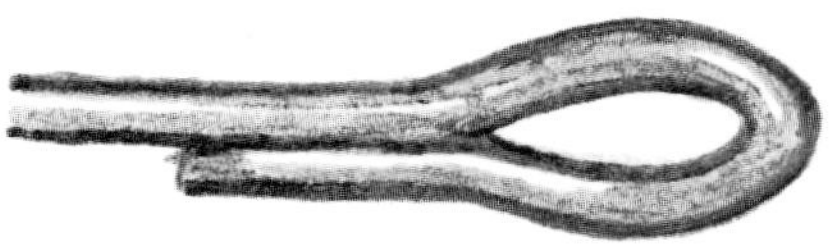

Loop

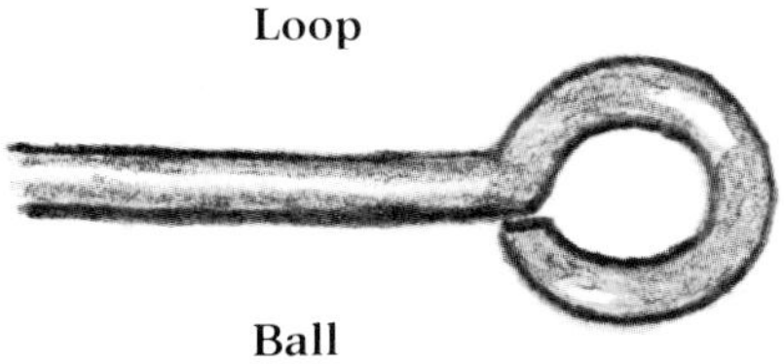

Ball

There are several hook manufacturers, including Partridge (England), Mustad (Norway), Wright McGill (America), and Tiemco (Japan).

Hooks account for the greatest expense in tying flies, but it matters little whether you spend five cents for a so-so hook or ten cents for the best. The added cost is negligible and fishing the best possible hook is another way to maximize your angling success. To better understand and select hooks for your particular needs, let's take a brief look at hook terminology.

Eye:

Few angler-tyers give hook eye design the attention deserved. Eyes that are not completely closed or those that have a rough closure easily cut leaders and make tying a neat head difficult. Check your hook eyes, they are important.

The most common eye designs are turned down (T.D.), followed by turned up (T.U.), and straight (ring) eyes. These designs may incorporate a tapered, loop, or ball design. The shape of the eye in conjunction with your leader knot helps determine how the fly will ride in the water.

I prefer to attach turned down and turned up eye hooks with a Turle knot. The Turle knot allows for a straight pull and will not rotate or swing around the eye like a clinch knot will. When the leader is not extending straight out from the eye, or hook shank, the fly is cocked at an angle and not swimming properly. The Turle knot also keeps your leader from becoming wedged into the corner of an improperly designed or manufactured eye where it is easily broken. The Turle knot secures itself *behind* the hook eye so it does not create a knot in front of the fly. A clinch knot tied on a size 20 hook can enlarge the imitation by over 25%.

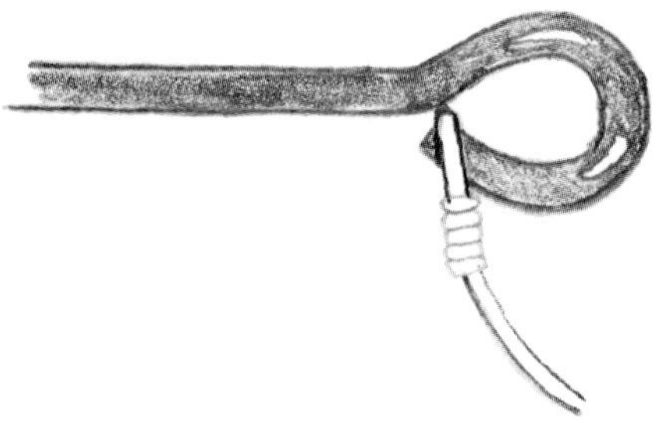

Point:

The point is the most fragile part of a hook and care should be taken to avoid damaging it, especially on back casts. When tying, hook points should not be buried in vise jaws. Most hook points need sharpening before you fish them and they should be checked often for broken or dulled points. A traditional method for determining if hook points are sharp is to drag the point across your thumb nail. If the hook leaves a scratch, it is fairly sharp. If it stops dragging, it is very sharp.

Clinch knot poised for breakage in the corner of an improperly closed eye.

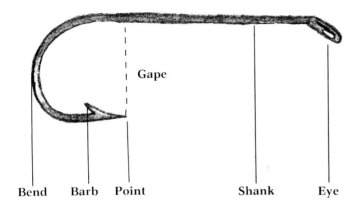

Gape

Bend Barb Point Shank Eye

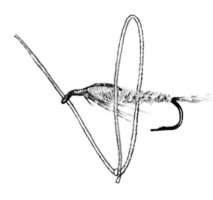

Gape:

For the most part, manufacturers adhere to a standard gape distance for each size hook. A standard hook shank length is roughly twice the hook gape. The smaller the number, the larger the gape, hence a size 4 hook gape is larger than a size 6. But, because hook shanks vary greatly in length, the "size" of a hook actually only denotes the gape size, not the overall length.

If a hook gape is too narrow, it will be difficult to hook fish. If it is too wide the hook point can penetrate a fish's brain or eye, neither of which is conducive to its survival. This is especially true when lead wire is added to the hook, for weighted hooks have a tendency to ride upside down. When fish accept an imitation in the upside-down position the hook becomes imbedded in the top of their mouth. If the hook has a wide gape there is a good chance it will enter the eye or brain. When tying stonefly, dragonfly, hellgrammite and forage fish imitations a 6x long hook should usually be used, *not* a 2 or 3x long hook. Mustad 9671 (2x), 9672 (3x), Tiemco 5262 (2x), and 5263 (3x) should be avoided. Mustad 9575 and 3665A, and Tiemco 300 are alternatives. English style bait hooks (Mustad 37140 and 37160 have been popularized for stonefly, caddisfly, and scud imitations, and, because of their extra wide gape, should also be avoided. Tiemco 200 is a reasonable alternative.

Wire Diameter:

Manufacturers have also *somewhat* standardized wire gauge, so a size 6 "standard" hook will have the same diameter wire regardless of its configuration or manufacturer. Extra light and extra strong wire are possible options and such deviations are also denoted with an "x" system. I have seldom found the need for extra strong or heavy wire hooks. It can be difficult to set or penetrate large diameter wire hooks into the tough, bony mouth of fish, especially when you are using a relatively light tippet (see "About Barbless Hooks"). For this reason lighter diameter wire hooks are used and lead is wrapped around the hook shank for weight before the fly is tied. The occasional "super fish" that straightens out a hook makes for a great story and leaves the fish to your enlarging imagination.

Extra light wire (small diameter) hooks are used for surface flies that are intended to be fished near, or on the water's surface. Examples would include the Chironomid Pupa and Floating Mayfly. If you do not tie such flies on light wire hooks you will have difficulty keeping them from settling below the feed zone.

A Turle knot alleviates the leader from becoming caught in the corner of the hook eye and allows for a straight pull. It is easy to tie.

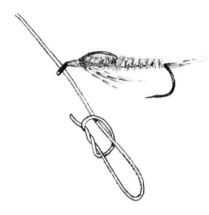

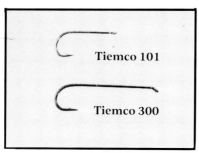

A standard length size 10 compared to a 6x long size 10.

Shank:

It is the length of the hook shank that ultimately determines the length or size of your fly. In other words, fish are concerned with the overall length of your fly, not the gape. A standard size 6 hook is about 3/4 of an inch in length. A size 6 hook with a 6x long shank is 1½ inches long! Hook shanks are designated by an "x" system. Because odd size hooks are also manufactured, each "x" denotes one size. A size 6 1x long means the hook shank is the standard length of a hook one size larger (1x long), which would be a size 5. A size 6 2x long denotes a standard size 6 gape with the shank of a size 4. A size 8 6x long denotes a standard size 8 gape with the standard shank of a hook 6 sizes larger, or a size 2.

A size 6 1x short would be the shank length of a size 7 hook. A 2x short shank would equal the shank of a standard size 8. Short shank hooks are seldom used when tying nymphs.

Hook Styles:

Originally I had hoped to explain and simplify some of the mass confusion and misconceptions surrounding hooks, but after exhaustive research I concluded that nothing short of a *complete* renovation would ease confusion. Manufacturers assign a number to all hook styles. Unfortunately these numbers tell you nothing about hook styles and are totally erroneous. Perhaps a standard numbering system should be implemented, with each number representing a particular standard feature, such as eye design, configuration, wire diameter, shank length, etc.

For various reasons, individual fly tyers will prefer one hook over another. As an example, various representations or patterns of the stonefly species *Pteronarcys californica* could call for 10 different hook styles! To simplify this confusion and alleviate tyers having to inventory 15,000 hooks, I have listed only the hooks I use. If you have the hook styles and sizes listed below you will be able to construct most nymph imitations and a great many adult (dry fly) and forage fish (streamer) imitations on what I feel are *currently* the most advantageous hooks.

Tiemco 101 sizes 12-20:	Standard extra light wire, ring eye surface hook suitable for midge pupa, surface nymphs and adults.
Tiemco 5262 sizes 8-18:	Standard wire, 2x long suitable for mayfly, caddis fly and scud imitations.
Tiemco 5263 sizes 8-18:	Standard wire, 3x long suitable for larger (longer) caddis and mayfly nymphs, and shorter dragon and stone imitations.
Tiemco 200 sizes 8-20:	Specially refined, 2x long, fine diameter wire hook suitable for mayfly, caddis, scud and adult imitations.
Tiemco 300 sizes 4-12:	Fine diameter wire, 6x long suitable for damsel, dragon, stone, leech and forage fish imitations.

All hooks are size 10 and are pictured actual size.

For those who already have a selection of hooks and do not wish to update themselves, I have prepared the following chart. This chart will allow you to see at a glance which hook styles are generally comparable in length to others, so it will be easy to locate a substitute.

HOOK COMPARISON CHART

Hook														
Tiemco 101 Standard Length									10	12	14	16	18	20
Tiemco 3769 Standard Length								8°	10		12°	14	16	
Tiemco 3761 1x Long								10	12		14	16		
Tiemco 5262 2x Long									12	14		16	18	20
Tiemco 5263 3x Long							8	10	12	14	16	18		
Tiemco 200 2x Long				4°		6°	8	10	12	14	16	18	20	
Tiemco 300 6x Long	2	4		6	8	10	12	14						
Mustad 94845 Standard Length									10	12	14	16		18
Mustad 94840 Standard Length									10	12	14	16		18
Mustad 3906 Standard Length							6°	8°		10°	12°		14°	16°
Mustad 3906B 1x Long							6°	8°	10	12	14		16	18
Mustad 7957BX 1x Long							6°	8°			10°	12°	14°	16°
Mustad 9671 2x Long					4°	6°	8	10	12	14		16		
Mustad 9672 3x Long		2°		4°		6°	8	10		12	14	16		
Mustad 79580 4x Long	2		4		6		8		10	12	14	16		
Mustad 79582 6x Long			6		8	10	12*							
Mustad 9575 6x Long	2	4		6	8	10	12*							
Mustad 3665A 6x Long	2	4		6	8									
Mustad 38941 3x Long		2°		4°		6°	8	10	12					
Mustad 36620 6x Long	2	4		6	8	10	12*							
Mustad 9674 6x Long	2		4		6°		8							

Read the columns vertically to compare hook lengths and to select a substitute hook.
Shading represents preferred hooks in relation to length-to-gape ratio.
Starred numbers represent hook gapes too narrow for tying most standard style nymphs.
Zeroed numbers represent hook gapes too wide for tying most standard style nymphs.
Tiemco 101 and Mustad 94840 and 94845 offer extra light gauge wire and are expressly designed for adult and surface film imitations only.

6

Setting Up
The Tying Bench

Most tyers begin tying on the kitchen table or office desk and it usually does not take very long to outgrow such quarters. A desk devoted solely to tying is ideal but a card table in the corner will also do nicely. It is important to keep your vise set up permanently so that you can take advantage of short periods of free time. If you just tie one or two flies here and there you will have about 500 flies in a year. If you were to buy them they would cost between $700 and $1,000! You will have no trouble stashing 500 flies into your fishing vest. I probably carry somewhere around 4,000 and a friend of mine takes two carrying bags filled with big plastic boxes of flies from which he restocks his vest or changes his inventory. You will *never* have enough flies. Back to setting up the bench. A light background will allow you to easily see hooks, tools and materials. A stark white background reflects too much light for my liking so I have settled on a light blue. Poster board is perfect. You will want a high intensity lamp, one that throws a concentrated light beam. You will also want a spare bulb. Be certain to keep any dangerous objects or materials away from children and pets. There are many handy improvements that can be incorporated into your tying bench and you will make many as you become familiar with your various needs. The important thing is to set up your work area and keep it set up. You will be surprised how often you sit down for a feather bending session.

7

Speed Tying

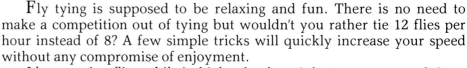

Fly tying is supposed to be relaxing and fun. There is no need to make a competition out of tying but wouldn't you rather tie 12 flies per hour instead of 8? A few simple tricks will quickly increase your speed without any compromise of enjoyment.

I began tying flies while in high school, mainly to support my fishing and tying habit and was to the point that either I had to produce more flies or get a real job. The prospect of a real job and a W-2 form was not exciting and about that time I received an order for 700 dozen flies or all I could do in 60 days. This figured out to about 12 dozen a day which seemed like an unattainable goal but I finished them and in the process increased my speed 25%. I knew I could speed up my tying even more and for the next couple of years I traveled around tying flies and fishing and never missed a chance to observe and tie with others. I picked up a hint here and an idea there and began to increase my speed considerably. At first I would attempt to tie a fly for every song on the radio, then a fly per song *and* commercial until I worked up to the newest station on the air, which played the most songs. Eventually I could tie two dozen per hour and easy flies went at three dozen per hour. In an average day I would tie twelve dozen by two o'clock. Tying alongside and racing with a fellow tyer will also pick up your speed. Following are some ideas that will get you tying a little faster.

1. Get into the habit of making your hands move faster. Turning the smallest diameter circle of thread will help immensely.

2. Minimize your thread turns, wrapping only what is needed to properly secure materials in place.

3. Organize your tying table and always put everything in the same place, especially tools and materials in current use. You should be able to reach for hooks, or anything else, with your eyes closed and certainly without thinking.

4. Get into the habit of carrying the scissors on your hand. A great deal of time is wasted looking for, picking up and setting down scissors.

5. Use half hitches and tie them by hand. If done properly, a whip finish is not needed. Half hitch directions are explained later.

6. Scatter your hooks where they are easily picked up and seen.

7. Clear an area around the vise and have only those materials laid out that are in current use.

Two methods of carrying the scissors in your hands as you tie. This may feel awkward at first, but you will quickly appreciate the advantages.

8. Set up for several flies of the same pattern.

9. Think ahead to the next step before the current one is finished.

10. Your tools should be in perfect working condition. If you have a dull scissors or if your vise is not holding the hook securely you will tie far fewer flies than you should and probably become a little frustrated, too.

11. Tie only with the best materials. Don't bother with road kills or untanned skins. These often become greasy or buggy and any dollars you save will be spent again and again. Hackles cause tyers more time and frustration than anything else. Use Metz and Hoffman and you know you have the best.

12. Tie under a high intensity lamp. Not only will you see better but you will be able to tie longer and feel better doing it.

13. Weight all hooks in advance.

14. Lacquer all heads at once, not one at a time.

15. Have extra bobbins threaded.

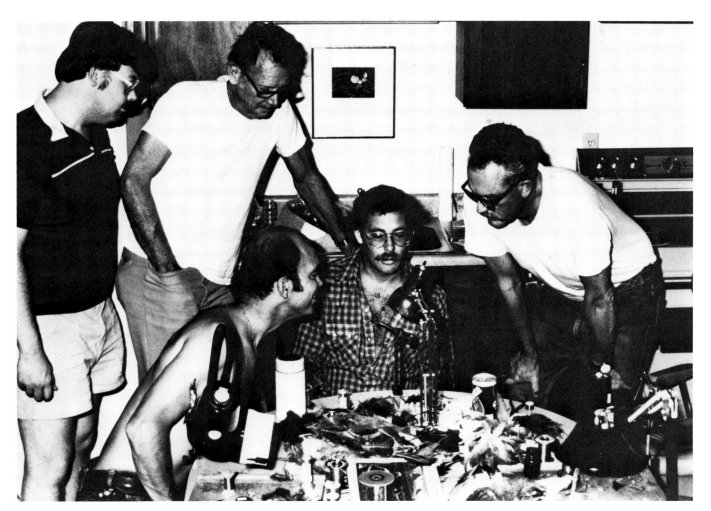

The author instructing fly tying at Maupin, Oregon. Such instruction will greatly speed your understanding and increase your enjoyment of the sport.

8

Basic Tying Techniques

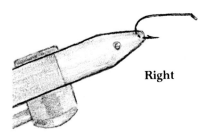

Right

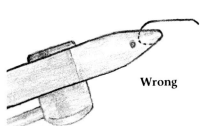

Wrong

Mounting the Hook

Before you mount the hook, check the point, eye, shank, hook temper and smash the barb. Hooks should be secured parallel to the table and mounted high in the jaws. As little of the hook as possible should be buried in the jaws. I like to insert only the lower bend of the hook in the forward topmost part of the jaws. By doing this you can more easily tie materials onto the hook. The point and barb should be exposed, as vise jaws can weaken a hook point. This is especially true of smaller hooks. The only disadvantage of this is that you must be careful not to hit your thread on the hook point. To avoid this, simply wrap the thread in an oblong circle thereby avoiding this razor edge. It should be noted that all directions are given for tying right handed. Left hand tyers will normally do the opposite, including turning the vice around and wrapping thread in the opposite direction. Flies that are tied left handed are easily spotted because the rib is slanted in the opposite direction.

This chapter explains the basic tying techniques needed to begin fly construction. They should be fully understood and practiced before beginning Part II.

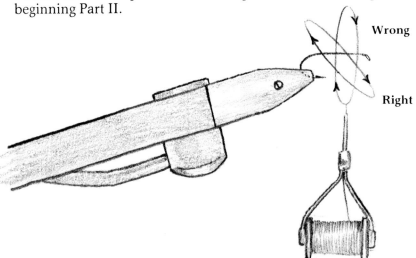

Wrong

Right

Wrap thread in an oblong circle, thus avoiding hitting the hook point with the thread. Thread is easily placed at the back of the hook if a short circle of thread is employed.

Securing Thread and Materials onto the Hook

This is a simple matter of wrapping thread over the top of the short end. Assuming you tie right handed, hold the end of the thread in your left hand and place it at a right angle over the hook. Keep tension on the thread and with your right hand wind the thread back over the short end and away from yourself. Thread should always be wrapped clockwise and always in the same direction. The same is true of materials, except for reverse rib.

Hook shanks are round, smooth and very slippery. If a thread foundation is not wrapped over the hook the finished fly will easily spin around the hook shank. Note the position of the thread on the hook shank. There is a slight space immediately behind the hook eye that is void of thread. This is referred to as the head area and *nothing* should be tied in this area until you are ready to finish the actual thread head. By leaving this front space clear you will have no trouble finishing off a neat, tapered head, which is usually the hallmark of a fine fly. Neat heads also allow you to easily tie a leader onto your fly. The thread should cover the remainder of the hook shank to just before the hook drops off in the back or to the rear position of the body. Carefully note this thread position. If thread is hanging between the barb and hook point of a standard style hook it is at the standard tail tie-in position. During construction it is not uncommon to break the thread. Simply resecure the thread as illustrated and continue tying the fly, being certain all materials are secure.

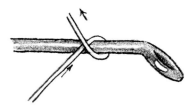

Step 1: Keep tension on both ends of the thread and place thread over the hook at a right angle to the hook.

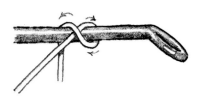

Step 2: Wrap the bobbin end of the thread back over the short end of the thread.

Step 3: Continue wrapping thread back over the short end for about six turns. Thread is now secured onto the hook.

Step 4: Trim or pull off loose end of thread.

The remaining pages in part I are crucial to understanding nymph nomenclature and construction techniques, and it is advised that you have a complete understanding of these pages before continuing on.

The following three pages, in particular, will explain how to properly tie-in and tie-off (secure) material onto the hook, how to wrap material around (onto) the hook, and how to form a neat, tapered head. These techniques will be required for *every* fly you tie.

Spend some time practicing, and if you have any problems, pay closer attention to the photo detail and instructional captions.

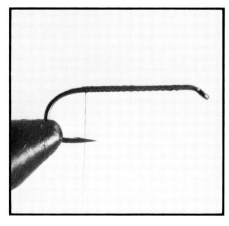

2. The position at which the thread hangs halfway between the barb and hook point, and where the hook shank usually begins to fall off onto the bend of the hook, is known as the *standard tail tie-in position*.

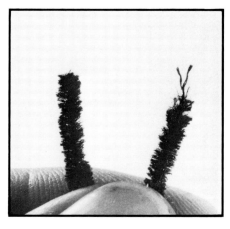

3. Select a 4-inch section of chenille and twist off the woven fibers, exposing the thread core. This will eliminate excess bulk at the tie-in area and make for an easier and quicker tie-in.

4. This is the wrong way to secure any material onto the hook, as the thread will "chase" the material around the hook almost indefinitely. Your fingers must be up close at the exact thread tie-in position.

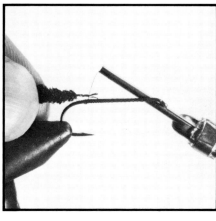

5. The chenille end has been twisted off properly, but the fingers still are not close enough to the tie-in position. Move forward a little more.

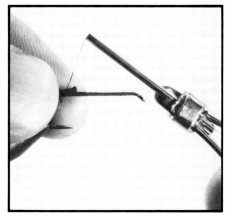

6. With your fingers in this position, the material being tied in place cannot possibly run around the hook, away from the thread. This is known as the *in-front-of-the-finger* tie-in technique. Begin with a loose wrap of thread downward from the position shown and cinch up on the tension. If the material should roll off to the side, push it back in position with your finger.

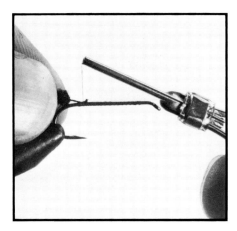

7. Once the first wrap or two of thread has "caught" and tied down the material end, back off your fingers and secure in place. A *half dozen* turns of tightly placed thread is sufficient. Exert the maximum amount of pressure on the thread.

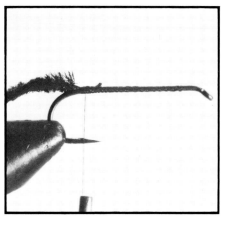

8. Chenille tie-in is complete and free of bulk. The first material (tail, body, back, etc.) to be tied in at this rear position is actually tied into place *slightly behind* the standard tail tie-in position, ensuring that no thread will show behind or underneath the tail or body. Compare this thread position with photo 2.

Up Between-Your-Fingers Tie-In Technique

Another method of tying-in or securing materials follows. It is known as the *up-between-your-fingers* tie-in technique and it is the most effective method of positioning and securing materials in place.

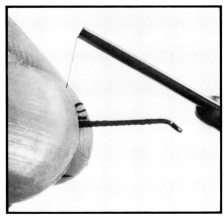

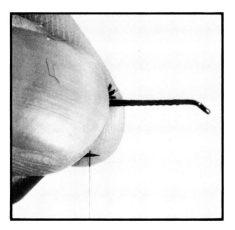

1. The thread hangs at the standard tail tie-in position. The chenille (or other material) is positioned where it is desired and the thumb and first finger encompasses it as shown. The exact tie-in position is denoted by the position of the thread.

2. Bring the thread up between the fingers. Do not remove or open up your fingers to accomplish this. If need be, bring the thread in front of the fingers and slide it back between them to the position shown here.

3. Bring the thread down, catching the material in place. Remember, material will be tied into place wherever you demand or are actually positioning it. If material is not where you want it, reposition and hold it where you *do* want it placed.

Over-The-Top and Hold-It Technique

Material is best wrapped around the hook with the *over-the-top and hold-it* technique. A little discipline, practice and finger control now will save you many frustrations later. The left hand will do *all the wrapping.* The right hand only holds the material at the bottom position until the left hand can come back over the top of the fly and continue another wrap around the hook.

Thread is always placed at the exact position material is to be tied onto the hook. Once the tie-in is complete, the thread is moved or positioned at the *tie-off position.*

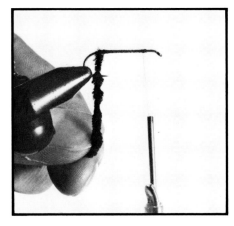

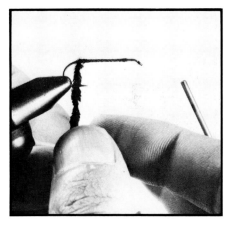

5. Continuing from photo 8 page 34, wrap chenille clockwise to this position with your *left* hand. *Constant tension must be kept on any material being wrapped around the hook,* or material will loosen or unravel, which means beginning anew. Thread is positioned at tie-off position.

6. *Before* you release your left hand, grasp the chenille with your right hand as shown. Notice the position of the bobbin. By allowing the bobbin to rest over the top of your right hand it stays out of the way, making this technique easy to accomplish.

7. Bring your left hand back over the top of the hook and take ahold of the chenille. Do not release the tension with your right hand until your left hand is in complete control. Bring the chenille over the top and back down to the bottom position.

8. The chenille has again been wrapped around the hook with the left hand, and the right hand is about to hold it in the bottom position, hence the "over-the-top and hold-it" terminology. Repeat these turns side by side until the body is formed.

9. The right hand is holding the thread in the bottom position and keeping the bobbin out of the working area. The left hand is ready to grab the chenille in this position and complete a circle around the hook back to this position, where the right hand will again hold the chenille.

Tie-Off and Tie-Down Technique

The following series of photos depicts how to *tie-off* or *tie-down* materials and trim off the excess. If properly accomplished, there will be no unnecessary excess material protruding from the fly and a neat head will be easy to construct. All materials will be secured or tied off in this manner.

2. Hold the material to be tied off in your right hand. The chenille is angled more to the right than necessary only to more clearly show the tie-down position. Keep tension on the chenille until it has been secured in place.

3. Hold the chenille very close to the hook shank and bring the thread up and over the top and down. Work the thread into and between the chenille fibers, catching the very core of the chenille. Take a half dozen turns of thread in this position and a couple more in front of the chenille.

4. Position the bobbin over the top of your hand and place the scissors' point against the body and make one clean cut. Notice that the tie-down is well away from the hook eye. After the cut remove any loose or unimportant fibers with your fingers.

5. Tie down is complete.

Thread Heads

Thread heads are a problem for tyers and throughout Part II there is constant mention of tying a neat, tapered head. A neat head is the hallmark of a finely-crafted fly. It also means that the leader can be easily threaded and attached to the fly. Before you begin actual fly construction it will be helpful to practice tying a thread head. By doing this you can easily understand what a neat thread head really is and what is required to construct one. You will see that it is very easy to do if enough room is left for the job.

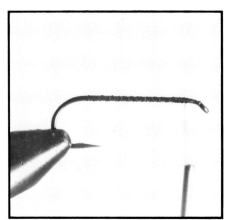

7. Thread has been positioned along the hook shank, forming a rough foundation. This would be the normal beginning of an actual fly and the thread would be wrapped back to the standard tail tie-in position. Notice that the area where the thread head will eventually be is *void of material. The entire fly will be constructed behind this bare spot.*

8. Let us assume that the fly has been constructed up to this bare spot. All that remains to be done is to finish off the thread head. Give it a try, it is easy when enough space is left. The head should be of small diameter and have a slight taper. It is not a question of bulk, but of a few turns of thread and two half hitches which finish off the fly.

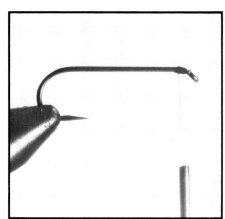

9. Properly constructed thread head.

Half Hitch

When properly executed, the half hitch is a quick, simple, neat and effective knot for tying off thread at the head of the fly. The half hitch is simply a loop that is thrown around the hook. I like to place *two* half hitches at the *rear* of the thread head area (one half hitch will not hold and three will not cinch up tightly). Proper placement will ensure a neat head. Before cutting the thread, cinch the two half hitches by pulling the thread around the hook (over the top from the back side). You will feel the two half hitches cinch together. Back off slightly on the tension and cut the knots close to the thread head so there is no loose end protruding from the thread head. Lacquer the entire head.

Note: a whip finish is very popular with many tyers but if done properly, the half hitch is just as durable, but quicker, easier, and neater. Those tyers who purchase whip finish tools will receive explicit directions.

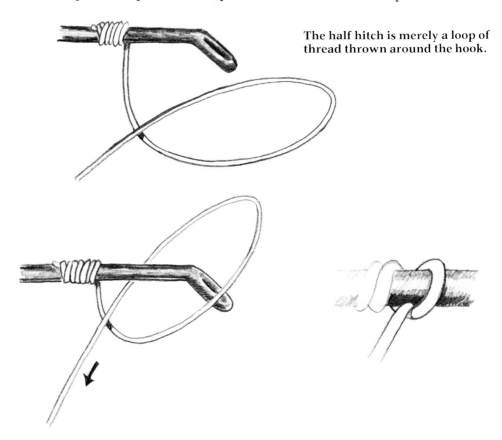

The half hitch is merely a loop of thread thrown around the hook.

1. Hold the thread between your thumb and first finger. Your third finger keeps downward tension on the thread from the vise. When in this position, the *back* side of your hand should be facing you. Hold the bobbin with your left hand, supplying tension as needed.

2. Rotate your hand clockwise 180 degrees, forming a loop. Now the *palm* of your hand should be facing you. Notice the position of the third finger, which continues to supply tension on the thread. Also, notice that the thread is positioned on the *tip* of the first finger, not halfway down the joint.

3. Place the loop around the hook, holding it in place on the far side of the hook with your first finger. Carefully note the position of the thread across the first finger.

 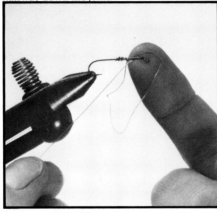 

4. Drop out your third finger. Keep your thumb in position as you draw the loop closed, holding the thread in *front and away* from any material at the head area. Drop off your thumb only when the loop is *nearly closed*.

5. The thumb has been dropped in this photo prematurely to show the half hitch loop. The first finger stays on the loop until it is *completely* closed, ensuring proper placement. Place *two* half hitches, cinch them tightly counter clockwise, back off slightly on the tension, trim thread and lacquer.

6. The half hitch tool helps some tyers better understand this technique and tie "hitches", but I recommend using your fingers as they are faster and exact placement is easier.

 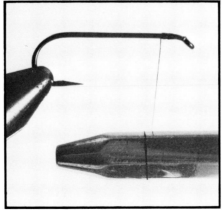 

7. Place the tool in front of the thread.

8. Take a turn around the tool.

9. Place the tool around the hook eye and slide off the thread. Repeat, cinch tight counter clockwise, trim the thread and lacquer the head.

10

Weighting Hooks

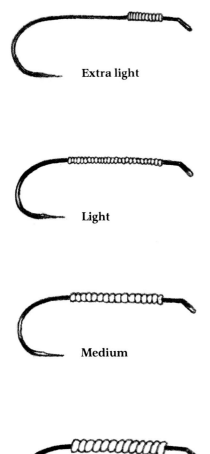

Extra light

Light

Medium

Heavy

When you buy a Hare's Ear, or any other weighted nymph, you do not have a choice as to the amount of weight and hence the sink rate of the fly. They are all the same. If that particular weight suits your needs, fine, but suppose it doesn't? Suppose you want to fish that Hare's Ear in the surface film, or over a weed bed that is two feet below the surface or, three feet deep in a fast current? How can one weight of fly cover these varied possibilities? It can't. But, when you tie your own, you can weight them tailored to your exact needs. This is a tremendous advantage non-tyers do not enjoy. It is a good idea to weight some flies in two or even three various weights. If you cannot tell them apart by looking at, or bouncing them in your hand, change the color of thread or make some other subtle change. You should have an idea of various wire diameters and which are best for particular hook sizes. For instance, .055 diameter wire would not fit on a size 16 hook. At the same time, .015 will not add much weight to a size 2 hook. Become familiar by wrapping various diameter wires onto different length hook shanks, viewing the weighted hooks from a weight factor and with finished proportions in mind. The larger diameter the wire the heavier and fatter the fly. If you are tying a damselfly and wish it to be lightly weighted you would use a fine diameter wire. Basically this is common sense but a brief mention will clear any doubts.

Lead wire is best wrapped over a thread base but if you are weighting hooks in advance forego the thread base. Lead should be placed on the forward area of the hook shank. This will allow the fly to ride on a reasonably even keel and there will be room behind the lead to work a taper into the fly body. The illustrations depict four ways to weight a standard nymph; extra light, light, medium and heavy. The heavy fly will be somewhat bulky, but this can be a worthwhile trade-off.

A heavily weighted fly tied on a long shank hook tends to roll or ride upside down in the water. A strip of lead wire tied along the underside of the hook will help keep the fly in an upright position. If a fish is hooked while the hook is in an upside down position the hook will be embedded in the top of the fish's mouth. If the hook has a wide gape it will puncture the fish's eye or brain. Needless to say, this is not conducive to any fishery. For this reason, we suggest the use of 6x long hooks when you are tying larger stonefly, dragon, hellgrammite and forage fish imitations. Refer to the chapter on hooks.

When a hook is weighted with a large diameter wire there is a rather abrupt drop-off to the hook shank. It is usually necessary to fill in and taper this area with thread or fur so the body can be more easily and properly constructed. When wrapping on lead, do not cut the ends with your scissors. The resulting sharp edge will easily cut your thread and lead is hard on scissors. Place your finger on the wrapped lead and grasp the loose end of lead with your finger close to the hook shank and *pull* it off. Fold and tuck any loose ends down. Secure lead in place by wrapping thread forward and backward until the lead will not spin around the hook shank. If you wish to create a flattened body you may crimp the lead flat with a *smooth* nose pliers *after* it has been secured in place. If you crimp it too tightly it will crumble.

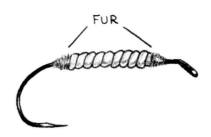

Dub a little fur in front of the lead wire, alleviating any abrupt drop-off to the hook shank and making a tapered body easier to construct.

A strip of lead secured along the underside of the hook helps the fly ride hook down, lessening the chance of hooking fish through the eye and brain.

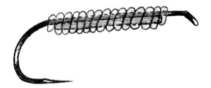

If more weight is desired, wrap lead around the hook shank over the previously placed lead strip.

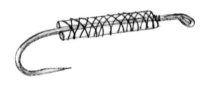

A wide, flattened body can be achieved by securing lead strips along each side of the hook.

11

Barbless Hooks

There are only positive reasons for fishing a barbless hook. There are no disadvantages. More fish (especially big fish) are hooked on barbless hooks because they have tough, bony mouths and barbed hooks have difficulty penetrating or sinking in. A barb forms a resistant wedge.

How many good fish have you missed on the strike? How many of those would you have hooked if the hook point was sharp and the barb smashed flat? Remember the last time you had a good fish on and the line suddenly went slack? Chances are the hook never penetrated and just fell out of the fish's mouth. The fish was never hooked — you were!

Pull a barbed and barbless hook into a piece of cardboard. You'll see and feel the difference.

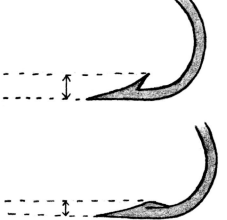

When a hook sinks to the bend of the hook (instead of only part way) you have the fish until you back out the hook exactly the way it went in or until it breaks through the skin.

Do you remember the last time you hooked your clothing or yourself? Smash the barbs and avoid the pain and frustration of being hooked yourself.

The best way to debarb a hook is to smash it flat using a *flat-nose* pliers. Be careful not to damage the hook point.

I have tested the fishing speed of barbed vs. barbless hooks several times. The angler fishing barbless hooks is able to release nearly twice as many fish as the angler fishing a barbed hook. The time consumed in handling fish, working out barbed hooks with pliers or forceps, plus the time required to properly revive fish handled in such a manner, drastically reduces actual fishing time and the catch rate.

I am confident you will find barbless hooks a pleasure to fish.

Dubbing

Dubbing material is any natural fur, such as rabbit, or blended synthetic nylon, such as Antron, or any other soft material that can be spun or rolled onto thread. Generally, a great many nymph imitations have dubbed bodies. Dubbed bodies are far superior to chenille, yarn and floss bodies, offering better animation, translucence and, when blended with various colors, superior light diffusion.

Smooth fur, such as rabbit, muskrat and blended hare's ear, is very easy to dub tightly. The more coarse the dubbing material, the more difficult it is to dub tightly. Goat that has not been blended with a softer fur will never dub tightly. When dubbing goat, do a little at a time and do not concern yourself with the fact that it is not tight. When you wrap it onto the hook, overlapping wraps will secure enough fibers and any excess can be pulled out.

Following is the best method of applying dubbing to thread I have found. If done properly it is very quick and easily accomplished. Pay careful attention to the following steps:

1. This clump of otter fur has been trimmed directly from the hide. Notice that all guard hairs are in place and that the fur is very dense, but soft. Such fur can be dubbed directly onto thread. It is very helpful to blend it before dubbing it.

2. Blended otter. Notice that the guard hairs are well scattered and the fur is not matted together. It is light and airy, and will be very easy to spread out along the thread in preparation for dubbing.

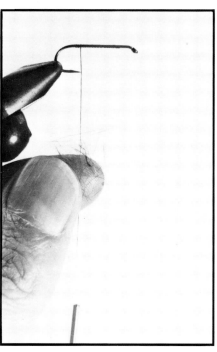

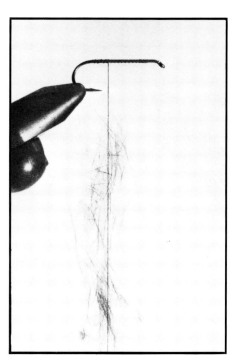

1. Dubbing can be applied directly onto 6/0 prewax thread without additional wax, but Wonder Wax is very tacky and will make dubbing much easier, especially for beginners. Apply wax to 2-4 inches of thread. Working with a longer amount can become unwieldy.

2. Begin with *very little* fur. Merely touch the fur to the waxed thread and it will adhere instantly. Begin this process about *one-inch down* the thread from the hook shank. If the dubbing is started too close to the hook you will be unable to roll the topmost fibers onto the thread.

3. Spread dubbing along the thread *evenly* and *thinly*. Remember, we are only *spreading* the dubbing out along the thread. To begin, cover the thread with just enough fur (dubbing) to show its color. Do not create *any* bulk. As you become more dextrous, larger amounts of dubbing may be applied, especially when tying larger flies.

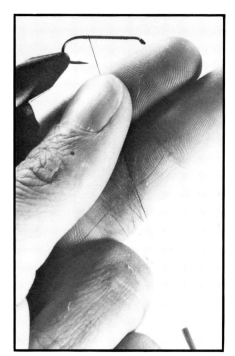

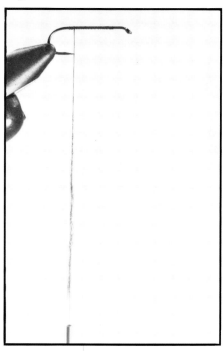

4. Beginning at the *topmost* fiber of dubbing, roll the thread and dubbing between your thumb and first two fingers. Begin this roll at the *base* of your first two fingers (more surface area covered), not at the finger tips. A great deal of pressure must be exerted between your thumb and first two fingers (they should turn white). At the same time, keep tension on the thread with your other hand.

5. One, perhaps two, rolls should press the dubbing tightly onto the thread. Roll dubbing in one direction only, not back and forth. Do not wet your fingers. Move down the thread and roll the next section.

6. A small amount of dubbing properly in place. Pictured is about 4 inches of thread. Notice the dubbing begins down from the hook about an inch, and the *topmost* dubbing fiber is *tightly* rolled onto the thread. Dubbing is *spread evenly* along the thread. If your dubbing does not look like this, try it again.

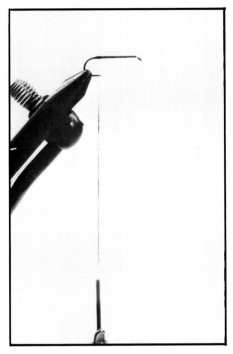

1. Thin application of dubbing. The less fur you attempt to dub onto the thread the easier it will be to accomplish. Begin with about 10% of what you think is necessary.

2. Medium application of dubbing. Dubbing should be looked upon as "heavy thread" and must be continuous and even in application.

3. Heavy application of dubbing. Suitable for large (size 8 and larger) imitations. Notice how even the distribution of fur is.

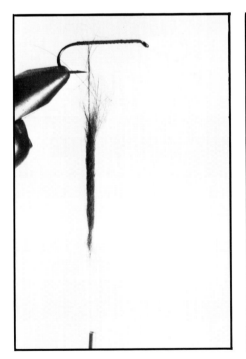

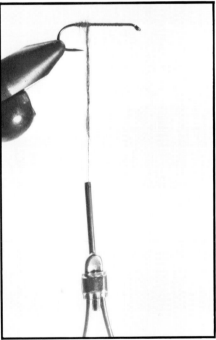

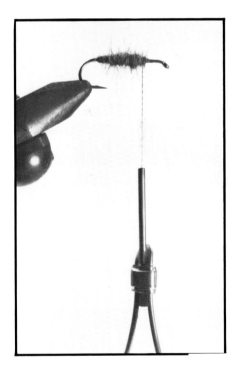

4. *Improper dubbing.* Dubbing is too close to the hook shank and the topmost fibers have not been tightly dubbed. Fur somewhat "spirals" around the thread and is not dubbed onto the thread tightly. This dubbing is easily picked off and adheres poorly to the thread. If your dubbing looks like this, try it again and pay closer attention to the instructions.

5. Once you have mastered the technique of dubbing, begin wrapping it around the hook shank, forming the body. A tapered shape is usually desired, with the body being smaller in diameter at the rear and larger toward the front. Dubbing can be wrapped either back-to-front, or front-to-back-to-front, or a combination of the two.

6. A medium dubbed body. Notice the starting position of the body and the taper. Both are standard guidelines. The guard hairs protruding from the dubbed body are usually desired when imitating nymphs. If a longer body is desired (when the thorax is absent) simply dub and wrap more fur, filling up the hook shank as desired.

13

Parts of a Nymph

An understanding of the various parts of nymph imitations will allow you to associate or visually "see" what the finished fly should look like. Once you have a complete understanding of the parts and how to construct them you will be able to tie most nymphs. Throughout this text, fly pattern dressings are listed in the order the materials should be tied onto the hook.

Tail:

For the most part, tails should be tied reasonably sparse, unobtrusive, and short (about the gape of the hook shank). Besides natural appearance, tails provide stability and therefore should be mounted on *top* of the hook. If they are tied onto one side the fly may not swim properly. The exception to this is strip goose tails, which are paired and tied in a "V" along each side of the hook. The most common materials used for tails include partridge, mallard, strip goose and hackle fibers.

Antennae:

Antennae are sometimes referred to as "feelers" and usually protrude from the front of the fly, but are also tied back over the top of, and beyond the length of the body. Common materials include stripped goose tied "V" style, such as seen on the Kaufmann Stone, and mallard fibers, which are usually tied back over the top of the fly, as seen on some caddis pupa imitations. Antennae length is determined by the natural being imitated.

Rib:

Ribbing is referred to as any material (other than hackle) which is wrapped around the body. Ribbing should be evenly spaced and wrapped tightly. If it is not wrapped tightly it will fall off the back of the fly. When checking the durability of flies I always test the rib. Ribbing is intended to "set off" the body, add a slight amount of flash, act as a reinforcer and depict segmentation. Ribbing is supposed to be a subtle addition; do not overdo it. Fine wire, oval and flat tinsel in gold and silver, thread, peacock and ostrich are all common ribbing materials.

Gills:

Gills are tied along each side of the body on some mayfly patterns and the effect adds a great deal of authenticity. Marabou, ostrich and filoplume are the most common materials employed. An example would be the Pale Morning Dun.

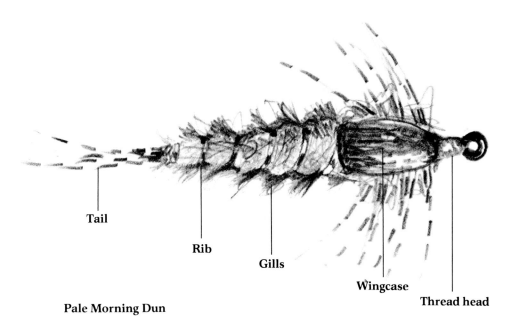

Tail

Rib

Gills

Wingcase

Thread head

Pale Morning Dun

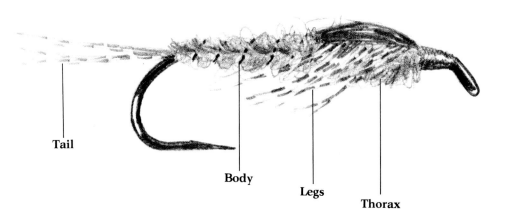

Tail

Body

Legs

Thorax

Back:

Commonly called a shellback or overbody, the back is any material tied in at the tail and pulled forward over the top of the entire body much like a wingcase. Backs are commonly constructed with heavy mill plastic, peacock, and lacquered turkey. An example is the *Gammarus-Hyalella* Scud.

Body:

The actual body of a natural nymph is divided into two parts, the abdomen and thorax. The abdomen is casually referred to by fly tyers as the body. Many nymph patterns call for both a body and thorax, others just a body. When tying those patterns that call for both, figure on the body filling up roughly 60% of the hook shank, sometimes slightly more, sometimes slightly less. Bodies should be constructed with a taper and be of much smaller diameter than the thorax. You will find it very difficult to form a neat, tapered dubbed body, and correspondingly larger diameter thorax, unless you begin tying a very small diameter body. Nymphs with only bodies (no thorax) include Trueblood Otter, Zug Bug, Timberline Emerger, and Woolly Bugger.

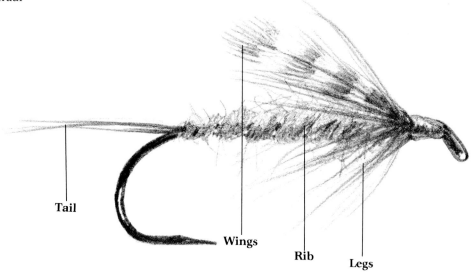

Tail

Wings

Rib

Legs

Timberline Emerger

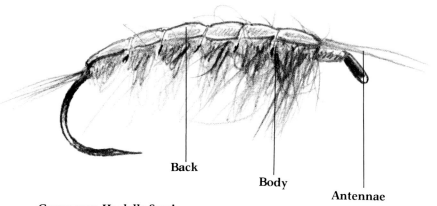

Back

Body

Antennae

Gammarus-Hyalella **Scud**

Thorax:

The thorax is representative of the forward section of the nymph body. It is at the thorax area that legs are often present and from this area the wings mature. As mentioned previously, the thorax is either a continuation of the tapered body or considerably larger in diameter. The thorax can be the same or different color than the abdomen or body. Dubbed thorax areas are often "picked out" in the hopes of trapping a few additional air bubbles, representing legs, and giving the fly an overall buggy appearance. The Hare's Ear, Soft Hackle, and Kaufmann Stone all have a thorax.

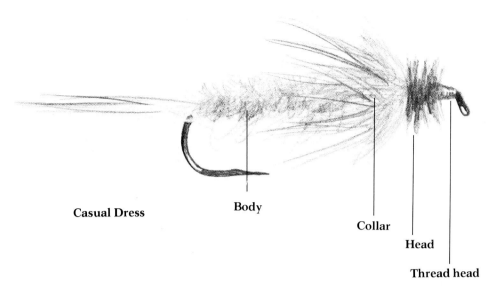

Casual Dress　　　　　　　　　**Body**

Collar

Head

Thread head

Wingcase:

In the eye of the angler a wingcase seems to put the finishing touch on a nymph. The wingcase, or wing pads as they are sometimes referred to, represent the area where wings will grow and expand and where insects such as stoneflies, mayflies, dragonflies and damselflies emerge from their nymphal case. To eliminate confusion and simplify tying instruction, a "wingcase" will be any material that is tied in ahead of the body and behind the thorax, pulled forward over the top of the thorax and tied off. The technique is the same as tying a "back," but the "wingcase" will only cover the top of the thorax, not the entire body. Standard materials include lacquered turkey, goose, mallard, and ringneck pheasant tail fibers. Gold Rib Hare's Ear, Matt's Fur, and Pheasant Tail patterns all depict this style of wingcase.

Wing:

Wings represent the more advanced stages of a "hatching," "emerging," or "pupating" insect, just prior to adulthood. Wings are often the last piece of nymph construction and should be tied *exactly* on top of the hook. If they are tied to one side the "keel" or action of the imitation can be affected. A common error is to tie wings too narrow and too long. They should not be longer than the body and usually *much* shorter. Common wing materials include Hoffman or Metz grizzly hen hackle tips, such as seen on the Chironomid Pupa and Timberline Emerger, and marabou as seen on the Marabou Damsel. Other "wings" are actually meant to represent the wingcase, but construction and technique are the same as tying wings. Examples include the Marabou Damsel, which incorporates marabou, and the Zug Bug, which incorporates dyed mallard. When such is the case, special mention will be made in pattern recipes.

Head:

This term will refer to the area immediately behind the thread head. "Heads" are often confused with a thorax, but are actually much smaller and a pattern may call for both a thorax and head. A perfect example of this is the A.P. series. Heads are usually constructed with dubbing but peacock (Filoplume Damsel) and ostrich (Casual Dress) are also used.

Collar:

A collar is usually a bunch of fur (but it can also be hair or hackle) tied in front of and encompassing the thorax in such a manner that it extends about 1/3 to 3/4 the length of the body. A perfect example is the Casual Dress.

Legs:

Most nymphs will have legs and they will usually be constructed with partridge, mallard, or hackle. There are six styles of legs that are commonly employed on nymph patterns, and they will be thoroughly explained in Part II. The following illustrations will help you become familiar with wing style terminology and their visual appearance.

1. Beard style, tied along the underside of the body (Trueblood Otter), side view.

2. Divided style, tied along both sides of body (Matt's Fur, Pheasant Tail), side and top view.

3. Tied full, or 360° around the body (Soft Hackle, Timberline Emerger).

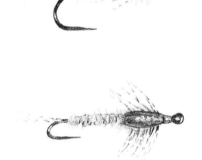

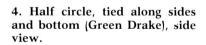

4. Half circle, tied along sides and bottom (Green Drake), side view.

5. Pulled over thorax (Pale Morning Dun), side and top view.

6. Palmer, tied through body, and/or thorax (Filoplume Damsel).

Thread Head:

The thread head is where the fly is finished off with a knot, just behind the hook eye, after which a drop of lacquer is applied. Heads should be neat and *smooth* in appearance with a *slight taper*. Beginning tyers tend to crowd the head and not leave enough room to finish off the fly. A crowded head makes a sloppy fly, often precludes threading your leader through the hook eye, and makes it difficult to tie a Turle knot properly. *A small space immediately behind the hook eye should be left completely bare* until you are ready to finish off the head. This will insure enough room.

Part Two

Tying Instruction

Part II illustrates in explicit detail the many and varied techniques required to construct nymph imitations. The thirty demonstration patterns have been selected for their tying technique, fishing versatility and angler interest. They encompass most major food sources of trout and many associated angling techniques are also discussed. Patterns and tying techniques follow a logical sequence, hence you should progress from start to finish without deviation. The photo instruction is, for the most part, very exact. Pay careful attention to all photo detail and your tying skills and enjoyment will increase dramatically.

14

Rubber Legs

Rubber Legs

It is difficult to find a sporting goods establishment in Montana that does not offer this pattern in a wide selection of sizes and colors. It is usually weighted heavily and bounced along the bottom in faster currents or used in conjunction with an extra fast sinking fly line and fished along willows and undercut banks. Some steelhead anglers have had good success bouncing a heavy Rubber Legs through deep runs and in small sizes it is an excellent panfish producer. Other, somewhat similar patterns include the Yuk Bug, Girdle Bug and Bitch Creek, all basically Montana patterns. The Rubber Legs is relatively easy to tie and makes a good start. Most of the basic techniques previously illustrated are incorporated into the Rubber Legs. If you encounter any questions refer to the "Basic Tying Techniques" chapter.

HOOK:	Tiemco 300, 2-10, weighted
THREAD:	Black
TAIL:	Two medium diameter white rubber strips tied "V"
LEGS:	Three pairs of medium white rubber strips spaced evenly along the body extending at right angles and clipped to desired length
BODY:	Black, yellow, olive, or brown chenille

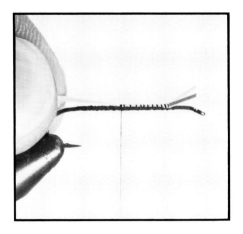

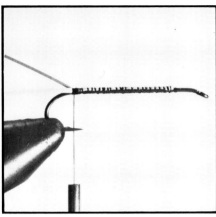

1. Position thread at front of hook. Secure two white rubber strips on *top* of the hook. Stretch strips backwards (less bulk and easier in-place tie down) and wrap the thread back to the standard tail tie-in position.

2. Trim the tail to the desired length: From the standpoint of naturalness and animation, naturally tapered materials such as hackle fibers, hackle tips, partridge fibers, etc., *should not be trimmed.*

3. Wrap the thread to the forward portion of the hook and again secure two white rubber strips on top of the shank. The strips can be easily secured with a figure 8 (criss cross in an "x") or whatever it takes to secure them in the desired position.

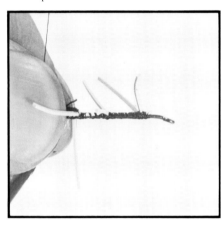

4. Working back, secure two more pairs of rubber strips and trim to desired length. Materials are often obstinate. Don't be afraid to "manhandle" them, positioning them where and how you desire. Note the smooth under-body, thus insuring a properly tapered body.

5. Cut a piece of chenille about 5 inches long. Twist the chenille off the woven core with your fingers (less bulk and easier to tie down). Chenille is best purchased on 144-yard spools as it is not matted or kinked as it is on paper cards.

6. Place the end of the chenille between your thumb and first finger. Bring the thread up between your fingers and down, securing the chenille exactly on top of the hook immediately in front of the tail. A half dozen turns of thread are sufficient.

7. Wrap thread forward to the head area. This is easily accomplished with 6-8 wraps. Wrap the chenille forward in-between the legs to the head area and tie off.

8. Secure chenille with about 6 turns of thread. Hold thread away from the area to be cut and trim chenille end *close* to the hook shank. Remove any fuzzy excess with your fingers and finish off a neat, tapered head.

9. One small drop of lacquer on the tip of your bodkin will penetrate the entire head. Clean any lacquer out of the hook eye. If you have any problems constructing this pattern, review the appropriate chapter.

15

Rhyacophila Caddis

Rhyacophila Caddis (Randall Kaufmann)

Rhyacophila are perhaps the best known and the most abundant of the free living caddisflies. They provide anglers with excellent fishing both when they lose their grasp and drift and tumble with the current and when pupae emerge. Over 100 species of the genus *Rhyacophila* are known to inhabit North America. They require cool, clean, fast waters, hence a great many western streams support large populations. During early summer it is common to collect several dozen in one net sampling from Oregon's Deschutes River.

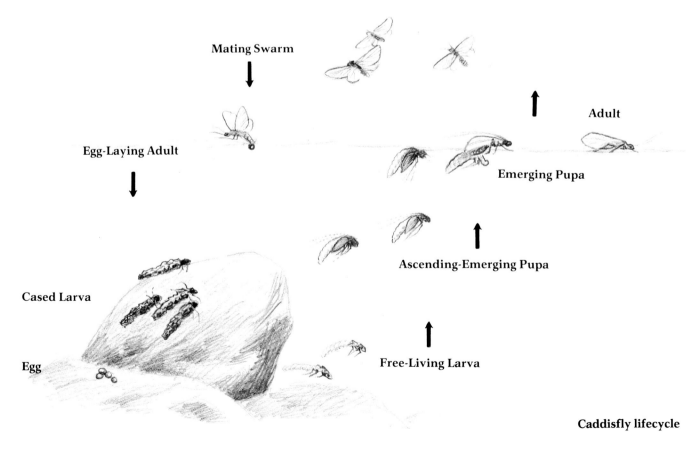

Mating Swarm

Adult

Egg-Laying Adult

Emerging Pupa

Ascending-Emerging Pupa

Cased Larva

Free-Living Larva

Egg

Caddisfly lifecycle

Prime *Rhyacophila* habitat, Deschutes River, Oregon.

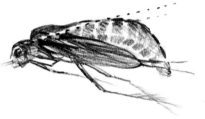

Caddis pupa

Ernest Schwiebert, writing in *Nymphs*, describes good hatches available to anglers throughout the east. *Rhyacophila* are commonly bright green, but dark olive, metallic blue-green, and even tan are common. It is believed trout "key" into the bright colors of particular food sources, such as *Rhyacophila*, more so than when feeding on other less colorful food sources of the same species. During such periods trout will move farther to ingest food but also seem to become more selective, hence a realistic representation and presentation is of utmost importance. It was for reasons such as these, and the fact that color variations occur from water to water that I became interested in a local workable pattern. It should be noted that this pattern differs little from many other caddisfly larva imitations, including Polly Rosborough's Green Rockworm and Gary LaFontaine's Caddis Larva.

The natural larva is basically worm-like in appearance and imitations are correspondingly simple. Drifting larvae will often have a curve to them, so it does not hurt to bring the body a little farther back onto the hook shank than normal. The Tiemco 200 style hook lends itself nicely to this application.

The technique to master with this pattern is the dubbing, rib, or ribbing and the head. Most nymphs will have some type of rib which will lend a slight amount of flash, represent segmentation and reinforce fragile bodies.

Caddis larva

HOOK:	Tiemco 200, 12-20, weight to suit
THREAD:	Black
RIB:	Fine green wire, thread, or floss twisted tight
BODY:	Antron caddis blend #5 (cream green)
HEAD:	Slight amount of black Hairtron blended with body material

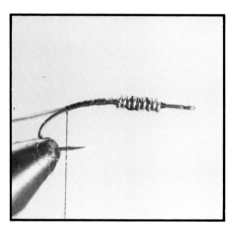

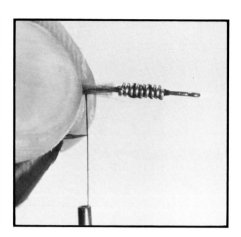

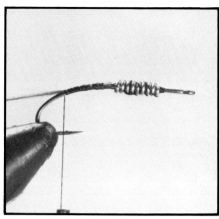

1. Secure the thread onto the hook and cover the shank. Install the lead wire and secure with thread.

2. Using the in-front-of-the-finger tie-in method, secure 4-5 inches of 2-to-4 strands of floss. The floss should not be tied on top of the lead, thus avoiding an uneven underbody.

3. Floss is properly secured in place *behind* the lead wire. Notice that the thread is slightly behind the standard tail tie-in position. This style hook (Tiemco 200) requires that the tail and body begin slightly behind the standard beginning position.

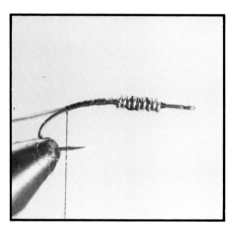

4. Dub on a thin strand of Antron Blend (out of view).

5. Wrap the dubbed body forward, creating a taper front-to-back as shown. The *Rhyacophila* will have a smaller than normal thorax (oftentimes referred to as a "head" on caddis imitations), but room must be left between the body and hook eye.

6. Hold the floss down from the hook shank and twist it tight. It should be twisted at the ends because it is easily soiled and dulled. Wrap the floss around the body, spacing it out at even intervals and keeping it tightly twisted. Use the over-the-top and hold-it technique.

7. Take an extra wrap of floss in front of the body and, holding the floss in your right hand, bring the thread behind and over the top of the floss, securing it down with about six turns of thread.

8. Floss is now secured in place. Notice there is ample room to accommodate the thorax and that the eye is not being crowded.

9. Position the bobbin over the top of your right hand so it is out of the way. Place the *tip* of the scissors up against the hook shank and, keeping tension on the floss, make a close, clean cut.

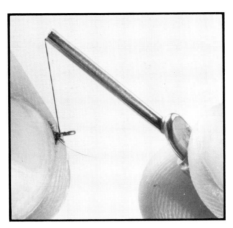

10. Dub and wrap the thorax. Notice that the thread is at the front of the thorax and that no thread has been overwrapped through the thorax. Notice that the head area is not crowded.

11. Sweep your fingers back from in front of the hook eye, encompassing all fibers and errant materials. Notice that one wild fiber still protrudes. Sweep your fingers back again and pull it out of the way, or trim it off very close to the shank.

12. A small thread head has been finished off. To give the imitation the appearance of having legs and added animation and translucence, score the thorax area with the scissors point.

13. Pick up a drop of lacquer on the *tip* of the bodkin and allow it to penetrate the thread head. Care should be taken not to lacquer the actual fly, except perhaps some wingcases.

14. Finished *Rhyacophila.*

16

Trueblood Otter

Trueblood Otter (Ted Trueblood)

This nymph was developed over 30 years ago by the late Ted Trueblood, noted Nampa, Idaho, angler, writer and conservationist, to represent scuds, freshwater shrimp, sowbugs and other underwater organisms. It has been popular ever since, often under the name Trueblood Shrimp or simply Otter nymph, and is one of only a handful of "old time" nymphs still in wide use today. Lake anglers cast it to opportunistic feeders and rely on it as a probe pattern. Stream anglers find it very useful in all types of water, especially back eddies and slower pools. The tan pattern is the most popular, but gray, brown and olive are also of value.

Backpackers descend from the Continental Divide in Wyoming to secluded lake basin.

Much of the fly's allure is due to its translucence and animation, and the great amount of light the body reflects. The standard pattern is a 50-50 mix of otter and cream goat, but muskrat and gray goat or any subtly colored fur mixed with a like color of goat will produce well. Hold one up to the light and you will notice numerous strands of somewhat coarse goat hair protruding from the softer underfur. I like to mix various colors of goat into many fur blends believing that the added translucence and animation is an important aspect of imitation.

A close variation of the Trueblood Otter is the Hare and Copper, which is identical except for the addition of heavy copper wire rib and perhaps a more robust and shaggy body. The popular Beaver is also very similar only it is traditionally tied more sparse and slender.

This pattern will facilitate your understanding of dubbing fur, securing tails and legs (beard style). It is easy to produce several of these flies in an evening.

HOOK:	Tiemco 5262, 10-16, weighted
THREAD:	Brown
TAIL:	Brown partridge
BODY:	Blend even parts of cream angora goat and otter or brown mink
LEGS:	Brown partridge tied beard style with fibers extending to bend of hook

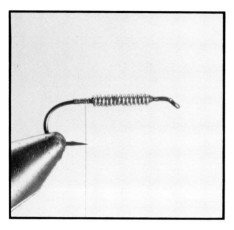

1. Secure thread, install and secure lead wire, and position thread at tail tie-in position. Thread should always be positioned at either the next tie-in or tie-off position.

2. Select a brown partridge body feather or mottled brown hen saddle feather. Select the fibers that are all about the same length and stroke or arrange them so they are at a right angle to the center stem.

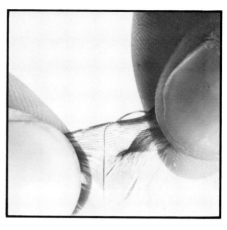

3. Grasp the *feather* tip with your right hand and the *fiber* tips, *half way* out from the stem, with your left hand. Pull or strip the fibers from the feather stem. All hackle, and/or feather fiber tails are prepared in this manner.

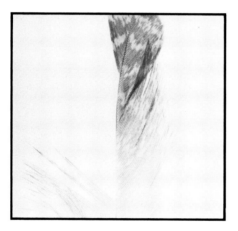

4. All the choice, well barred or mottled, and even-length fibers have been stripped from the center stem. If you desire a thicker tail, remove more fibers from the other side of the feather.

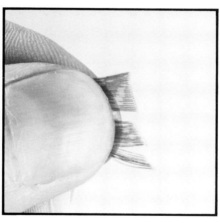

5. The unseen fiber *tips* between your fingers and the visible fiber *ends* are both even. The fiber ends should protrude from your fingers far enough to allow an easy grasp when you change hands. Don't allow the fiber tips to become uneven during the hand change.

6. The fiber tips are now held in your right hand. If the above steps are accomplished properly the tail fibers should look like this.

7. The thread should be positioned at the standard tail tie-in position. Adjust the tail length until it is in the proper position. Generally, nymph tails should be about as long as the hook gape is wide.

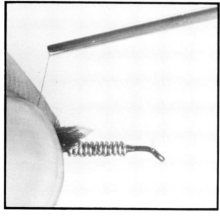

8. Without changing the position of the tail, grasp the fibers with your left hand and secure the tail with the thread-between-your-fingers technique.

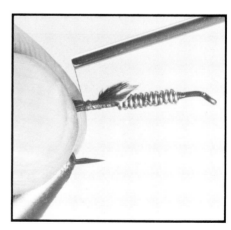

9. Once the tail has been tied in place, back off your fingers slightly and if the tail needs to be tied back more, or adjusted to either side, hold the fiber tips in position and secure exactly on top of the hook shank. There should be *no* thread showing behind the tail.

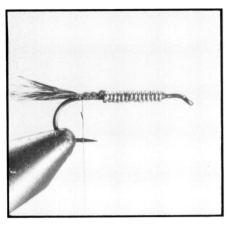

10. Tail is properly secured *behind* the lead wire. Such positioning forms an even under-body and more easily allows for construction of a properly tapered body.

11. Dub fur onto the thread and form the body. Depending upon your needs, bodies can be of various diameters, but are always tapered larger toward the front. Bodies can be wrapped front-to-back-to-front, or back-to-front as demonstrated here.

12. Finished tapered body of medium-large diameter. No thread should be visible between the tail and body, and the body should not encroach upon the hook eye. Notice the bare hook area in front of body which will eventually become the thread head.

13. Prepare another bunch of fibers like the tail. Holding the fibers in your right hand, position them along the underside of the hook so tips extend to hook point and thread is positioned *immediately* in front of the body. Some tyers like to turn the hook upside down for this tie-in.

14. Without changing the position of the legs, change hands and bring the thread *up*, catching the fibers along the underside of the hook, positioning the fibers with your thumb or first finger as needed. Secure and trim the ends.

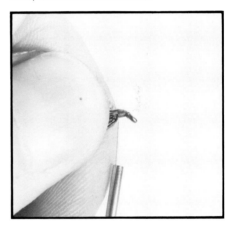

15. When legs are tied immediately in front of the body away from the hook eye, it is easy to trim off excess materials, thus making it easy to finish off a neat head. Stroke *all* fibers back out of the way when tying off the thread head.

16. Proper leg placement. Leg fibers are evenly distributed along the underside of the hook in a symmetrical arc, allowing the fly to ride properly in the water.

17. Finished Trueblood Otter.

17

Soft Hackle

Soft Hackle

The book, *The Soft Hackle Fly*, by Sylvester Nemes, brought soft hackle patterns to the attention of 20th century anglers, but the first mention of soft hackle flies dates back almost 500 years! Because the fly is so simple, it is doubtful it has evolved too terribly much in five centuries. The term soft hackle denotes many patterns tied with partridge, grouse, or soft hen hackle in conjunction with slender floss, thread, or fur bodies.

Soft hackle patterns are suggestive of many food forms, alive, bedraggled, or dead, and over the years they have become my back eddy standby. I especially favor soft hackle patterns in the Deschutes River which offers what I consider the best back eddy fishing in the west. Deschutes back eddies are numerous and range in size from tiny foam line swirls to eddies large enough to swallow a house. Back eddies can, and usually do, trap anything that happens to come within their swirling domain, including tiny nymphs, assorted debris and even boats! One back eddy of renown is referred to as "beer eddy." On holiday weekends one can usually count on finding a six-pack or two bobbing around the pool's vortex, courtesy of some unfortunate boater who picked the wrong route among the many boulders and suck holes in Whitehorse Rapids.

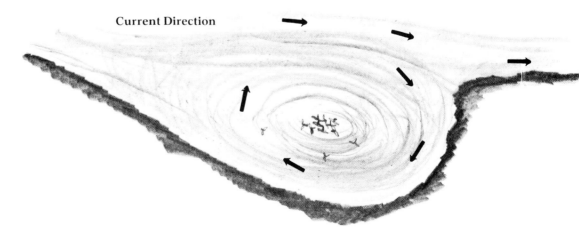

Current Direction

Back eddies flow in the opposite direction from the main current and, because fish always face upstream, should be approached accordingly.

Aerial view of middle Whitehorse rapids. Notice the huge back eddy in the upper middle of the photo.

One can only imagine how many insects become trapped, and like a revolving door, are helplessly paraded past hundreds of greedy trout. Indeed, back eddies are the smorgasbords of rivers, and much of the menu is served near the surface.

Soft hackles fish effectively in all types of water and are called upon to imitate caddis pupa, mayfly nymphs, emergers, and many other smaller, somewhat nondescript foods. They can be retrieved slowly, dead drifted, or fished as an insect rising toward the surface. Soft hackles create lots of animation and popular colors include green, olive, black, orange, and yellow floss, along with peacock and hare's ear. Soft hackles are fun and fast to tie and offer practice tying partridge legs, tied full style, and twisting floss.

HOOK:	Tiemco 5262 or 200, 10-18
THREAD:	Color to match body
BODY:	Floss or fur. Olive, green, black, orange, yellow, and brown are most useful. Fine wire or thread rib is optional, and usually omitted
THORAX:	Blended hare's ear
LEGS:	Gray or brown partridge, tied full. Soft hen hackle can also be used, color to suit

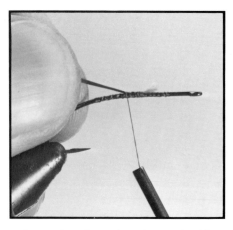

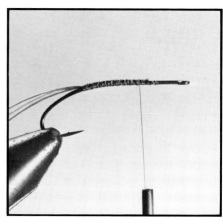

1. Secure about five inches of 3 strands of floss at the thorax area. Holding the floss over the top of the hook, wrap the thread back to the standard tail tie-in position, securing the floss. Wrap the thread forward to the thorax area.

2. Note the perfectly level underbody, or floss tie-in. If floss, and other such materials, are not secured in this manner it is usually difficult to construct a nicely tapered body.

3. Floss is spooled 4-strand. For this fly 3-strands are about right for creating the desired body diameter in relation to the hook size.

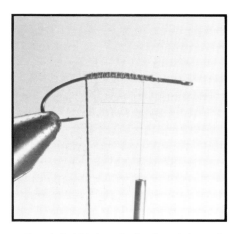

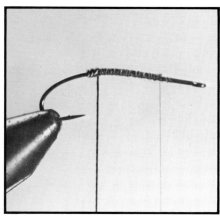

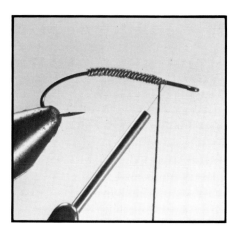

4. Floss is held below the hook and the ends are twisted together with your fingers (or hackle pliers) until it begins to kink. Twist the floss only on the ends as it becomes easily soiled and dulled.

5. Beginning of segmented, twisted floss body. Floss can be wrapped with the over-the-top and hold-it technique, or with the right hand only. With respect to the latter, each complete circle requires the bobbin to be positioned over your right hand.

6. Finished body, ready to be tied off with thread. Note the position of the thread. Thread must always be positioned in advance at the exact location materials are to be tied in place and tied off.

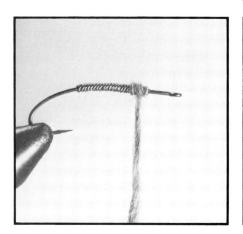

7. Fur is dubbed onto thread and the thorax is constructed. All body parts must blend together. No thread or inconsistencies should be visible.

8. Finished body and thorax. Thread is properly positioned to tie in the legs, *immediately* in front of the body, and back from the hook eye. Remember, there must be bare hook shank where the thread head will be positioned.

9. Hen saddle hackle feathers are similar to partridge body feathers, but partridge is smaller, less dense, and more difficult for beginning tyers to handle, but it creates an *excellent* effect. When tied in place, fibers should extend to hook point.

10. Hold the *extreme tip* of the feather with one hand and stroke the individual feather fibers downward with your other hand.

11. Position the feather tip as shown and tie onto the hook. Carefully note the finger position in relation to the feather tip and thread.

12. Properly secured hen saddle hackle before excess is trimmed.

13. Position the thread over the top of your hand so it is out of the way. Grab the feather tip and pull it back, *away* from the eye, and, using the *extreme* point of the scissors, make one clean cut.

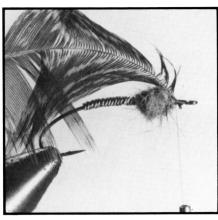

14. We are now ready to wrap the hen saddle hackle feather around the hook, forming the legs. Hackle legs are always wrapped from the back to the front, each turn *immediately* in front, if not on top, of the preceding turn. This allows for maximum fiber density in a small area.

15. The winding technique is over-the-top and hold-it.

16. After each turn it is necessary to stroke the fibers back out of the way. Notice position of the first turn; it is well back from the eye, *immediately* in front of the thorax.

17. Three turns of the feather is considered medium-heavy and will provide plenty of legs. Notice that there is still bare hook shank in front of the legs, ideal for tying a neat head. Tie off the hen hackle and finish the thread head.

18. Finished Soft Hackle.

Filoplume Mayfly

Filoplume Mayfly (Randall Kaufmann)

The Filoplume Mayfly is especially valuable when fishing small ponds and slow streams for ultra selective trout, which are best approached during hours of dim light. Usually, such locations and conditions demand a long, light leader and slow retrieve, hence a fly that casts easily, comes alive under slow motion, and attracts attention from a distance is preferred.

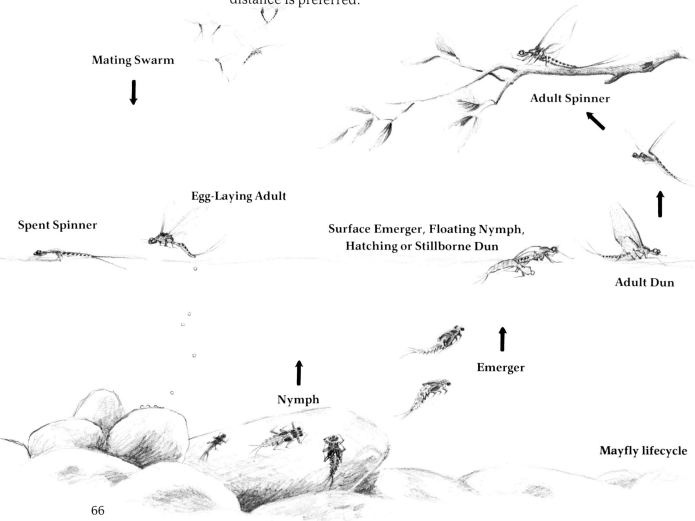

Mating Swarm

Adult Spinner

Egg-Laying Adult

Spent Spinner

Surface Emerger, Floating Nymph, Hatching or Stillborne Dun

Adult Dun

Emerger

Nymph

Mayfly lifecycle

There are times and places when *anything* will entice fish, even a bare hook, but more often than not, fish are selective. Meadow waters, such as this remote stream in Yellowstone National Park, often require near exact, animated imitations and proper presentation.

A recent addition to my fly box, the Filoplume Mayfly offers exceptional animation and is versatile enough to represent many species of mayflies. Drop this fly in a bowl of water or view it up close from underwater. It seems to be moving even when it isn't. Whenever I take the time to observe its irresistible coloring and action, I am amazed at its attractability.

From a tying aspect this is a classic nymph, purporting a tail, body, rib, wingcase and thorax. This particular style of fly is synonymous with nymph imitations. If you can tie this pattern and the following Hare's Ear you will be able to construct numerous other patterns.

I prefer to tie the Filoplume Mayfly on a Tiemco 200 hook. If you do not fall in love with this hook visually, you certainly will when you begin to fish it. The preceding patterns have covered all necessary techniques (tail, rib, body, thorax) to construct this pattern with the exception of the wingcase. This is a standard wingcase and they should usually be constructed in this manner.

HOOK:	Tiemco 200, 12-20, weight to suit
THREAD:	Color to match body
TAIL:	Marabou color to match body, tied short and full
RIB:	Copper wire
BODY:	Marabou of desired color, olive, brown, black and gray
WINGCASE:	Peacock sword fibers
THORAX:	Filoplume, color to match body

1. Secure thread on the hook and position at the thorax area. From a marabou feather, select a section of fibers in the same manner as for the Trueblood Otter tail. Marabou feathers are very soft and usually come from domestic turkeys.

2. A selected bunch of marabou fibers have been removed from the main feather. These will form the tail. Marabou will slim down to a fraction of its size when wet, so plan accordingly.

3. Pull out any loose or short fluff that will not contribute to the actual tail. Such fluff creates extra bulk and can make a mess.

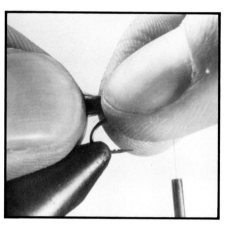

4. Tie down this clump at the thorax position and secure back to the standard tail tie-in position. The natural ends of the marabou should point backwards.

5. Because marabou is so fine and fluffy, it is difficult to gather a short dense clump. Do not trim the ends with a scissors as such ends are too abrupt and unnatural. When evened up with your fingers, marabou, unlike most other materials, is acceptable.

6. Notice tail length and level underbody. Tie in the rib material at the tail and bring the thread forward to the thorax area.

7. Select a *small* bunch of marabou and, pulling out any short fibers, tie the tips onto the hook at the thorax area. Secure the fibers on top of the hook back to the standard tail tie-in position, then bring the thread forward to the thorax area.

8. Wrap the marabou fibers around the hook, forming the body. Continue forward to the thorax area and tie off.

9. Wrap the rib through the body, tie off at the thorax area and trim off any excess body and rib material.

10. Tail, body and rib in place.

11. Depending on fly size, select 4-10 peacock sword fibers and tie fibers onto the top of the hook at the thorax area. Note that fibers are tied directly on top of the actual body. This will ensure that no interruption occurs in the transition from body to thorax.

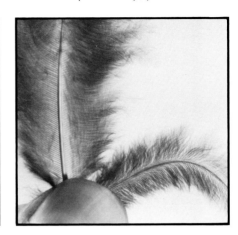

12. Filoplume feathers are secondary shafts. Some are more developed than others. Select a mature filoplume feather and tie in at rear of thorax area. Filoplume feathers are *very* fragile so care must be exercised when winding them into place.

13. The thorax should usually be of larger diameter than the body. While filoplumes fluff out when dry, they slim down remarkably when wet. To beef up the thorax, dub and wrap a little fur prior to wrapping the filoplume thorax.

14. If one filoplume is not enough to complete the thorax, tie a second feather where the first feather left off. Wrap the second filoplume feather, completing the thorax.

15. Dampen your left fingers and stroke the filoplume thorax back away from the eye and the wingcase tie-down position.

16. With your right hand, pull the wingcase over the top of the thorax. It should be pulled over tightly and pinched in place at the hook eye with your right thumb and first finger.

17. Continue holding the wingcase in position with your right hand. With your left hand, secure the wingcase in place without tying down any filoplume fibers in the head. After a couple of secure turns are in place, wrap thread with your right hand.

18. Finished Filoplume Mayfly.

19

Gold Rib Hare's Ear

Gold Rib Hare's Ear

It is difficult to pick up a fly fishing magazine or catalog and not come across the name Gold Rib Hare's Ear or Hare's Ear, as this fly is commonly referred to. The Hare's Ear is available at any fishing establishment and will be found in almost any angler's collection of nymphs. It is the most popular nymph pattern in the fly fishing world today. It can be fished anywhere, anytime, with just about any method and the angler will have a reasonable chance of hooking trout. Much of the success of the Hare's Ear is attributed to its good general imitation of mayfly nymphs, but it also passes for a host of other food sources. Over the years this fly has been so effective for me that I tailored the colors to more closely match the natural mayfly nymphs where I fished, including *Baetis*, *Ephemerella* and *Siphlonurus*. Olive was the first color variation and now there is a series of several colors which I refer to as the Kaufmann Hare's Ear. It is identical to the original pattern with the exception of the body color and I prefer heavy copper wire for the rib. Oftentimes I will tie a peacock herl or peacock sword wingcase. If this pattern is tied in five sizes (8-16) and five colors you will quickly figure that 25 flies is only one of each! One hundred assorted Hare's Ear nymphs will barely get you into the water, but they are easy to tie. I figure on tying one per minute, but be content with ten per hour after you have become proficient at handling the materials.

With respect to technique, the Hare's Ear is identical to the Filoplume Mayfly except it is tied with a dubbed body and different materials. Experience is also gained tying with flat tinsel, which is two sided-gold and silver. Both flies incorporate a tail, rib, body, wingcase, and thorax. With these and the next few patterns you will get varying perspectives of technique and mayfly imitation.

HOOK:	Tiemco 5262, 8-18, weighted
THREAD:	Brown
TAIL:	Hare's ear fur
RIB:	Oval or flat gold tinsel
BODY:	Blended hare's ear
WINGCASE:	White tip turkey tail segment
THORAX:	Blended hare's ear, picked out

1. Secure the thread, wrap the lead, and secure it in place. Notice the position of the lead. There is plenty of space behind to form a taper and it does not crowd the head. Position the thread at the exact position you intend the tail to be tied in place.

2. Trim a bunch of hare's ear from the center of the mask, which will form the tail. This fur is quite short and difficult for beginners to handle.

3. Pull out the short, dense fur, leaving a manageable bunch to secure in place. Grasp the butt ends with your right hand, then reposition your left hand on the tips and secure in place.

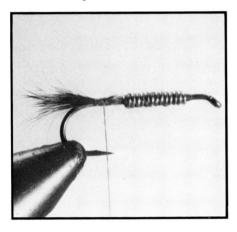

4. Notice the tail length is about the width of the hook gape and the tail has been secured *behind* the lead wire. Absolutely no tail material should be tied on top of the lead, as this makes the underbody uneven and it becomes difficult to form a tapered body.

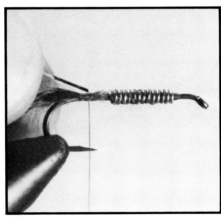

5. Select a 4-inch piece of flat tinsel, and with the gold side facing you, secure it on the opposite side of the hook. Position your fingers up close to the thread and secure in place. When the tinsel is wrapped clockwise the gold side will show.

6. Dub the fur and wrap the body, keeping a neat taper. Standard style nymphs generally have a body about 60% of the overall hook length. The thread is positioned at this point, where the rib will be tied off and the thorax tied in place.

7. Wrap the rib around the body, spacing it out and being certain it is tightly wrapped. If you can pull it off the back of the hook it is not tight. Notice the position of the bobbin as the tinsel is wrapped with the over-the-top and hold-it technique.

8. Take an extra turn of tinsel (rib) at the tie-off area and secure down with the thread. Trim off the excess close and clean. Notice that the thorax area is not being encroached upon.

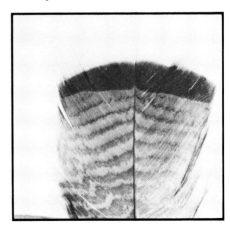

9. Shown is a white-tip turkey tail feather that has been lacquered, which will ensure against the fibers splitting during fly construction and add durability to the finished fly. Turkey is commonly used for wingcase construction.

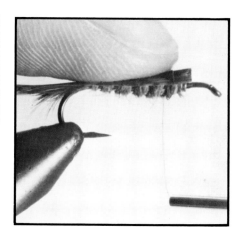

10. Trim out a section of feather, which will be used for the wingcase. Feathers such as these will be more coarse close to the center stem. Sometimes they will be too coarse to use, but the tips will be okay. Coarse fibers split more easily and have more bulk.

11. Removed section of turkey feather. The width is mostly judged by your eye as there is no consistent comparison. It is better to cut it too wide as it can always be reduced when positioned in place.

12. With your left thumb, position the wingcase feather flat over the top of the hook. Notice that the thread is loosely wrapped over the top. Now it will be pulled down tightly. Also notice that the thumb and thread are both positioned at the exact tie-in area.

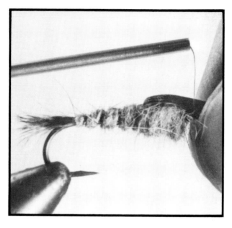

13. Properly secured wingcase feather. Notice the wingcase has been secured back to the 40% mark on the hook shank and that the head area has been left free of clutter.

14. The thorax looks like it has been wrapped back to the 50% mark, but when the wingcase is pulled forward the distance will shorten to 40%. Therefore, a turn of fur should always be taken back over the wingcase feather, ensuring continuity and proper proportion.

15. Pull the wingcase forward tightly over the top of the thorax with your right hand. I like to pinch the eye of the hook, thereby ensuring it is properly placed. Secure at extreme rear of thread head area, immediately in front of the thorax.

16. Hold the excess with one hand *away* from the hook. With your other hand, trim excess with the very *point* of the scissors, close as possible. If not done properly, It will be very difficult to form a neatly tapered head.

17. Finish off the thread head. With your bodkin, pull out the thorax fur to create the appearance of legs and help add extra animation. Pull out the fur at a cross angle to the thread wraps. Lacquer thread head.

18. Finished Gold Rib Hare's Ear.

1. Secure, or tie in, the tail and copper wire rib. Notice the tail length and thickness.

2. Dub the body, keeping it level or forming a slight taper. The thread is positioned at the rear of the thorax area.

3. Bring the copper wire through the body and, taking an extra wrap, tie it down securely. If the body was dubbed too loosely, the rib will sink into the fur and not be visible. When such is the case, stroke the fur body forward immediately in front of each turn of rib.

4. Secure in place 2-4 choice peacock fibers on top of the hook at the rear of the thorax area.

5. Dub and wrap a buggy thorax, taking an extra turn back over the top of the body beyond the peacock herl tie-down, and be careful not to crowd the head.

6. Pull the peacock fibers over the top of the thorax with your right hand and secure in place immediately in front of the thorax. Trim off the excess herl very carefully, being certain no fibers protrude into the thread head area. Finish the thread head.

7. Finished Kaufmann Hare's Ear. Once mastered, the Hare's Ear pattern is very quick to tie. Because so many color variations are possible and because it is so effective, you will almost certainly find yourself stocking several dozen in your fly boxes.

20

Matt's Fur

Stonefly

Damselfly

Mayfly

Matt's Fur (Matt Lavell)

In my tying class, I usually follow the Hare's Ear with this fly. The tying technique is the same with the addition of legs. As I so often mention, if you can tie a few patterns incorporating a variety of often used techniques, you can tie many, merely by varying materials and technique. This fly is another good example of a classic style nymph, having all the important parts, including a tail, rib, body, thorax, wingcase, and legs. The Matt's Fur is also a good example of a pattern which, depending on how it is constructed, can double for numerous food sources. The three styles of tying a Matt's Fur pictured here will give you some insight into the many possibilities. Tie it slender and perhaps vary the color and you have a damsel imitation. Bulk it up and you have a stonefly or perhaps a dragonfly. Tie it on a shorter shank hook and a mayfly nymph comes to mind. The standard pattern calls for a 50-50 mixture of otter and cream goat, but other mixes and plain hare's ear fur are also popular. I like to tie it with dyed hare's ear. Experiment a bit!

Golden trout seldom come easy. They only inhabit icy waters in high, spectacular mountain areas, mostly in California and Wyoming. Like the country they live in, they are the most beautiful of all trout.

Originally I found the Matt's Fur to be especially effective in rainbow riffles, but my most memorable experience occurred at a high rock bound lake at the head of a long canyon in the High Sierra mountains north of Bishop, California. Large golden trout were known to inhabit its lonely ice blue waters, but in two days of casting I had yet to even see one! The evening of the second day my companions decided to cook dinner and relax about camp, but I opted for one turn around the lake. Across from camp I hit a pocket of eager goldens and the Matt's Fur seemed to be just what they wanted. I stood in my original boot prints in the crusty snow and released several 1-2 pounders until the cold shadows were replaced with a numbing October chill. My companions' repeated pleas of "dinner's on" went unheeded, echoing on deaf granite spires high above the lake. Finally, after dark and back at camp I described the great action but was met with "oh sure," "how many?" They humored me through dinner but at daylight I heard the scrufflings of two anglers hopping shifting boulders down along the lake shore.

New techniques include tying divided style legs and in varying proportions.

HOOK:	Tiemco 300, 6-12, weighted
THREAD:	Brown
TAIL:	Mallard dyed woodduck
RIB:	Oval or flat gold tinsel
BODY:	Blend even parts of cream angora goat and otter or brown mink tail
WINGCASE AND LEGS:	Mallard dyed woodduck. Leftover tips of wingcase are pulled back and tied divided style along side of body or beard style underneath body. Legs should extend to hook point
THORAX:	Same as body

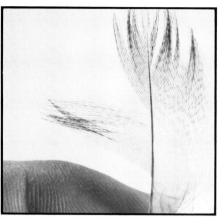

1. Select a mallard feather that has even, un-frayed tips. The smaller feathers can be used for tails and the larger feathers for wingcases.

2. Pull off the unusable fuzzy fluff at the base of the feather and mend together a bunch of fibers as shown, being certain the feather tips are the same length.

3. Grab the tips with your left hand and the feather top with your right hand. Pull the fibers *down* off the stem with your left hand.

4. The mallard fiber tail is in your left hand.

5. Grab the butt ends with your right hand.

6. Notice the fibers are all even and are held in the right hand. If more fibers are desired, re-peat the process and bunch them all together. Place tail fibers in position, measuring the proper tail length which is about the length of the hook gape.

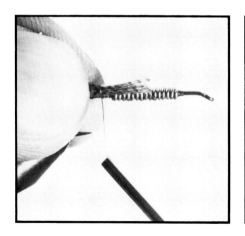

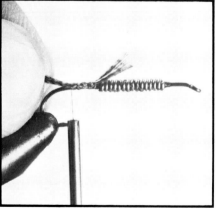

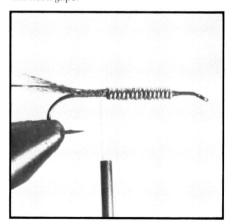

7. Change hands again, holding the tail fibers in place at the standard tail tie-in position. Using the "up between the fingers" tie-in technique, or the "in front of the finger" tie-in, as demonstrated here, secure tail in place *behind* the lead wire.

8. Hold the tail between your fingers over the top of the hook while thread is wrapped back to the extreme end of the body. Keep fibers on top of the hook shank. Notice that the tail has not been secured on top of the lead. Trim off the ex-cess butt ends of the tail close to the hook shank.

9. Secure a 3-inch piece of flat tinsel along the opposite side of the hook with the gold side facing toward you. Notice how close the excess tail fibers were trimmed off and that the tinsel was also secured behind the lead at the tail tie-in position.

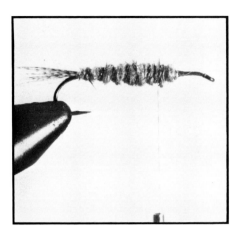

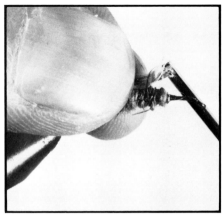

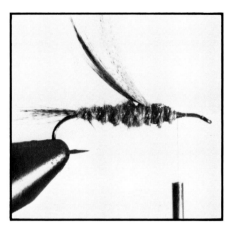

10. Dub and wrap the body, then wrap the tinsel through the body. Notice that the thread has been wrapped back over the last turn of rib and is positioned at about the standard thorax tie-in position.

11. Select a bunch of mallard fibers as you did for the tail. Hold and position them in your right hand over the top of the hook thorax area, being certain fibers extend to the end of the tail. Change hands, secure in place.

12. Wingcase properly secured in place with tips extending to the end of the tail. They should be placed exactly on top of the body and secured down to the very *rear* of the thorax area. Notice this position carefully.

13. Dub and wrap the thorax, which should be about twice the diameter of the body. Do not crowd the head. Position thread immediately in front of the thorax as shown.

14. With your right hand, pull the wingcase over the top of the thorax and hold in position as shown. Bring the thread over the top with your left hand and secure the fibers in place.

15. Wingcase secured in place. Notice that the thread head area of the hook is void of any thread. The fibers extending out the front of the hook will become the legs. They could be a little longer, but not shorter.

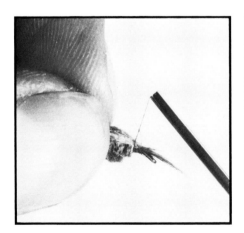

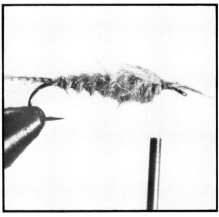

16. Pull half of the fibers back along the side of the fly and tie down with the thread.

17. Half of the fibers have been secured along one side of the fly. Repeat the process along the opposite side of the fly. The fibers should not extend beyond the hook point.

18. Finished Matt's Fur.

21

Pheasant Tail

Pheasant Tail (Al Troth)

The tiny creek slipped through a quiet New Zealand sheep pasture, hidden in a small draw from all but the most inquiring eyes. Today, as yesterday and the day before, the spring creek moved about its aquatic business undisturbed by visitors. Undisturbed, that is, until we arrived. Foreigners from America, armed with all the current high tech tackle and enough state-of-the-art flies to create our own hatch. Fortunately, nature had complied and supplied the hatch, with hundreds of tiny mayfly duns gliding the slick currents, eventually lifting off and disappearing into the tangle of vegetation so common along such waterways. Not a trout was seen feeding on the surface bonanza, but creeping close and peering through the canopy of brush revealed 16-22 inch rainbows feeding wildly on rising nymphs. The water was glass smooth and equally clear. I was so close that I could see individual nymphs and watch as trout grabbed them!

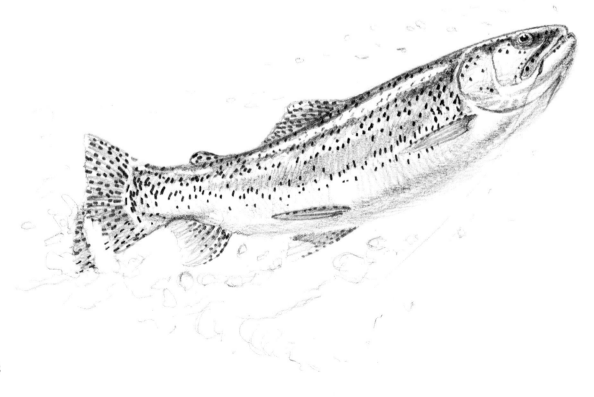

Duane Grayson about to land and release a beautiful rainbow from an unnamed spring creek in New Zealand.

After a careful survey of the situation it was determined the fish were best approached from downstream, but it would only be possible to lead them by the length of the tippet. A longer cast showing a leader knot would spook them. The fly would need to sink to a depth of 2-3 feet and be lifting up from the bottom when it approached the fish. A size 16 heavily weighted Pheasant Tail was knotted on. The cast was, luckily, right on, the drift deep and the take easy. Instantly, upon feeling the resistance, the 18-inch rainbow bolted into the air higher than my head, not once but three times! It was no disappointment when the tiny hook tore loose. There would be more feeders mistaking the Pheasant Tail for something edible.

My research has revealed that English tyer Frank Sawyer is credited with tying the original Pheasant Tail, but this particular version is from master Montana angler and ace tyer, Al Troth. Al is one of the most exacting tyers to ever bend a feather and my mounted and framed collection of his beautiful flies always attracts rave reviews. Al currently rates the Pheasant Tail his best selling subsurface fly. It is certainly a good representation of *Ephemerella* mayfly nymphs. Personally, I carry over 100 of these in my fly boxes. You are probably wondering how any sane angler can use 100 flies of a pattern, especially after I have already suggested you have 100 Hare's Ears? Easy. First, there are probably no sane angler-tyers. Second, you will never *use* them all, but not using some is better than not having any when you need one. If you have four colors in six sizes with some weighted light, medium and heavy, you will only have one or two of each style, which means your selection is minimal at best. You'd better get another fly box and start filling it up. Besides, collecting and tying is great fun!

The Pheasant Tail is a perfect follow up to the Matt's Fur. The tying techniques are identical but the materials change.

HOOK:	Tiemco 5262 or 200, 10-18, weight to suit
THREAD:	Brown
TAIL:	Ringneck pheasant tail fibers
RIB:	Gold wire
BODY:	Same as tail
WINGCASE AND LEGS:	Same as tail. Leftover wingcase tips are tied divided style
THORAX:	Peacock

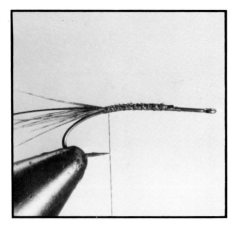

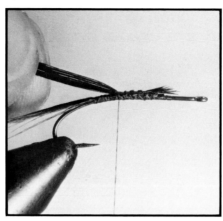

1. Tie in the tail and copper wire rib. Tails should usually be as long as the hook gape is wide, but some nymphs, especially mayflies, may require a longer tail.

2. Position thread at thorax area and tie in a small clump of pheasant tail fibers by the tips. Wrap the thread back, tying down the tail to the standard tail tie-in position. Wrap the thread forward to the thorax area.

3. Wrap the pheasant tail fibers around the hook, forming the body, and tie off at thorax area. Bring the rib through the body and tie off. Trim off pheasant and wire rib excess.

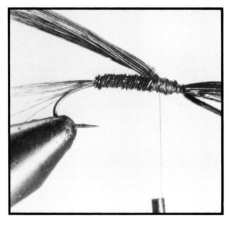

4. Tie in a fair-sized bunch of pheasant tail fibers by the butt ends. When tied in place, the fiber tips should extend about to the end of the tail. This distance is critical because the tips will ultimately form the legs.

5. Tie in one or two peacock herls at the rear of the thorax area and wrap them to the front, forming the thorax. Tie off and wrap thread through thorax. This reinforces the fragile peacock.

6. Pull the pheasant fibers over the top of the peacock thorax, forming the wingcase. Secure in place at the extreme rear of the thread head area.

7. Divide the pheasant tail tips, pull half of the fibers back and secure along one side of the fly. If the original tie-in length of the wingcase was not judged properly the legs will not be the proper length.

8. Legs secured in place. Next, secure the remaining pheasant tail fibers back along the opposite side of the fly and finish off a neat, tapered head.

9. Finished Pheasant Tail.

22

Emergent Sparkle Pupa

Emergent Sparkle Pupa (Gary LaFontaine)

Under laboratory and field conditions, Gary LaFontaine, noted Montana angler-author, concluded that the most realistic portrayal of the important pupa stage of caddisflies is best imitated with Antron yarn. Antron yarn is three sided, highly reflective, and individual fibers do not cling together. This means that each and every fiber retains an air space around it. Air bubbles clustered around a fly make it both an attractor and imitator.

But, the correct pattern alone is not enough to consistently fool trout. The fly must also react and be presented in a natural manner. Until recently, the general belief was that trout chased ascending caddis pupa and caught them mid current.

From underwater observations, Gary learned that the ascent is not one rapid movement and that trout do not chase pupa. There are two moments of feeding activity on the pupa. First, when the pupa initially cuts itself free of the cocoon and drifts along the stream bottom, and second, just subsurface where the pupa hangs on the underside of the surface film as it struggles to split and shed its pupal shuck.

In order to capitalize upon these two points of vulnerability, Gary devised the Emergent Sparkle Pupa and the Deep Sparkle Pupa.

The pattern recipe for the Deep Sparkle Pupa, Diving Caddis, and Caddis Larva is listed in the pattern directory. Those anglers interested in more caddisfly insight and fishing strategy should read Gary's award winning book, *Caddisflies.*

New techniques include construction of an overbody and installing a deer hair downwing. Hair incorporated into tails and wings should be cleaned and "stacked," or evened up, with natural tips all being a uniform length. The specialized method described to weight this fly helps it ride right side up.

HOOK:	Tiemco 200, 12-20
THREAD:	Brown
OVERBODY:	Strands of rust or gold Antron yarn tied in at end of body and pulled forward somewhat loosely around body and tied off at head
BODY:	Blend 1/2 rust or gold Antron yarn and 1/2 brown fur
WING:	Light deer hair tied sparse and extending to bend of hook
HEAD:	Brown marabou or brown fur

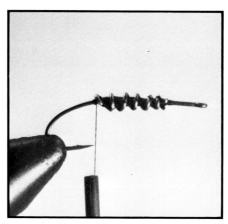

1. Secure a strip of lead along the underside of the hook, positioning it about in the center of the shank.

2. Wrap the lead forward, spacing it out, unless a very heavy fly is desired. As the lead is wrapped forward, it might be necessary to hold the under-strip of lead in place. The under-strip helps the fly ride right side up.

3. Cut a 2 or 3-inch piece of 4-strand Antron yarn and carefully unravel it. Each of the four strands will be tied onto the hook, one on the top, bottom, and each side. Dub and wrap some fur, creating a tapered underbody.

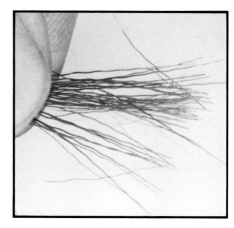

4. Dub and wrap the body.

5. Pull one strand forward loosely over the top of the body with your right hand. Change hands and secure in place. Repeat, tying all 4-strands so they completely encompass the body. One strand will be over the top, another along the underside, and one along each side.

6. Select a bunch of well barred deer hair fibers. Hold by the *tips* and pull out *all* the loose underfur and short fibers.

7. Properly prepared hair with all underfur and short fibers removed. This quantity of fibers is okay for small flies, but use more for larger flies.

8. Place the *natural* tips into the bottom of the stacker.

9. Place your fingers over the top of the stacker, and holding the bottom in place, tap it on a hard surface. Moose fibers stack with one or two taps. Properly prepared, small bunches of deer will stack in about half a dozen taps. The thicker the bunch, the more taps are required.

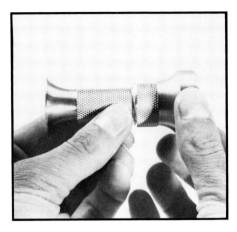

10. Hold the stacker in a horizontal position with the closed end pointing slightly up. The even, or stacked, tips are at this end and they should not be allowed to slip backwards or fall out the front when the closed end is removed.

11. Slowly remove the closed end of the stacker and grab the even tips with your right hand. With your left hand, grab the uneven butt ends and pull out any short fibers with your right hand.

12. Now, grab the even tips with your right hand, and the center section of fibers with your left hand. Release your right hand, and grab the trimmed butt ends with your right hand. You are now ready to position the fibers over the top of the body with your right hand.

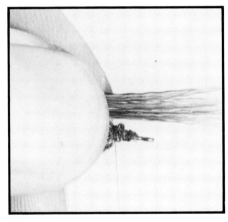

13. Change hands and secure in place. Notice the position of the thread in relation to the finger tips. A loose turn over the top and a tight downward pull of the thread will secure the fibers in place, or use the thread-between-the fingers tie-down technique.

14. Wing secured in place. A half dozen turns properly placed should be plenty. Notice that the wing has been secured immediately in front of the body and that it does not extend beyond the body.

15. Excess wing ends have been trimmed. Notice that there is an abrupt drop in front of the wing. Either build this area up with thread or a little fur, creating the proper foundation for the head.

16. Tie in a few marabou or ostrich fibers by the tips and trim off any excess.

17. Twist the fibers (often referred to as flues) together and wrap over the thread area, forming the head. Tie off, trim excess and finish off a neat thread head.

18. Finished Emergent Sparkle Pupa.

23

Green Drake

Formerly classified as *Ephemerella grandis*, this mayfly is now known as *Drunella grandis*. This change has caused some confusion, with *Ephemerella* and *Drunella* references being used interchangeably.

Green Drake (Mike Lawson)

The Green Drake, or *Ephemerella grandis* hatch excites trout and anglers like few other western hatches. The insect is large and very beautiful. Adults produce about two weeks of angling, but nymphing is good much longer. Most trout waters throughout western America offer Green Drakes, including Oregon's Metolius and Deschutes Rivers, but the Yellowstone area offers the strongest hatches, with Henry's Fork hosting the most angler attendance.

Green Drakes begin hatching on Idaho's Henry's Fork the latter part of June and I have experienced very strong hatches on the upper Yellowstone in mid July. Fred Arbona, writing in *Mayflies, the Angler and the Trout*, reports that the most impressive hatches seem to occur during the coldest, darkest days between the hours of one to four o'clock in the afternoon.

Anglers who plan on fishing this hatch should be aware that Green Drakes are somewhat slow and clumsy in emerging, hence this stage can offer very fine angling. The Green Drake Emerger, also developed by Mike Lawson, Henry's Fork angling authority, and the Surface Emerger, developed by Idaho angler-artist Rene Harrop, can produce phenomenal surface takes just prior to and during the hatch. The Floating Mayfly, described later, in the proper size and color can also entice surface takes.

This pattern incorporates legs tied half circle, plus other techniques previously discussed. The natural insect is somewhat robust, and imitations should be tied accordingly.

HOOK:	Tiemco 5262, 10-12, weighted
THREAD:	Olive
TAIL:	Mallard dyed wodduck
RIB:	Fine copper wire
BODY:	Blended hare's ear with slight amounts of dyed gold and olive hare's ear
WINGCASE:	White tip turkey tail segment
THORAX:	Same as body
LEGS:	Brown partridge, tied half circle or beard style

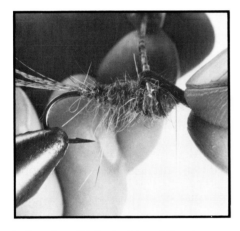

1. Secure lead wire, tail and rib material in that order. Dub and wrap the body, then wrap the rib over, or around the body. Tie off the rib.

2. Select a section of lacquered turkey in the same manner as described for tying the Gold Rib Hare's Ear and secure it over the top and at the rear of the thorax area. Note that the wingcase is positioned at about the 40% mark slightly over the body.

3. Dub and wrap the thorax, remembering to create a taper and leaving plenty of room at the head.

4. Sometimes it is best not to pull the wingcase tightly over the thorax. To leave a little space and give the appearance of a "folded" wingcase, fold the pre-lacquered wingcase over the bodkin. With your right hand, pinch the wingcase at the eye, holding it in place.

5. Remove the bodkin and continue holding the wingcase in position with your right hand. Note the thread position. It is immediately in front of the thorax at the rear of the thread head area.

6. Secure the wingcase in place and trim off all excess.

7. Select a brown partridge feather or hen saddle and secure at the rear of the thread head area, as explained in tying the Soft Hackle. Trim off the excess protruding from the front of the fly.

8. Wrap the feather 2-3 turns, tie off and trim excess. Stroke all feather fibers *back and down* alongside the fly so there are no fibers extending over the top of the fly. Secure in place. This will create a half circle effect of legs.

9. Finished Green Drake.

The Yellowstone River supports numerous aquatic insects, including *Ephemerella grandis* and *Ephemerella infrequens*.

24

Pale Morning Dun

Pale Morning Dun (Ernest Schwiebert)

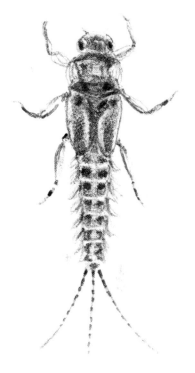

The Pale Morning Dun, so named because of its pale yellow colors and time of emergence, is the common name associated with the mayfly *Ephemerella infrequens*, a widespread western specie that provides much enjoyable angling throughout the early and mid summer months. Many anglers confuse *infrequens* with other *Ephemerella* and, as imitations, all but the most selective feeders will be fooled. Provided you have stationed yourself in an area offering slower water and weed beds, nymphs usually produce well for about two hours beginning in the morning. A dead drift technique produces the best action and it is usually best to begin fishing a weighted imitation around bottom debris. Emergers and duns follow an hour or two later.

There are many Pale Morning Dun imitations, but this particular pattern comes from the book *Nymphs*, by Ernest Schwiebert, a genius of the sport and certainly one of the most knowledgeable anglers of our time. All students of the sport should read *all* of his books. This pattern was selected for its gill and over the thorax leg application. It should be remembered that, unlike any other aquatic insect, mayfly nymphs have wavy filament gills along their abdominal (body) segments and any imitation can be so adapted. Marabou, ostrich, filoplume and other soft feathers produce the desired effect.

HOOK:	Tiemco 5262, 12-14, weight to suit
THREAD:	Brown
TAIL:	Mallard dyed woodduck
RIB:	Gold wire
GILLS:	Brownish amber marabou (color with Pantone pen)
BODY:	Amber-brown fur
WINGCASE:	Brown turkey tail
LEGS:	Pale brown partridge, pulled over thorax
THORAX:	Amber-brown fur

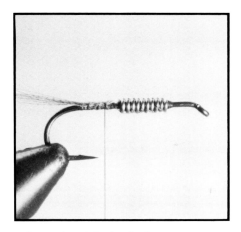

1. Secure thread, lead and tail.

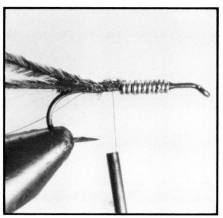

2. Secure wire rib and two ostrich herls, positioning one on each side of the hook. These will form the gills. Remember to tie all materials onto the hook *behind* the lead wire, not on top of it.

3. Dub and wrap the body. Next, pull one ostrich herl along one side of the body and tie off at the thorax area. Repeat the process with the other herl.

4. Wrap the rib through the body and gills. Be careful not to tie down too many of the gill fibers and keep the gills positioned along each side of the body. Pick out gill fibers with the bodkin if necessary. Tie off rib at thorax area.

5. Tie in a section of lacquered turkey quill at the rear of the thorax, which will form the wingcase.

6. Prepare, as shown, a partridge body feather or hen saddle feather. Be certain to select a feather with the proper width fibers, about the length of the body.

7. Secure at the rear, and on top, of the thorax. Feather should be tied flat over the top of the body, not on its side.

8. Dub and build up the thorax.

9. With your right hand, pull the hen feather over the top of the thorax. You will want to incorporate as many of the fibers as possible so stroke them back as shown. Carefully note this photo.

10. Before releasing your right hand, grab the feather with your left hand, encompassing all fibers and securing in place. Once a couple of turns are in place, remove your fingers and, if need be, reposition the legs in place.

11. Top view of "over-the-thorax" leg placement.

12. With your right hand, bring the wingcase over the thorax and legs. Carefully notice the thread position in relation to the eye and the space available to complete the head.

13. Tie down wingcase, trim off excess and finish the thread head.

14. Finished Pale Morning Dun.

25

Gray Drake Wiggle

Gray Drake Wiggle (Fred Arbona)

The Gray Drake, or *Siphlonurus occidentalis*, is one of the most unusual mayflies anglers are likely to encounter. In its nymphal form, it looks and acts somewhat like a minnow, being streamlined in appearance and very animated. Just prior to hatching into an adult, nymphs literally crawl out of the water before the dun emerges, much like a stonefly. Because the Gray Drake crawls out of the water in preparation for emergence, they are especially vulnerable to foraging trout along shallow, shoreline areas.

Fishing a wiggling imitation with a darting motion is very effective. In order to more effectively capitalize upon this angling bonanza, Idaho angler-author Fred Arbona, Jr. designed the wiggle nymph series. This style of imitation best duplicates the wobbling, side-to-side swimming or burrowing action characteristic of many mayfly nymphs. Fred spends a great deal of time pursuing hard fished trout in the Sun Valley, Idaho, area, and claims refusals to the wiggle series are usually the exception.

Gray Drakes do not occur in all waters, but where they do, populations are usually moderately dense. Slow, weedy, nutrient-rich waters of western America shelter major populations, including the Big Hole, Yellowstone, Bitterroot, South Platte, Snake, Big Wood and Hat Creek. Many western lake waters also provide excellent angling during migrations of Gray Drakes. Nymphs become active in the morning and adults begin hatching by early noon. August and September are the prime months. Anglers interested in learning more about Gray Drakes and the other three oversized mayfly species indigenous to the American west should read Fred Arbona's excellent book, *Mayflies, the Angler and the Trout.*

HOOK:	Tiemco 5262, 12
THREAD:	Gray
PLANER:	Clear plastic trimmed from a coffee can lid
TAIL:	Three dark moose fibers, 1-1/2 length of hook shank
EXTENDED BODY:	Gray dun ostrich herl
WINGCASE:	Gray goose wing quill section
BODY:	Gray dun ostrich herl

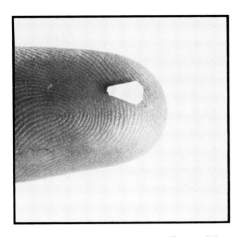

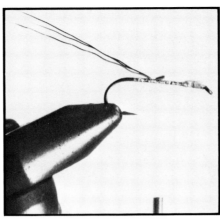

1. Trim a piece of plastic from a coffee can lid as shown and secure on top of hook, immediately behind the hook eye. Half of this piece will protrude out the front of the fly, the other half will be secured down. Insert a slight groove in the plastic for easier tie down.

2. Secure three dark moose fibers for the tail perpendicular to the hook point. The fibers should be even and extend about 1½ times the hook length.

3. At the same position, secure three thick ostrich herls by their tips. Most feathers, herls, etc., have a natural taper to them, wide at the base, narrower at the tips. A tip first tie-in helps ensure a nice taper.

4. A third hand is nice for this next step, otherwise . . . hold the moose and ostrich at the end of the tail with your left hand. With your right hand, wrap the thread around the tail fibers and ostrich back to about the halfway point along the tail. Don't let go of the tail with your left hand.

5. Wrap the thread forward onto the hook shank, positioning it at the original tail tie-in position.

6. Hold the end of the tail with your left hand and wrap the ostrich forward over the extended tail and onto the hook. This is awkward but possible. Again, a third hand would be nice. Trim off the excess ostrich.

7. Secure a section of goose wing quill perpendicular to the hook point by the tips. Build up a fur underbody if needed. Next, secure three ostrich herls by the tips, twist them together, and wrap forward around the hook, forming the body.

8. Once the ostrich herl body is formed, pull the goose segment forward over the top of the body, forming the wingcase. Secure in place and trim off the excess.

9. Finished Gray Drake Wiggle.

26

Peacock

Picture this page as a section of peacock quill (herl). The herl would only cover half the page. Inspect a quill carefully and you will notice that the actual herl only extends from one side of the quill. The bare portion should precede the herl portion when it is being wrapped around the hook. Also, carefully inspect the top and bottom of the quill, as one side will offer longer herl. Often two or more herls will be required to provide the desired hook coverage.

Peacock

Peacock has been a long time favorite tying material. Its iridescent, metallic colors and soft, buggy characteristics make it very attractive to both fish and fisherman.

Peacock should be purchased by the complete tail and only the choice herl should be considered. Examine the herl along the complete tail and you will see the thick, wide herl begins immediately below the "eye" and extends for about four inches.

Peacock herl only grows on one side of a flat quill or stem. To construct a juicy looking body it is imperative that the smooth, herl-less side of the quill precede the herl side as you wrap it around the hook. If not, then succeeding wraps of bare quill will over-wrap or cover the preceding turns of thick peacock. Two, three and even four herls may be tied at once, but they must all be properly aligned. Sometimes it may be necessary to build up a fur underbody in order to construct a proper diameter peacock body. This is especially true when tying on a long shank hook.

Peacock herls have a *slight* taper from tip to butt and when two or more *choice* herls are used they can be tied in tip first. The resulting body is very nice and quick to construct, but not as thick as tying herl in at the butt.

Peacock herl is extremely fragile and should always be over-wrapped with thread or fine wire.

Peacock sword are the shorter, narrower and more metallic uneyed tails. Nymph tyers mostly use sword for tails, such as on the Zug Bug, or for wingcases, as seen on the Filoplume Mayfly.

1. Select and secure one to three choice peacock herls at the rear of the hook. Herls must be positioned so the unherled portion of the quill precedes the herled portion when wrapped.

2. Dub and wrap a fur underbody, creating the desired taper.

3. Wrap the peacock forward, forming the body. Wrap all herls at once, but do not allow them to spread away from each other. Hold them together with your fingers close to the hook shank. Reinforce peacock with wire, thread, etc.

4. A peacock body that did not have an underbody and herls were not positioned properly. Remember to use only the choice herls, which are located two-to-four inches *directly below* the peacock eye. Strung peacock herl should not be used for body construction.

Peacock sword   **Peacock eyed tail**

27

Zug Bug

Zug Bug (Cliff Zug)

The Zug Bug is definitely a flashy fly and when the fly box is opened it seems to almost jump to life saying, "pick me, pick me!" I often have a difficult time not selecting one and whether I do or not, they will at least get a nodding glance and consideration. As a youngster when fishing unfamiliar alpine lakes or riffled Montana and California streams, I would always count on the Zug Bug to entice a few fish. Over the years it has remained, if not commanded, an important niche in my fly box and I still look forward to viewing its regal and beautiful iridescent colors.

Today the Zug Bug is very popular with lake and stream anglers, being suggestive of many food forms. It is available from most outlets and commonly fished in size 10 to 14. Rick Hafele and Dave Hughes, in their excellent book, *Western Hatches*, recommend it as a pattern for *Rhyacophila* caddis larvae. Tie up a dozen of assorted sizes and give them a cast or two.

Many of the peacock tying techniques previously discussed can be put into practice on the Zug Bug. The "wing" actually represents a wingcase. Most commercial flies will have a trimmed wingcase but if you arrange the mallard feathers so they do not need trimming the wingcase will look more professional and natural. Remember to wrap the peacock and tinsel rib tightly as such bodies slip and slide off the back of the hook very easily.

HOOK:	Tiemco 5262, 10-14, weighted
THREAD:	Black
TAIL:	Peacock sword, 3-6 fibers
RIB:	Silver tinsel
BODY:	Peacock (build up underbody if desired)
LEGS:	Brown or furnace hackle, tied beard style or half circle
WING:	Mallard dyed woodduck, extending 1/3 length of body (represents wingcase)

1. Select a few peacock sword fibers, even up the ends, and holding them in your right hand, place them over the hook so the tail extends the desired distance beyond the hook. Again, by tying in the tail beginning at the front of the hook the underbody remains level.

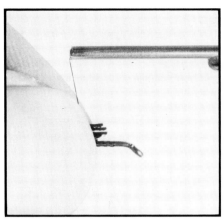

2. Grab the tail with your left hand, bring the thread up between your fingers and tie the tail down by wrapping the thread back to the standard tail tie-in position.

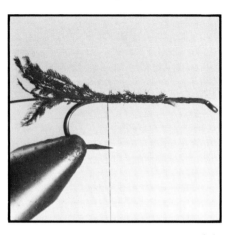

3. Tie in the flat tinsel on the far side of the hook with the silver side facing you. The silver side will show when you begin wrapping it clockwise.

4. Build up a fur underbody so the ensuing peacock body will have some bulk and a nice taper.

5. Depending on the fly size, tie in 1-4 thick peacock herls and wrap the thread to the front of the hook where the peacock will be tied off.

6. Wrap the peacock toward the front of the hook, keeping it tight. It is best to grab the peacock close to the hook shank each time you come around the hook, as this helps keep the individual herls from separating.

7. Wrap the flat tinsel rib up to the front. Tinsel is notorious for slipping off the back of the hook. Be absolutely certain it is wrapped tightly from the start, and is tied off securely.

8. Tail, body and rib complete. Notice the nice taper, evenly spaced rib and forward position of the body.

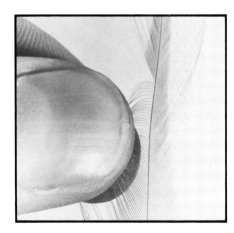

9. Pictured is a rooster saddle hackle. Hold the feather tip with your right hand and with your left hand, grab and strip off a suitable bunch of fibers that will become beard-style legs. (See Trueblood Otter.)

10. With your right hand, place the selected bunch of hackle fibers along the underside of the hook, making certain the fibers do not extend beyond the hook point.

11. Change hand positions, holding the fibers on the underside of the hook with your left hand. Secure in position with thread and trim off the excess.

12. Notice the position of the thread-bobbin, the butt-ends to be trimmed, and the point of the scissors.

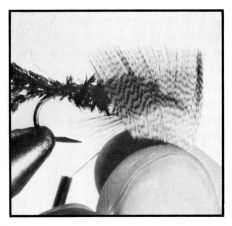

13. Select a mallard feather with fairly even tips. Strip off any short and flimsy fibers from the center stem.

14. Stroke the feather fibers together.

15. Place on top of hook at rear area of head with your right hand. Keep the wingcase (wings) short, about 1/3 the body length.

16. Change hands. The tip of your thumb should be *exactly* where you plan to place the thread tie-down wraps at the rear of the thread head. Don't allow the wingcase to roll to one side. Secure, trim ends, and stroking all the tiny peacock fibers back, finish off the thread head.

17. Finished Zug Bug.

All Purpose
(light)

All Purpose
(medium)

All Purpose
(dark)

A.P. Black

Assam Dragon

Baetis

Beaver

Bitch Creek

Black Drake

Black Hellgrammite

Black Martinez

Blue Quill

Blue Wing Olive

Breadcrust

Brook's Stone

Brown Bomber

Brown Drake

Caddis Larva

Caddis Pupa

Carey Special

Carrot

Cased Caddis

Casual Dress

Cate's Turkey

Catskill Canadensis

Catskill March Brown

Chironomid Pupa

Crayfish

Cream Variant

Dark Caddis Emergent

Dark Hendrickson

Dave's Red Squirrel

Deep Sparkle Pupa

Diving Caddis

Dun Variant

Early Black

Emergent Sparkle Pupa

Emerger

Emerging Callibaetis

Ephemerella

Filoplume Damselfly

Filoplume Dragonfly

Filoplume Leech

Filoplume Mayfly

Fledermouse

Floating Caddis Pupa

Floating Dragon

Floating Mayfly

Gammarus-Hyalella Scud

Golden Stone (Troth)

Golden Stone (Rosborough)

Gold Rib Hare's Ear

Gray

Gray Drake Wiggle

Great Leadwing Drake

Green Drake

Green Drake Emerger

Hairy Brown Leech

Hare and Copper

Hellgrammite

Hendrickson

Hendrickson Emerger

Hendrickson Wiggle

Kaufmann Hare's Ear

Kaufmann Stone

Kemp Bug

Lake Dragon

Latex Caddis Pupa

Leib's Bug

Light Cahill

Lingren's Olive

Little Green Caddis

Marabou

Marabou Damsel

Marabou Leech

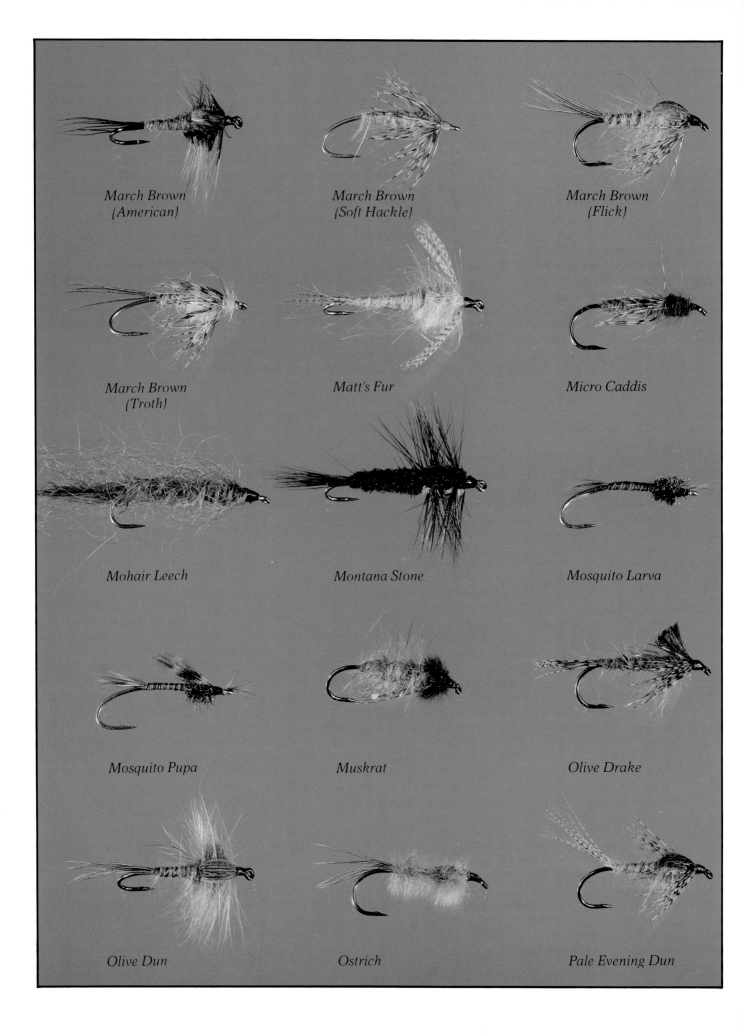

March Brown
(American)

March Brown
(Soft Hackle)

March Brown
(Flick)

March Brown
(Troth)

Matt's Fur

Micro Caddis

Mohair Leech

Montana Stone

Mosquito Larva

Mosquito Pupa

Muskrat

Olive Drake

Olive Dun

Ostrich

Pale Evening Dun

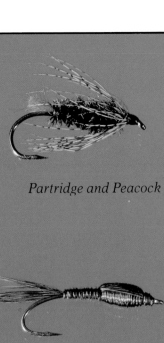

Partridge and Peacock

Peacock Matt's Fur

Peeking Caddis

*Pheasant Tail
(Sawyer)*

*Pheasant Tail
(Troth)*

Prince

Quill Gordon

Randall's Caddis

Randall's Caddis Pupa

Red Brown

Rhyacophila

Rubber Legs

Rubber Legs Brown Stone

Simulator

Siphlonurus

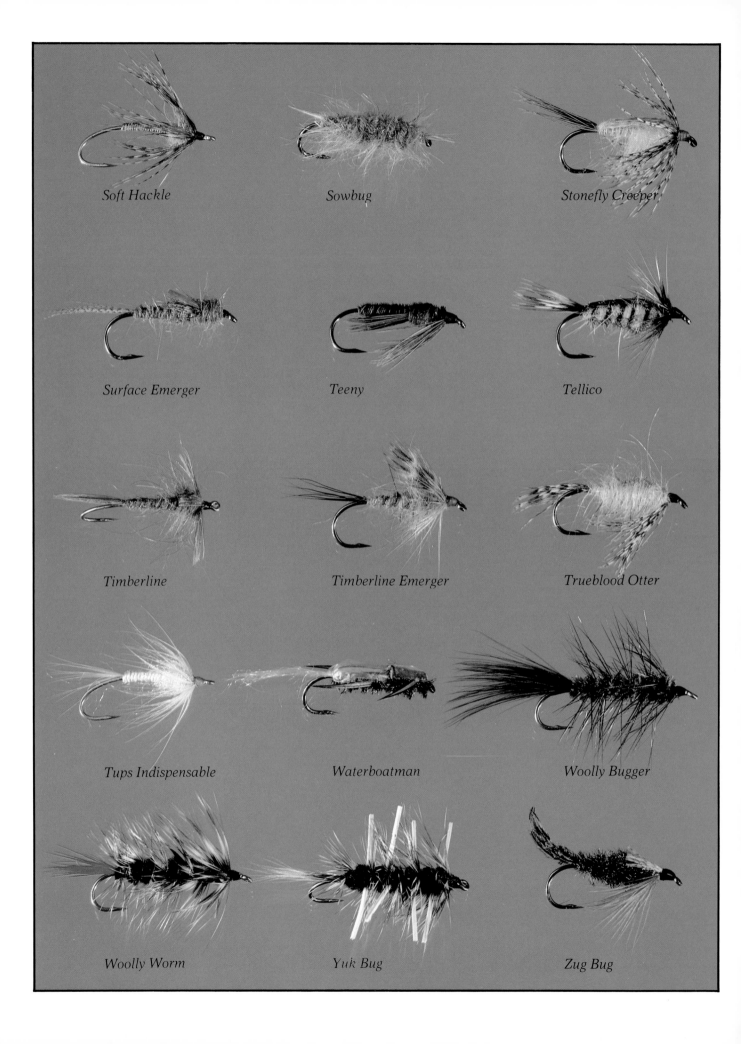

Soft Hackle

Sowbug

Stonefly Creeper

Surface Emerger

Teeny

Tellico

Timberline

Timberline Emerger

Trueblood Otter

Tups Indispensable

Waterboatman

Woolly Bugger

Woolly Worm

Yuk Bug

Zug Bug

28

Gammarus-Hyalella Scud

Gammarus-Hyalella Scud (Randall Kaufmann)

In the not too distant past, anglers would fish their entire life without ever investigating the revealing and fascinating subaquatic environs. Casual observation was, for the most part, casually avoided. The pace of innovation moved at the speed of the geologic time clock. It was not until the mid '60s that anglers began investigating and questioning old truths and rearranging the experimental basis from which all gospel angling facts evolved.

I would be embarrassed to admit how many times I cast a "shrimp" pattern, not really knowing what freshwater shrimp looked like or if they even existed where I was fishing.

It was only out of sheer frustration that I got my first look at scuds in the wild. The Glacier Divide in Humphrey's Basin outside of Bishop, California, cast its cold morning shadow over our bleak 11,000 foot high campsite. Arising early and scavenging the lake area for wood (there were not enough campers to deplete scant wood supplies even slightly above timberline 20 years ago), I noticed several 12-inch goldens feeding along shoreline shallows. After an hour of fruitless casting, the sun emerged bright and warm and the brilliantly colored fish suddenly faded into the icy depths. Frustrated, I waded barefoot into the numbing water in an effort to discover what food had summoned the goldens to breakfast. I soon found hundreds of pale olive scuds, about a size 16. It would be many years before I learned to equate healthy scud populations with obese trout and shallow shaded areas with scuds, but just poking below the water was a start. The creature I had observed certainly did not resemble the flies I had been tying and fishing, but I had plenty of ideas for the next outing.

Taxonomically, scuds, shrimp, sowbugs and crayfish are not "nymphs," but Crustaceans. They do not undergo a transformation from larva to pupa to winged adult. Scuds belong to the Order Crustacea and the Suborder Amphipoda. There are several genera, of which *Hyalella* and *Gammarus* are the most important to trout anglers. *Gammarus* are the largest but *Hyalella* are the most widespread.

This current scud pattern has undergone many refinements over the years and will undergo more. I am currently experimenting with a marabou tail and antenna and filoplume bodies. Whichever pattern you

Prolific Scud populations produce oversize rainbow for the few intrepid anglers lucky enough to visit this beautiful lake near Yosemite National Park.

decide to stock in your fly boxes, consider tying a color selection of olive, gray, tan and combinations thereof. Best sizes are 10 to 16 but a few 8 and 18 should also be available. New techniques demonstrated include a back, antennae and the picking out of dubbing to simulate legs and gills.

HOOK:	Tiemco 200 or 5262, 10-18 weighted
THREAD:	Color to match body
TAIL:	Hackle fibers, tied short, color to match body
ANTENNAE:	Same as tail
BACK:	Heavy mil plastic strip
RIB:	Clear monofilament, .006-.007 diameter
BODY:	Blend of angora goat and Hairtron. Best color combinations are olive-gray, tannish-gray, yellow-olive, brown-olive and gray-gray

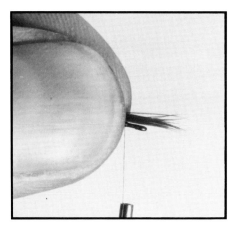

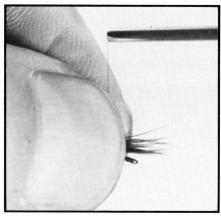

1. Select a bunch of olive hackle fibers in the same manner tail fibers were selected for the Zug Bug legs. The antennae look like a tail, only the fibers face out the front of the hook.

2. Secure antennae in place by bringing the thread up between your fingers.

3. If the antennae roll to one side, simply reposition them and secure. Notice the slight space between the eyes and where the antennae are tied in. Depending on body positioning, the head can be placed here, or in front of the antennae.

4. Tie the antennae ends down on top of the hook shank.

5. Trim off excess ends, nice and neatly. Notice how even and smooth the tie-down is.

6. Beginning where the antennae leaves off, secure the tail. It is desirable for the Scud to have a *slight* curve to the body, so secure the tail a *little* beyond where you normally would.

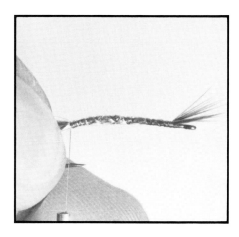

7. Notice the tail and antennae length and the even underbody.

8. Cut a 2-inch strip of heavy mil plastic (the type fly tying materials are packaged in) about 1/8- to 1/4-inch wide.

9. Secure plastic strip and monofilament rib.

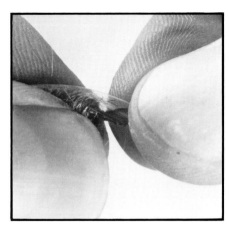

10. Dub and wrap the body, being certain to wrap extra dubbing in the thorax area. Because the body will need to be picked out it is best not to dub the body too tightly.

11. With your right hand, bring the plastic over the top of the body, forming the "back." The back should fold down slightly over the side of the body.

12. Stroke all fibers away from the tie-down area and secure the back.

13. The Scud is now ready to be ribbed.

14. The monofilament rib has a tendency to catch and bind body fibers over the top of the plastic back and to roll, or push, the plastic off to one side. To avoid this, pull fibers down out of the way and hold the plastic in the proper position.

15. Monofilament can be difficult to secure. Be certain it is tightly wrapped and tied down securely before you trim off the end.

16. Finish off a small thread head. If the body was originally tied closer to the eye the head could have been tied small and unobtrusive in front of the antennae.

17. Using the bodkin, pick out the underside of the body. Pull out fibers at a right angle to the wraps. Notice direction and position of bodkin.

18. Finished Scud.

29

Marabou Damsel

Marabou Damsel (Randall Kaufmann)

Water bubbles rose between my feet as I cautiously waded through dense weeds along the boggy margin of the lake. Hundreds of newly hatched damselflies clung to exposed vegetation, pointing with the wind. Numerous unhatched nymphs crawled up my waders and along my arms searching for a suitable place to transform into adults. Occasionally a huge swirl would expand the water, denoting one less damselfly and one slightly heavier trout. A decent rainbow showed itself twice along a feeding path that roughly paralleled my position. I cast about 20 feet ahead of the moving, but unseen predator. My hand twist retrieve suddenly tightened and an awesome power pulled the line from my fingers and reel. A football size rainbow arched four feet, then five feet in the air, and the hook pulled free. I was ecstatic. I made an immediate

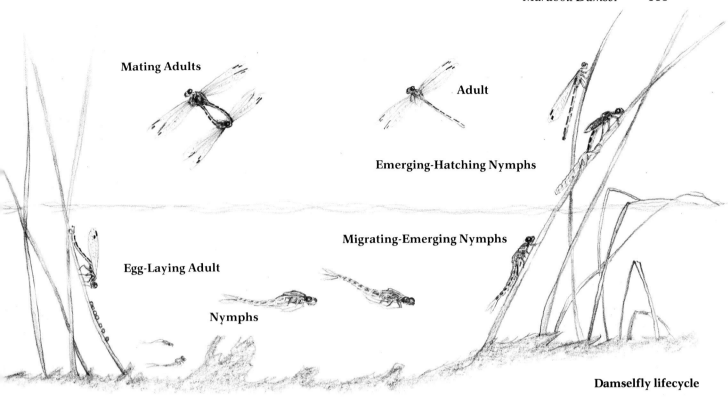

Mating Adults

Adult

Emerging-Hatching Nymphs

Migrating-Emerging Nymphs

Egg-Laying Adult

Nymphs

Damselfly lifecycle

blind cast, a cast born only from the excitement of a lost fish and the hopeful anticipation of another. Instantly, another rainbow tore out line, jumping six or seven times. My brother, Lance, estimated it at seven pounds. I didn't get too close to that one either, but long line releases are best for fish and I was wild with excitement! And so the day went, stalking, hooking, and releasing hefty rainbow in shallow, shoreline areas. We were in the right place at the right time with the right fly, a Marabou Damsel.

In doing research for my book, *Lake Fishing With A Fly*, I had ample opportunity to observe damselfly nymphs and they did not look like damsel imitations I saw in stores! A slender fly incorporating animation seemed to be needed, and if it was easy to tie so much the better.

Marabou can be used to represent many parts of nymphs and incorporated into most food source imitations. The Marabou Damsel demonstrates this versatility well and explains how to construct a nicely tapered marabou body, and the best way to even up marabou tails and wings on smaller nymphs.

HOOK:	Tiemco 200, 8-10, weight to suit
THREAD:	Olive
TAIL:	Olive marabou
RIB:	Copper wire or olive silk thread
BODY:	Olive marabou tied in by the tips. Leftover ends can form the wing. Pull off ends to 1/3 body length with fingers
WING:	Olive marabou (actually represents advanced wingcase)

1. Secure thread on the hook and position at thorax area. Select a bunch of fluffy marabou fibers for the tail. Remember that marabou slims down considerably when wet, so a thick bunch should be selected for the tail.

2. Secure marabou onto hook at the thorax area.

3. Trim ends and secure marabou back along top of hook to the standard tail tie-in position.

4. With your fingers, pull or tear the marabou to the desired length.

5. Photo shows tail after shortening. The wire rib has been tied in place and the thread moved forward in preparation for the next tying step.

6. Select another, but smaller, bunch of marabou fibers and tie in tip first at the thorax area. Secure down just like the tail, back to the tail position. Trim off the ends and wrap the thread forward to the thorax area.

7. Wrap the marabou around to the front of the hook, forming the body.

8. Finished body with rib ready to be wrapped forward.

9. Tying off the rib. Notice space at head. The marabou wing will be installed here, followed by the thread head.

10. Select another fair-sized bunch of marabou fibers, clean out any excess fuzzy bulk and secure immediately in front of the body.

11. Wing secured in place. Note position of wing and thread in relation to the hook eye.

12. Trim off wing excess and finish off the thread head.

13. With your fingers, pull off the wing fibers to the desired length, about one third the length of the body.

14. Finished Marabou Damsel.

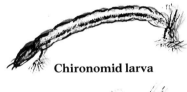

Chironomid larva

Chironomid pupa

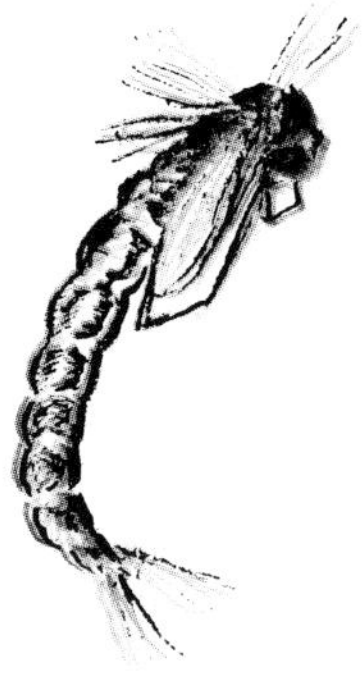

Chironomid Pupa

Chironomid Pupa (Randall Kaufmann)

Chironomids are commonly called midges and belong to the Order Diptera. They are probably the single most important food source of trout and they can hatch out every day of ice free water. Their numbers are staggering, their diversity unbelievable. Midges have an undeserved reputation of being a slow or still water insect but fast waters also have large populations of midges that often frustrate anglers as they do in lakes. The uninitiated angler takes a casual glance and either observes nothing or figures fish are feeding on adults, which is seldom the case. Because of their usually small size the observer will need a nymph net to make positive identification. Deschutes anglers are constantly querying us about the mystery surface activity where fish are showing tails and fins and appear to be feeding on the surface but no insects are seen. Much of the time these anglers are experiencing a midge hatch. A small

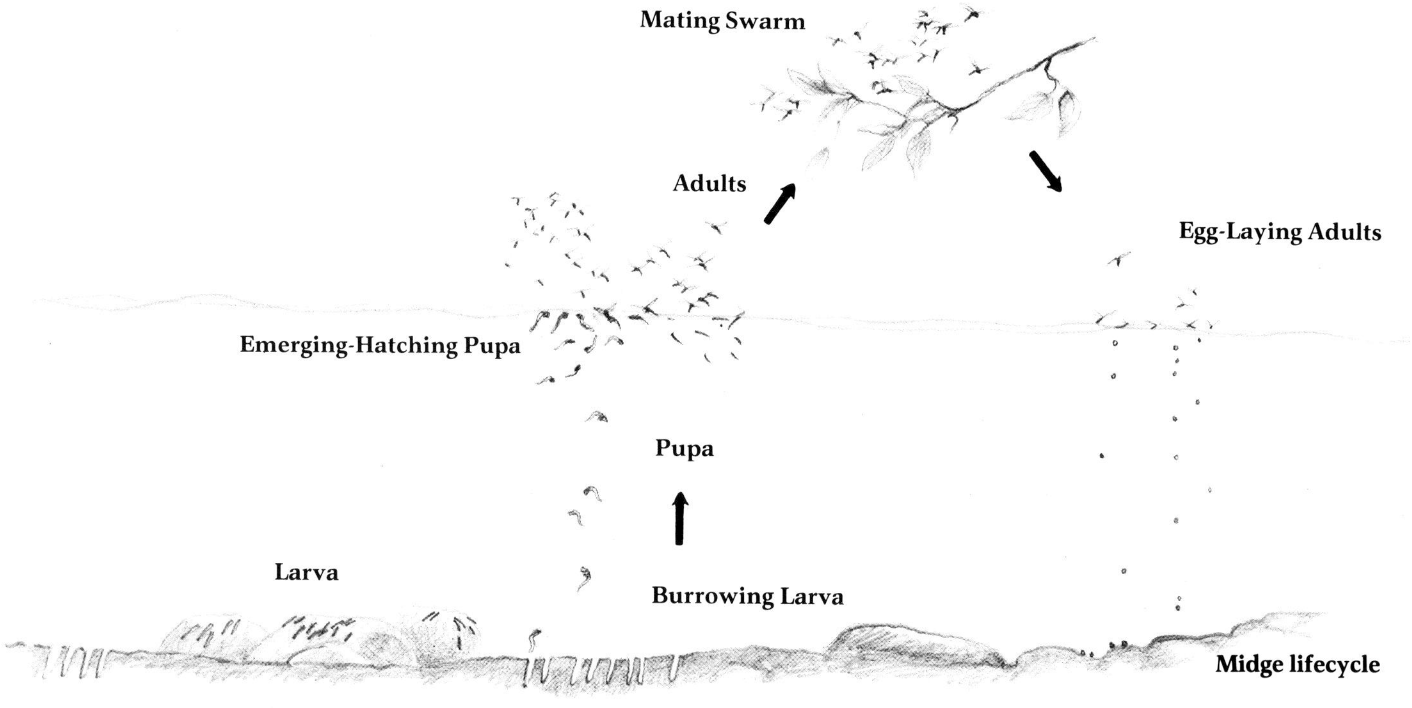

Mating Swarm

Adults

Egg-Laying Adults

Emerging-Hatching Pupa

Pupa

Larva

Burrowing Larva

Midge lifecycle

Midge pupa often present themselves in uncountable numbers, creating selective feeding habits. Reading and projecting riseform locations are a great aid in becoming an effective midge angler. Patience also helps.

Chironomid Pupa is in order but few anglers believe they can hook fish on a size 20 nymph in riffled water. Over the years I have become reasonably familiar with midging trout and I look forward to casting small imitations to voracious feeders. If everything is in order, it is common to experience two or more strikes per cast. When such is the case I will break off the hook point and cast only to specific fish. The "take" is discernible and oftentimes fish will not let go of the pointless hook until they have run some distance! Such small fly, rough water fishing demands a little expertise and the only way to acquire such skills is to fish under such conditions. It should be noted that not all midges are small. Hook size 8 and 10 midges are common in some waters.

I have had the best success with a black or olive body ribbed white. When tying Chironomids it is crucial to keep the body very skinny as the hook shank is already too large in diameter. Observe these mysterious creatures for yourself and you will have a better idea of their proportions. Also, an extensive treatment of midges will be found in my book, co-authored with Ron Cordes, *Lake Fishing With A Fly*.

The Chironomid Pupa demonstrates hackle tip wings, and practice tying a *slender* body and antennae. As a general rule, unless you are attempting to imitate an oversize insect, nymph imitations should be constructed on the slender or sparse side. Imitations dressed in such a manner more closely represent the natural, and they are able to penetrate the water's surface and swim or come alive much more easily than bulky counterparts. I *very seldom* see flies tied sparse enough, especially representations of midges, mayflies, and damselflies.

HOOK:	Tiemco 101 or 200, 12-24
THREAD:	Black
TAIL:	Clear Antron fibers tied short, not to extend beyond bend of hook
ANTENNAE:	Clear Antron fibers, not to extend beyond eye of hook
RIB:	White silk thread
BODY:	Hairtron, black, olive, browns, etc. Bodies must be *slender*
THORAX:	Black Hairtron
WINGS:	Grizzly hen hackle tips tied 1/3 body length

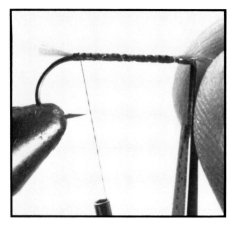

1. Beginning at the hook eye, secure a strip of Antron fibers back along the hook shank to the standard tail tie-in position. Hold the fibers securely with one hand and trim short so they do not protrude beyond the hook bend and eye, forming the tail and antennae.

2. Secure the rib material, then dub and wrap a *very thin* body. The hook shank is already too large in diameter. If you cannot dub a thin body, use thread.

3. Bring the rib through the body and secure at the back of the thorax area, which will only be about 30% of the overall length of this fly.

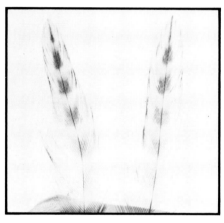

4. Dub and wrap the thorax. Position the thread immediately in front of the thorax, where the wings will be secured in place.

5. Select two identical grizzly hen hackle feathers. The hackle tips will form the wings and they should be wider than you might think, as only the extreme tips will be utilized on these normally small nymphs.

6. Face the shiny sides toward each other so they flare out from the center. The tips must be *exactly* even. Trim off the butt ends and any unnecessary fibers that will only be in your way.

7. Position the feathers (hackle tip wings) over the top of the fly with your right hand, making certain the wings do not extend beyond the halfway mark of the body.

8. Keeping the wings in the same position, change hands and secure in place. Wings must be positioned squarely over the top of the fly and not cocked off center. Trim the excess, being careful not to accidentally trim the antennae.

9. Finished Chironomid Pupa. Finish off a small thread head behind, or on top of the antennae.

31

Mosquito Pupa

Mosquito Pupa (Randall Kaufmann)

Mosquitoes belong to the family Culicidae which is included in the insect Order Diptera. Therefore, both Culicadae (mosquito) and Chironomids (midge) imitations and fishing techniques are very similar. As with midges, most mosquitoes are ingested by trout subsurface before they transform into winged adults. If you observe trout disturbing the water's surface when numerous mosquitoes are present, do not prematurely assume adults are the object of attention. Take a really close look and you will probably discover trout are feeding slightly subsurface or in the surface film itself. In many alpine lakes trout feed so heavily on midges and mosquitoes that they seem to be conditioned to accepting them even when none are showing themselves. For this reason, I will often employ the Mosquito Pupa as a general search pattern. Present it subsurface in conjunction with a *slow* hand twist retrieve.

The Mosquito Pupa demonstrates the technique for tying a combination stripped peacock quill and herl body using the same peacock herl. Midge patterns may also be tied with this technique. Experiment a bit.

HOOK:	Tiemco 101 or 200, 14-20
THREAD:	Olive
TAIL:	Grizzly marabou, tied *short*
RIB:	Gold or copper wire through body and thorax
BODY:	Stripped peacock quill
THORAX:	Peacock herl. If judged properly the thorax can be the same quill as the body. Strip off just enough herl to form the body and continue wrapping herl to form the thorax
WINGS:	Grizzly hen hackle, tips tied 1/3 body length

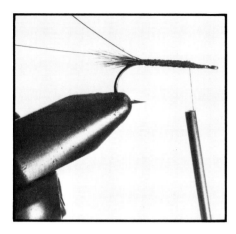

1. Select a clump of soft grizzly hackle fibers and, beginning at the thorax area, secure down along the shank to the standard tail tie-in position. Notice the smooth underbody and short, even tail. Wrap the thread forward to the thorax area.

2. Select a choice peacock herl and with your thumbnail and first finger, strip off the herl along the lower 2 or 3-inches of the quill. This bare peacock quill is referred to as a stripped peacock quill.

3. Beginning at the thorax area, secure the peacock quill, tying it down evenly back to the standard tail tie-in position. Bring the thread forward and repeat the tie-in process with the fine wire rib.

4. This is a close-up view of the last photo, number 3. Notice the smooth underbody over which the flat peacock quill will be wrapped. If the underbody is uneven, the finished body will also be uneven.

5. If the peacock herl was stripped off the proper distance along the quill, the stripped section of the quill will fall into place as the body, and the herl will fall into place forming the thorax. Do not trim off the excess until the rib is in place.

6. Wrap the rib through the body and thorax, secure and trim off all excess. Space must be left to accommodate the wings and thread head. Position the thread immediately in front of the thorax where the wings will be tied in place.

7. Prepare the hackle tip wings and secure in place. Wing tie-in placement is clearly visible. Notice how the wings are initially secured back from the eye, immediately in front of the thorax.

8. Wings are tightly secured. It is a common error for tyers to take too many turns of thread. A half dozen tightly wrapped turns should be sufficient. Always exert *maximum* pressure on thread. Notice how close and clean the excess was trimmed off!

9. Finished Mosquito Pupa. It is easy to complete a neat thread head when there are no excess feathers in the way and when ample space is available. Notice how the thread was wrapped back over the wings slightly, slanting them back over the body.

32

Hackles and Hackling

Left to right: Saddle hackle (rooster), neck hackle (rooster), hen neck hackle, hen saddle hackle

Hackles and Hackling

"Hackles" are the feathers found on birds and fowl. "Hackling" is the act of tying hackle in the construction of a fly. In relation to nymphs, hackles usually represent legs and possibly wings, gills and other nondescript parts. "Hackles" can, and usually should, play a lead role in animation.

Unless otherwise noted, the term *"hackle" denotes domestic chicken feathers, either rooster or hen.* There are two types of hackle: neck and saddle.

Neck hackle is commonly referred to as hackle, neck hackle, gamecock neck and rooster neck. Rooster hackle is much stiffer, longer and narrower than hen hackle, and is *always* used for hackling dry flies, but is also used for nymphs and other style flies. Hen hackle (both neck and saddle) is soft, webby, wide, and short. It is used for hackle tip wings (Chironomid Pupa, Timberline Emerger), and legs and tails.

Saddle hackle is referred to as saddle or saddle hackle. Saddle hackle is perfect for dry flies but it is rarely found in any quantity suitable for hook size 14 and smaller. Saddle is also much longer than neck hackle and is preferred when a palmer style hackle is needed (Woolly Bugger, Filoplume Damsel, Simulator).

Left: Hen saddle patch (back)
Right: Hen neck

Left: Rooster saddle patch
Right: Hen saddle patch

Until the last decade tyers had to be content with hackles imported from Asia. Asian necks were, and still are, not worth owning. Today there is no reason to subject yourself to their frustrations.

During the mid 1960s Henry Hoffman began developing a strain of grizzly hackles (barred rock, black and gray) that today are the best obtainable, but production is very limited. About the same time Buck Metz was gearing up a flock of birds spanning every color desired and today offers an abundance of the finest hackles in assorted colors on the market. Metz are readily available and there is no reason to buy any others.

Besides Metz and Hoffman neck hackles, you will also want a color selection of Metz hen hackles and saddles. At present, Metz saddles are mostly too wide for most nymph tying, running mostly size 6-8, some 10s and 4s. Hoffman grizzly saddles are the narrowest available, mostly size 10-12, some 14s and are ideal for tying nymphs and dry flies.

There is a shiny and dull side to all hackle. If you cannot visually tell the difference you can tell by the curve of the feather. All bird feathers curve off their backs toward the ground. The shiny side always faces out, or up. Just like the entire feather, individual fibers themselves also curve or face a particular direction. Depending on which direction they face when wrapped onto the hook, they will either curve forward or backward. Surface flies (dries) should always be tied with hackles facing forward as fibers facing this direction will better support a fly on the surface. Subsurface patterns (nymphs, forage fish imitations) should be constructed with hackle fibers facing or curving backward over the fly. When tying nymphs and other subsurface flies, hackle is usually "tied back," whereby the thread head is wrapped slightly back over the hackles, forcing or slanting the fibers back along the sides of the body. Subsurface flies should be sparsely hackled as they will more easily penetrate the surface film, sink quicker, and look and act more natural.

Close-up of prime grizzly neck hackles.

Saddle patch (saddle hackle) offering an abundance of long, narrow feathers ideal for both nymph and adult imitations.

Feather curves downward, shiny side faces up.

Same feather at left only inverted. Feather curves up, shiny side faces down.

Note: If the feathers at left were held vertically on edge they would either face forward or backward, as they do on the actual fly.

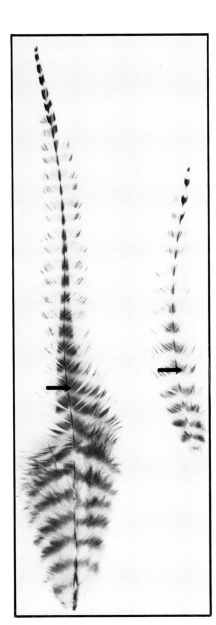

Left: Saddle hackle
Right: Neck hackle
Feathers are actual size. Note the shaded area extending outward from the stems, gradually disappearing toward the tips. Arrows point to the trim point. The usable feather above this point is mostly free of web, of universal width and offers a narrow stem. Notice the difference in the two stems. Generally, saddle hackle offers a narrower center stem.

Note: *Usually*, the term "hackle" denotes a rooster feather. Hen hackle is usually referred to specifically as hen hackle.

When selecting hackles the following criteria should be carefully considered.

1. The length of usable feather. Will the hackle be long enough to complete the number of turns desired? Nymph tyers should always be able to make do with a single hackle, but dry fly tyers may use two or more.

2. Judge the width of the feather carefully. Proportions are critical and hackle should be matched very closely to hook size. To judge the width of a hackle, bend the stem or gently stroke the fibers down at a right angle to the stem. When you bend the stem remember that hackles will appear slightly narrower than they actually are. When you are selecting or inspecting hackles on the skin be certain not to bend the entire skin as they are often brittle and break very easily. A broken neck is difficult for a retailer to sell and if you break one, you should offer to buy it. Hackles on the skin are best checked by selecting one hackle (do not remove it from the skin) and bending it. Standard hackling on a nymph usually does not extend beyond the hook point but particular patterns can vary.

3. Select a thin stem. Thick stem hackles are difficult to maneuver and take up too much space at the head of the fly, being impossible to pack tightly. Stems graduate in thickness, becoming thicker toward the base of the feather. Oftentimes the base of the feather can be trimmed off and the top section of hackle used. If the entire stem is unusually thick or flat do not use it for hackling.

4. Check for fiber resilience. Most hackles will have a tapered shadow area extending out from the stem. This shadow area is soft hackle and is referred to as web. The web is widest at the base and narrows toward the hackle tip. Dry fly hackle *must* be stiff, but nymph hackle can be soft or stiff, or a combination of both. Some nymph tyers prefer stiff (rooster) hackle, believing it retains its shape better underwater. Others prefer soft (hen) hackle, believing it slims down along the side of the imitation and breathes better.

A compromise of the above criteria will tell you where to trim off the butt section of hackle.

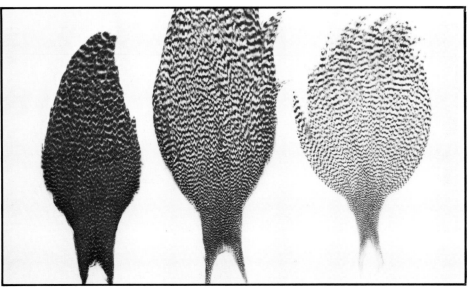

Hen Neck   **Metz Rooster Neck (grizzly)**   **Hoffman Rooster Neck (grizzly)**

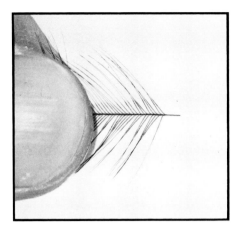

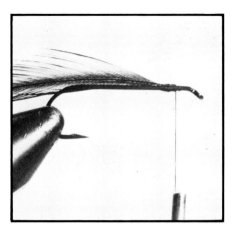

1. Select the proper width hackle and strip off the fibers along the center stem about 1/16-1/8 inch. This will avoid unwanted, wild fibers from "laying down" back along the hook (see photo 8).

2. Using the in-front-of-the-finger tie-in technique, secure the hackle slightly behind the thread head area.

3. Hackle properly secured in place. The shiny side is facing you. The first turn of hackle will be in a clockwise direction with the shiny side facing toward the front of the fly, or toward the eye of the hook.

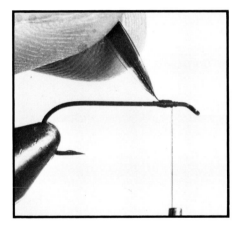

4. Using the over-the-top-and-hold-it technique, begin wrapping the hackle around the hook. Hackle is always wrapped *back-to-front*, with each turn of hackle *immediately* in front of the last wrap.

5. As you wrap the hackle, constant tension must be applied. Notice that hackle fibers extend at right angles from the hook shank and no wild fibers are present.

6. Four turns of hackle have been packed into a short space. They have been tied off, and the excess trimmed off, very neatly. Again, notice there are no out-of-place fibers.

7. Two or three turns of hackle are usually plenty for nymph imitations. Sweep all fibers back between your fingers and wrap the thread slightly back over the hackles and they will lie down, or slant back in the proper manner.

8. Poor hackle tie-in. There is no bare hook shank area for a neat head. Hackle is tied onto the hook too far back from the eye. The stem was not stripped of fibers and the hackle is too wide.

9. If your hackle looks like this, read the instructions again and pay more careful attention. This hackle is not wrapped tight, fibers have been tied down at the head, and the head area is too crowded!

33

Timberline Emerger

Timberline Emerger (Randall Kaufmann)

During the mid '60s when I began to fish the High Sierra back-country, it became apparent that a subsurface pattern was required if I was to be reasonably consistent in hooking trout in timberline lakes. I observed what looked to be surface feeding trout, but after only fair success with a floating fly and a closer inspection of riseforms, it became apparent that a subsurface pattern was in order. Standard "wet" flies of the day turned over fish, but it was not until I began experimenting with what was to become the Timberline Emerger that my success increased dramatically. I don't believe that the Timberline Emerger is an exact representation of a caddis pupa or hatching mayfly, but, as is often the case with mostly unsophisticated lake feeders, a subsurface pattern of *reasonable* size, shape and color, in conjunction with a slow hand twist retrieve, is sufficient to engage many trout.

In one of the lakes in the Mammoth Lakes chain, I could bank on the Timberline Emerger enticing a fish nearly every cast. During the day I would tie flies in a couple of local sport shops, either Kittredge's or Ernie's. From time to time, friendly, but skeptical tourists would goad me into taking them to the spot to "prove" I wasn't telling another mountain tale. Sometimes I would accommodate them, but always with a dinner wager attached, and, as I knew the best eating establishments in the area, I usually ate very well! The visitors felt they were getting in on a local "hot spot," and they were, but I do not recall any that could cast the required distance to reach the proper area.

I contribute a great deal of the Timberline Emerger's success to the natural grizzly hen hackle tip wings. The subtle barring effect coupled with the soft, water absorbing qualities and wide outline of the hen hackle wing seem to be a winning combination. Recently, I have replaced the moose tail with marabou, which offers more animation. Gray, olive and tan all produce well.

This is the first "hackle" pattern we have tied. It is important to note the space required for hackle and the distance it extends back from the head area. Hackle generally represents legs, and too much creates the wrong effect and inhibits the sinking and swimming qualities. Keep hackle sparse. Hackle should usually extend to the hook point.

Lance Kaufmann with a healthy Mt. Hood, Oregon area rainbow, hooked, quickly landed and released during an October snowstorm.

HOOK:	Tiemco 5262 or 200, 12-16, weight to suit
THREAD:	To match body
TAIL:	Dark moose, sparse, or marabou, short and heavy
RIB:	Copper wire
BODY:	Blend of angora goat and like color of Hairtron. Best colors are olive, tan, brown and gray
LEGS:	Brown neck hackle or color to match body
WINGS:	Grizzly hen hackle tips natural color or dyed to match body. Wings should be tied short, about 1/2 length of body

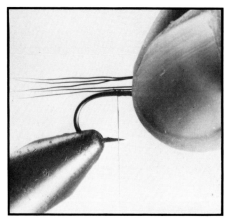

1. Heretofore, tails have been wrapped onto the hook beginning at the front of the hook and secured with thread *back* to the standard tail tie-in position. Tails can also be tied down in the opposite direction. Select a few moose fibers, stack them and place in position.

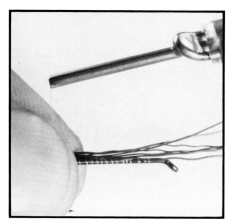

2. Bring the thread up between your fingers and secure with the standard tie-down method.

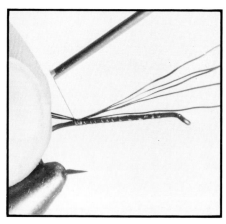

3. Hold the fibers up and back and take a couple turns of thread toward the rear position. These wraps will slim down the tail and bring individual fibers closer together. If you wish to flare or spread apart the tail fibers, take a turn behind the tail. This will also give it some "lift".

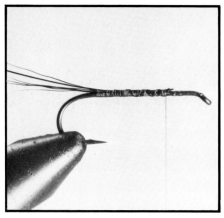

4. Tail is in place. Tie in rib. When you secure materials in a forward direction you will need to follow the thread closely with your thumb, keeping the material aligned along the top of the hook.

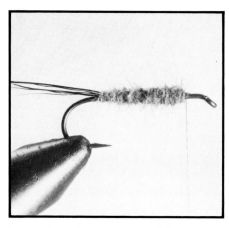

5. Dub fur onto the thread and form a neat taper as shown.

6. Wrap the rib forward, evenly spaced and tight. Tie off.

7. Select a hackle and install as described earlier. The first turn of hackle is placed immediately in front of the body. Carefully note the hackle position, thread position, and vacant head area. Hackle is wrapped forward to the thread position as seen here.

8. Two-to-three turns of hackle is about right. Again, carefully notice the position of hackle and thread in relation to the hook eye.

9. Stroke all fibers back out of the way and tie your thread *slightly* back over the hackle. There should be no stray fibers; the head area should be neat, just as you see it. The hackle, or legs, should lie down, or slant back.

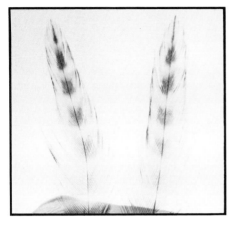

10. Select two matching grizzly hen hackle feathers which will form the wings. The shiny side is in view. Besides being less expensive than neck hackle tips, hen hackle tips are wider and therefore create a more desirable wing.

11. The shiny sides should face together, toward the inside. Be certain the tips are *exactly* the same length. Trim off excess feather length and strip off excess fibers at the base of the feather.

12. Hold the hackle tips in your right hand and place in position. It is important that wings are not cocked to either side. They should extend one to three quarters the length of the body.

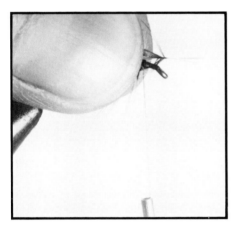

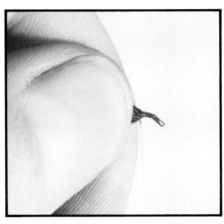

13. Holding the wings in position, change hands as shown here. Secure in place with the thread between the fingers technique and trim off excess.

14. Stroke *all* fibers back away from the head area and complete the thread head.

15. Finished Timberline Emerger.

16. Finished Timberline Emerger with marabou tail.

34

Floating Mayfly

Floating Mayfly

Some of the most beautiful rivers I have seen tumble and slip away from icy headwater mountains on New Zealand's South Island, creating dreamy, transparent runs and riffles where arm long trout are the rule. Today, they were the exception and four of us had tramped five miles of wild, seldom seen river and hooked only a handful. The evening was breathlessly still but damp and warm. Light had all but left the canyon and we were quickening our pace to put a nasty swamp behind us, thus avoiding hideous visions of three foot eels attacking us in the quiet darkness. The last river pool before the swamp was wide, exposed, and 2-3 feet deep and not a rock broke its smooth surface. During bright daylight, it was water you wouldn't bother to scout, but tonight was different. At least a dozen 3-5 pound browns were up for a hatch of mayfly duns, or so it appeared. After twenty minutes of refusals a belated net

In slow, crystalline waters, trout are finely tuned to their surroundings. Trout have ample opportunity to inspect offerings, and the slightest infraction into their territory alerts them. A long, well-placed cast is sometimes necessary. Charlie Miller in New Zealand.

sampling revealed a multitude of nymphs drifting in the surface film and fish were keyed to these easy marks. When we figured the reason for our lack of success it was near dark, but we were properly prepared the next night, eels or no eels! The basic lesson here is think, collect, and observe *first*, then fish. It seems to be a lesson we all learn – and forget – many times. Floating mayflies represent that stage of mayfly nymphs just prior to hatching into adults. This stage is often preyed upon by trout and overlooked by anglers. Most useful colors include olive, tan, brown, yellow and gray.

New techniques include split tails and a "ball," or floating wingcase. This wingcase can also be folded loosely over the thorax area, creating a slightly lower riding imitation. This "folded over" wingcase also traps air bubbles in the space between the thorax and case, perhaps adding a bit more realism.

HOOK:	Tiemco 101, 12-20
THREAD:	To match body
TAIL:	Split dark dun hackle fibers (or color to match body)
RIB:	Silk thread or floss to match or slightly contrast with body
BODY:	Antron, your choice of color
WINGCASE:	Dark dun poly dubbing shaped into "ball" and secured on top of body at thorax area
LEGS:	Same as tail, tied divided style

1. Secure and position the thread at the thorax area and dub dark dun poly onto about four inches of thread. Slide the dubbing down the thread with the bobbin, over the top of the hook at the thorax position, forming the floating wingcase.

2. Form a ball and secure in place by wrapping thread in front, behind and horizontally around the base of the poly ball.

3. Select half a dozen stiff saddle hackle fibers and secure slightly forward of the standard tail tie-in position.

4. Dub body material onto thread *thinly* and begin the body behind the tail. Stop wrapping body immediately behind the tail.

5. Position half the tail fibers along one side of the fly. Unless you use *very little* dubbing it is best to secure the tail with thread and cover the bare wraps with dubbing later.

6. Secure tail fibers along one side and then the other side of the fly.

7. Dub a tapered body up to and in front of the poly ball.

8. Select the proper size hackle and tie in immediately in front of the poly ball.

9. Wind two-to-three turns of hackle and tie off. Note the position of the hackle and thread in relation to the poly ball and hook eye.

10. Stroke all the hackle fibers back out of the way with your fingers and wrap the thread slightly back over the hackle fibers, pulling all hackle fibers alongside and underneath the body. Finish off fur head and thread head.

11. Finished Floating Mayfly with ball style wingcase.

13. Directions follow for constructing a "folded over" floating wingcase. This style of wingcase is preferred by some anglers as it traps air bubbles in the space between the thorax and wingcase. Omitting the poly ball wingcase, proceed to step 7 as above.

14. Unravel a 3-inch piece of 4-strand Antron (poly yarn is also used) and tie in 2-4 pieces at the rear of the thorax position. Dub more body material onto the thread and form a standard thorax.

15. Pull the Antron pieces loosely over the top of the thorax and secure in place, forming the wingcase.

16. Tail, body, thorax and wingcase complete.

17. Select, prepare and tie in a suitable hackle. Wrap 2-3 turns, tie off and slant back. Dub a little more fur onto the thread and form the fur head. Now, finish the thread head.

18. Finished Floating Mayfly with folded over style wingcase.

35

Palmer Hackle

Palmer hackle is very common in nymph construction and usually refers to the winding of hackle through or over the entire body or thorax. Hackle is spaced at even intervals much like rib and should not be wrapped too closely together. Fine wire or thread rib is usually over-wrapped for durability.

There are two methods for tying a palmer hackle, *tip first* and *standard* palmer.

Tip first is employed when palmer hackling a thorax area that does not have a rib. Tip first palmer will allow hackles to slant or lie down toward the back of the fly and taper wider toward the front of the fly, both of which are desired traits on nymphs. Tip first allows the use of a slightly shorter feather because you can use the unusable bottom portion of the feather as a handle when winding the hackle that would otherwise be trimmed off. Examples of thorax tip first palmer hackled flies include the Montana Stone, Prince Hellgrammite and Bitch Creek.

Standard style palmer hackling is employed when there is an over rib and generally is more easily accomplished without tying down hackle fibers when the rib is wound through. There will be a nice natural taper front to rear with standard palmering, and if the dull side of the hackle is facing toward the back the hackles will angle backwards. Examples of standard style hackled flies include the Simulator, Woolly Worm and Woolly Bugger.

1. Select the proper length and width hackle, which is determined by hook size and application. The longer the hook, the longer the hackle must be to wrap forward around the hook. Longer hooks require a saddle hackle.

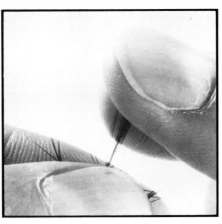

2. Grasp the *extreme tip* of the hackle with your thumb and first finger. Immediately below, grasp all the hackle fibers not being held by your two fingers and *gently* stroke the fibers down and away from the hackle tip.

3. If prepared properly, the hackle tip will look like this. Notice that no fibers are out of place. The point at which the fibers separate is where the feather will be secured onto the hook.

4. The fibers held between the fingers will become part of the fly and should not be tied down with thread. The thread should secure the feather onto the hook immediately in front of this position, as shown.

5. Once the hackle has been secured onto the hook you can release your fingers. Notice the neat tie down and that no hackle fibers are out of place. If your tie down looks like this you are ready to continue.

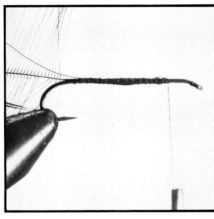

6. Tie in the rib material (fine wire) at the rear area and tie down the hackle tip along the hook shank, keeping an even underbody. The thread is now positioned at the hackle tie off area.

7. Begin wrapping the tip first palmer hackle around the hook. The tip of hackle stems are fragile and care must be taken during the first couple of turns not to break it, but at the same time the hackle must be tightly wrapped. Use the over-the-top and hold-it technique.

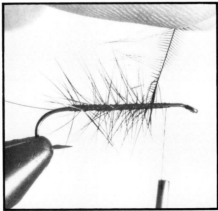

8. Space the hackle evenly along the hook shank up to the head area. You will find that a long feather is necessary. Take a couple of extra turns of hackle at the tie off area. Normally tip first style hackle is wrapped through the thorax only, and without a rib, but this is good practice.

9. Once the hackle is securely tied down, trim off the excess. Notice that the *point* of the scissors is resting *on* the hook shank, thereby ensuring the closest possible trim, and that the thread is in no danger of being cut.

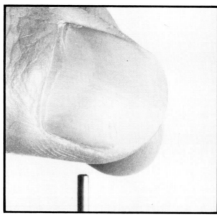

10. Wrap the rib through the body, using the over-the-top and hold-it technique, being careful not to tie down too many fibers. Notice that the rib is handled very close to the hackle fibers. It is a good habit to work close to the fly, not at a distance. Tie off the rib at the front of the hackle and trim off the excess.

11. This next series of three photos will explain how to sweep materials away from the tying area. Look at photo 10 and notice all the errant hackle fibers. These must be held out of the way to ensure a neat, clean tie off. Position your thumb and first finger a fair distance in front of the hook.

12. Sweep the two fingers up and toward the rear, being certain all fibers are captured between the two fingers.

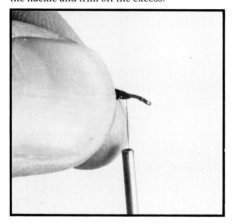

13. Continue sweeping the fingers back until they are in the proper position. The thread can now be wrapped slightly back over hackle fibers, slanting them toward the rear, and a neat, clean head can be easily formed. Notice the bare hook shank in front of the hackle.

14. Tip first palmer hackle is complete. Notice that all fibers slant toward the rear and that the thread head is neat and tapered. Practice this technique until you have mastered it.

1. Secure rib material at the standard tail tie-in position. Next, select a long hackle and trim off the bottom to the desired starting position (see page 122). Palmer hackle *usually* extends 1-1/2 times the hook gape.

2. Strip off the end fibers, exposing about 1/16-inch of center stem. Individual fibers should not be secured with thread, eliminating any wild fibers.

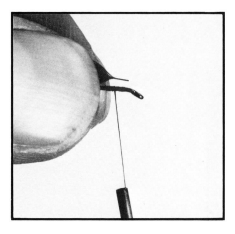

3. Using the in-front-of-the-finger tie-in technique, secure the hackle immediately behind the thread head area. The shiny side should be facing you.

4. Proper hackle tie-in. The hackle will be wrapped clockwise incorporating the over-the-top and hold-it technique. Be certain the shiny side faces forward.

5. Wrap the hackle back toward the standard tail tie-in position, spacing each turn the desired distance apart. This photo sequence depicts a *heavy* palmer hackle. It is usually more sparse.

6. When you have reached the standard tail tie-in position, keep tension on the hackle with your left hand.

7. With your right hand, take a couple of turns of rib around the hackle. When it is secured in place you can release your left hand and continue wrapping the rib forward.

8. A fine wire rib is easily wrapped through the hackle without tying down individual fibers. If not, move the rib in a sideway motion as you wrap it.

9. Tie down the rib at the head area and trim off the hackle tip. Note that this hackle became wider toward the hackle tip. This is not a desired effect. Hackle is usually wider at the base of the feather, and hence, wider at the head area, narrower at the tail.

36

Woolly Bugger

Woolly Bugger

The fish catching capabilities of the Woolly Bugger are matched by very few other flies. It can be effective in *all* types of water for just about *all* freshwater gamefish. Western anglers employ it on large rivers for rainbows and browns where it is dead drifted, retrieved or twitched, both along the bottom and just subsurface. Alaska anglers favor it for charr and rainbow and it is not uncommon to release several 2-8 pound and larger fish in a day's fishing. Anglers frequenting Argentina, Tasmania and New Zealand also rely on the Woolly Bugger to entice big rainbows and browns. The Woolly Bugger can be a reasonable representation of forage fish, dragonfly, leech and stonefly nymphs. Its unusual size makes it a good mouthful, while at the same time provoking cranky, curious and territorial response. Its dark color creates good visibility and the marabou

This obese rainbow fell for a four-inch long Woolly Bugger. It was carefully released back into its secluded, icy home high in the Wyoming Rockies, a long two-day backpack from nowhere. Angler, Don McCollum

tail provides animation, making it an excellent probe and chuck-and-chance-it fly. To underscore its appeal, allow me to relate an incident that occurred high in the Wyoming Rockies at an unfamiliar and unnamed lake. One of our party began walking the shoreline casting a heavy size 2 black Woolly Bugger, while the rest of us napped. After about an hour an inquisitive rainbow followed the fly back nearly to our friend's feet, casually turned and aimlessly finned away. The fly was slopped back into the path of the fish and it gently turned and inhaled the fly. The fish was a very real seven pounds and was landed and gently released!

This is not a fly to dismiss lightly. A few dozen belong in every angler's box. The standard pattern is tied with chenille but I like a mixture of rabbit and goat. My favorite is dark brown rabbit mixed with rust, purple, blue, amber, black, and brown goat palmered with dark dun saddle hackle. The overall effect is dark, rusty brown with numerous highlights. Make up your own mind on the goat vs. chenille. Hold one of each up to the light and view them from below, silhouetted against the sky, much like they appear to fish.

Palmered hackle is the important technique to master here. It is simple, yet creates an interesting effect, especially to those who have never seen it done.

HOOK:	Tiemco 300, 2-10, weighted
THREAD:	To match body color
TAIL:	Black marabou or to match body color (black, olive, and brown are most common colors)
LEGS:	Saddle hackle palmered, black or color to match body. Take 1-2 extra turns at front of body
BODY:	Black, olive or brown chenille; fur mixes are also good

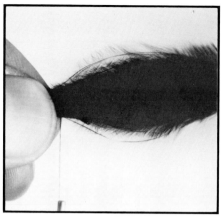

1. Secure and position the thread at the front of the hook. Select a complete marabou feather that is relatively straight across the top. Slim it down and, with your right hand, position it for the tail. The tail should be about the length of the hook shank.

2. Change hands and secure the marabou feather at the front of the hook. Marabou offers an irresistible breathing effect when twitched through the water, hence it is important that the Woolly Bugger tail be thick. If necessary, use two marabou feathers.

3. Wrap the thread back, securing the marabou tail at the standard tail tie-in position. Trim off the excess.

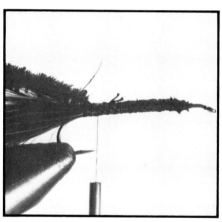

4. Notice the perfectly level underbody secured along the top of the hook. Secure the rib at the tail area.

5. Twist off the woven chenille fibers and tie in place. Notice that the thread core of the chenille does not add any additional bulk to a fly this size.

6. Wrap the chenille forward and tie off at the head area. Select a proper width saddle hackle and prepare as previously explained under "standard style palmer hackle."

7. Take a couple of turns of hackle at the head area, using the over-the-top and hold-it technique, and wrap the hackle back to the tail. Notice the spacing. Hold the hackle tip in your left hand, and with your right hand, secure the hackle tip with the rib.

8. Once a few turns of wire rib have secured the hackle, wrap the rib forward in the standard manner and tie off at the head area. Stroke the hackle fibers back and finish off a neat, tapered thread head.

9. Finished Woolly Bugger.

37

Simulator

Simulator (Randall Kaufmann)

The Simulator is patterned after the Woolly Worm, Charles Brooks' "tied in the round" style of stonefly, and Polly Rosborough's Nondescript pattern. It came about in a late evening effort to streamline and hasten the tying of the Kaufmann Stone. Three of us were embarking on a four day Deschutes River float, and for some reason I was supposed to tie all the flies. I have since learned that it is best to teach others to tie their own, or at least point them to a place where they can purchase a few of their own! The Simulator does not quite produce grabs like the Kaufmann Stone, but it is, nonetheless, very successful. I quickly adapted the Simulator to other food sources, tying it in various sizes and colors.

Today, ten years later, the Simulator is one of the most versatile flies you can tie and fish. It can be a reasonable imitation of many food sources at the same time, or, it can be appropriated toward one or two specifics. Stoneflies, caddisflies, mayflies, craneflies, hellgrammites, dragonflies, alderflies, damselflies, leech, and water beetles are all possibilities. The Simulator may not be the *best* imitation of all these food sources, but when you are unsure or caught without *exactly* what you need, you will welcome a wide selection of these! The photos here depict the Simulator as a stonefly, damsel and caddis. Tying sequence is identical; only the colors, material, and style of tying varies. As you construct your flies, keep these ideas in mind. Sizes 6-12 in four colors (black, brown, olive, peacock) cover a lot of aquatic country.

This pattern offers excellent insight into variation on the theme. Strip goose or marabou tails are good and hackle can be palmered and left as is, or trimmed for a special effect, or it can be palmered only through the thorax area. Experiment yourself; that is part of the enjoyment of fly tying.

HOOK	Tiemco 300, 4-10, weight to suit
THREAD:	To match body
TAIL:	Strip goose "V," or marabou to match body
RIB:	Copper wire
LEGS:	Saddle hackle, palmered standard style through body, clipped to shape if desired, or palmered through thorax only
BODY:	Blend of several colors of Angora goat and predominant Hairtron color. Pick out fur at thorax area

1. Pictured is a strip goose quill. This has been stripped off the short side of the leading, or first flight quill from a goose wing. Only the first flight quill offers stiff fibers. Stripped goose is often referred to as goose quill fibers, barbules and biots.

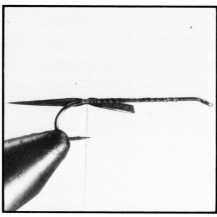

2. A single fiber has been removed and secured along one side of the hook, curving toward the outside, or away from the hook. Tie another fiber along the other side of the hook and the "V" tail is complete. Another method follows.

3. Select two fibers and arrange them so they curve away from each other, toward the outside. Tips should be exactly the same length.

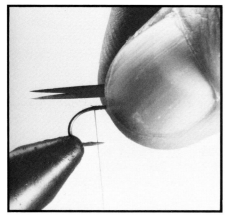

4. With your right hand, position them for length. Notice the thread position.

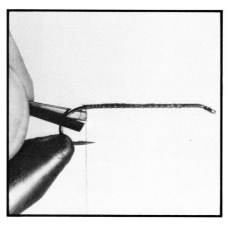

5. Change hands and slip the fibers along each side of the hook. Secure in place with the thread-between-the-fingers technique. Two at a time is the faster method, but if you have trouble handling two at a time, tie each fiber in separately.

6. Stripped goose "V" tail in place. Such tails should usually be very short.

7. Secure the rib and the tip-first palmer-style hackle, as previously illustrated. I prefer softer hackle for the Simulator and like the front turns to extend halfway back along the body.

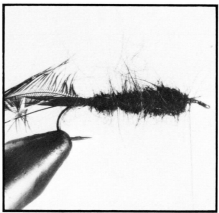

8. Dub and wrap the body forward to the head area. There should be a taper to the body and if you intend to pick out the thorax area, extra dubbing, loosely wrapped, should be applied.

9. Wrap, or palmer the hackle through the body, taking a couple extra turns in front, and tie off at the head area. Notice the hackle spacing. It is easy to wrap too many turns of hackle.

10. Wrap the rib forward through the body and hackle, which reinforces the hackle and adds a little flash. The rib can be worked in between the hackle fibers, or the fibers can be picked out from under the rib with a bodkin.

11. Stroke all materials back away from the eye and finish a neat, tapered thread head.

12. Remove the Simulator from the vise and trim the hackles at an angle, or to a cone shape. If the proper hackle length was selected, the front turns of hackle should not be trimmed.

13. Return the Simulator to the vise and using a bodkin, pick out the thorax area. Dubbing is best picked out at a right angle to the original wraps (the bodkin points the same direction as the hook when you are picking out the fur).

14. Finished Simulator.

15. Another style of tying a Simulator. This fly would perhaps imitate a damsel or other slender, underwater life form.

16. A middle of the stream dressing, imitative of many underwater organisms. Experiment on your own, tailoring this style of fly to fit your particular needs.

38

Filoplume Damsel

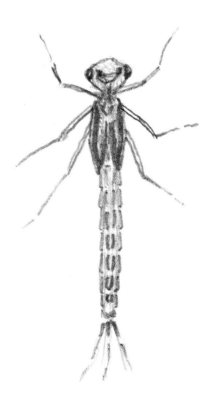

Filoplume Damsel (E.H. Gene Armstrong)

There are a great many new fly patterns that emerge from the vise. A very few find their way into print and fewer still catch on and become current standards, flies you commonly find in use and available over-the-counter.

Gene Armstrong, innovative Seattle area tyer and angler, has developed a series of "filoplume" nymphs (damsel, dragon and leech) that exude life-fullness, are attractive and very productive. Gene can often be found behind the counter at Kaufmann's Streamborn in Bellevue, Washington. He has supplied the store with filoplume patterns and they have become extremely popular. Only the damsel is detailed here, but the others should be self-explanatory and are pictured in the color pattern directory.

A filoplume feather is the secondary shaft that accompanies primary feathers on many game birds, the most useful of which are ringneck pheasant. Fly tyers have overlooked and discarded filoplumes for years, paying little attention to their slender, almost formless shape. Gene describes the filoplume as, "A soft and wispy feather that activates with a minimum of surrounding disturbance. The minute currents in bodies of still water, caused by minor flows, temperature variations, or movement of objects in or on the water, will move the filaments of this feather similar to the movement of the gills of the damselfly nymph."

This pattern incorporates palmered hackle legs, which on some patterns have a wingcase pulled over the top. The Filoplume Damsel will be a valuable addition to your collection.

HOOK:	Tiemco 200, 8-10
THREAD:	Olive, or color to suit
TAIL:	Olive marabou strands or other color to suit
RIB:	Silver wire, reverse wrapped through body, thorax and head
BODY:	Same as tail
LEGS:	Silver or silver badger saddle hackle palmered through thorax
THORAX:	Filoplume, color to match body
HEAD:	Peacock herl

1. Secure the marabou tail as previously illustrated with the Filoplume Mayfly. The tail should be short, but thick.

2. Secure the wire rib and a few long marabou fibers by the tips. Position the thread at the tie-off area (rear of the thorax area) as seen here.

3. Wrap the marabou fibers around the hook, forming the body, and tie-off at the rear of the thorax area, which is generally at about the 40% mark back along the hook shank from the eye.

4. Tie in a silver badger saddle hackle tip first (previously illustrated under "tip first palmer hackle") at the rear of the thorax area.

5. Select a filoplume feather, tie it in by the butt end at the back of the thorax and wrap it forward, forming the thorax. A second filoplume feather will often be required to complete the thorax.

6. Finished tail, body, thorax and legs. Notice the position of the thorax in relation to the hook eye. There is just enough room to complete the peacock head and the thread head.

7. Tie in a select peacock herl immediately in front of the thorax. Remember to position the peacock herl so the bare side of the quill precedes the herl side. Keep the actual thread head area clear.

8. Wrap the peacock herl forward, forming the head. Tie off the peacock herl and trim the excess. Next, bring the wire rib forward and tie off at the front of the hook. Form a neat thread head.

9. Finished Filoplume Damsel.

39

Kaufmann Stone

Kaufmann Stone (Randall Kaufmann)

For many anglers, stoneflies offer the most exciting fishing of the season, especially the huge *Pteronacys californica* and *Acroneuria californica*. These beautiful aquatic insects are common throughout the west, and streams such as the Deschutes and Madison can offer outrageous action.

Stonefly nymphs become available to fish as they migrate along the bottom rubble and when they lose their grasp and drift and tumble with the currents. Optimum stonefly habitat is quick riffle water, which provide nymphs with ample oxygen and cover. Trout lying among bottom debris are surrounded by a mosaic of ever changing currents, dancing light patterns, uncountable iridescent water bubbles, and assorted stream matter.

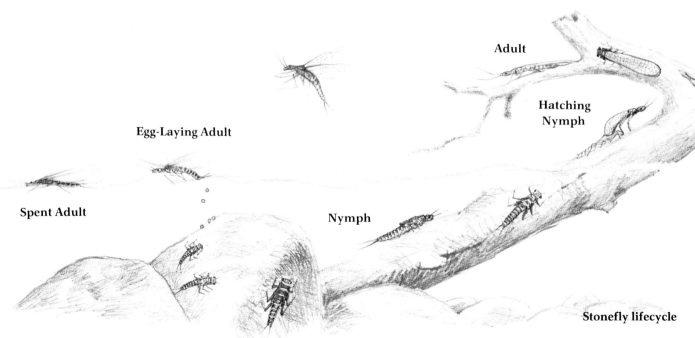

Spent Adult

Egg-Laying Adult

Adult

Hatching Nymph

Nymph

Stonefly lifecycle

Stonefly nymphs crawl from the water to hatch into adults, hence streamside vegetation and shoreline rocks are a good place to locate abandoned cases. This particular boulder was spied along the Middle Fork of the Salmon River in Idaho.

Under such conditions, trout often only have a split second to decide what is edible and what is not. From what little we perceive it would seem logical that stonefly recognition consists of the following "keys": size, shape, color, animation and presentation. The more "keys" you have the higher your rate of success. With these thoughts in mind the Kaufmann Stone was created. It has since become one of the most popular and effective stonefly nymph patterns, with black, brown, golden brown, and tan being the best colors.

Tying instructions involve quite a few steps, but it is not difficult to tie. Perhaps the most common mistake is not judging the proportions properly and ending up with too much room or, as usually is the case, not enough room to accommodate the thorax. Look at the photo carefully and note that the first wingcase is tied in about halfway along the body.

When you blend the body color, keep in mind that your rabbit fur will create the dominant color; the goat is only for highlights. Hence, you will not need very much. I usually figure 50% rabbit, 50% goat. New techniques include working with Swannundaze, and shaping and installing a triple wingcase.

HOOK:	Tiemco 300, 2-10, weighted and flattened
THREAD:	To match body
TAIL:	Strip goose to match body
ANTENNAE:	Strip goose to match body
RIB:	Swannundaze to match body
BODY:	Mixture of several colors (claret, amber, orange, rust, black, brown, blue, purple, ginger) of angora goat (50%) and predominant color of Hairtron (50%). Black, brown, tan and golden brown are the most popular colors
WINGCASE:	Three separate sections of lacquered turkey clipped to shape before tying in. The wingcase should occupy 1/2 of hook shank length. Each thorax is tied in separately alternated with thorax fur
THORAX:	Same as body
HEAD:	Same as body

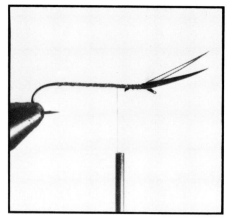

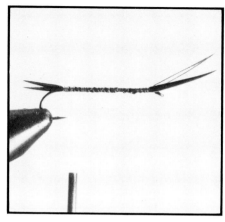

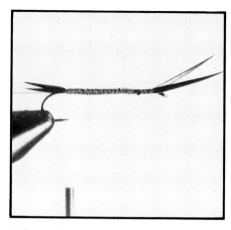

1. Select two strip goose fibers, flare apart and secure along each side of the hook, forming the antennae. Be certain the two tips are the same length. One half the body length is about right for length. See Simulator for detailed instructions.

2. Select two more strip goose fibers and secure along each side of the hook, forming the tail. Tail length should be short, about the gape of the hook.

3. Secure Swannundaze along the opposite side of the hook. It should be tied down along the entire length of the body area back to the tail.

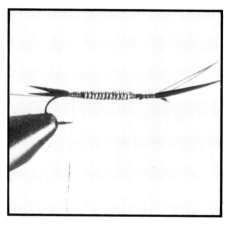

4. Install the lead wire, beginning slightly in front of the hook point and ending in the thorax area. Secure lead in place with thread and smash flat. By installing the lead at this time it is easy to cover up the Swannundaze and strip goose.

5. Begin wrapping the body dubbing, forming a quick taper at the back and rapidly forming a robust body.

6. Continue wrapping the dubbing to the thorax area, forming the body.

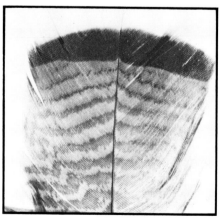

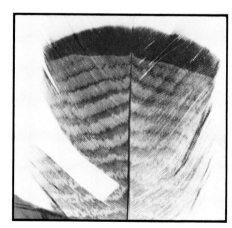

7. Wrap the Swannundaze forward, taking an extra turn in front of the fur body. Tie down securely, wrapping the thread back to the extreme back of the thorax area where the first of three wingcases will be tied in place.

8. Lacquered turkey tail feather.

9. Trim out section of tail feather at a right angle to the fibers.

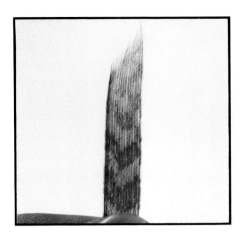

10. Section of turkey tail feather, about ¼-inch wide.

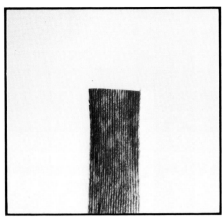

11. Trim the tip even.

12. Fold in half and cut at a 45-degree angle. If desired, trim the "V" wingcase points slightly so they are flat on top, or shape to suit.

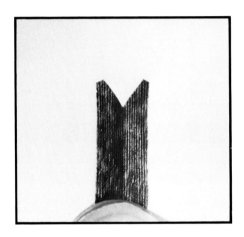

13. Prepared stonefly wingcase.

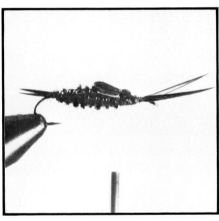

14. Secure over the top of the body at the rear of the thorax. Wingcase should fold *slightly* down over the side of the body. Trim off excess. First wingcase should look and be positioned as shown. Notice that the thorax area is not crowded.

15. Dub and wrap a little more fur, being certain the thorax is of larger diameter than the body. Dubbing should be wrapped right on top of the wingcase tie down and slightly on top of the wingcase feather itself. Trim off the excess. Tie in another wingcase as before.

16. Dub and wrap more fur, remembering not to crowd the head area. Each succeeding wingcase is secured slightly on top of the preceding thorax fur.

17. Tie in place the third and last wingcase, trim the excess and dub on the third and final section of fur, which will finish the imitation right to the antennae. When viewed from the underside the thorax should be continuous fur. Pick out fur along sides and bottom of thorax.

18. Finished Kaufmann Stone.

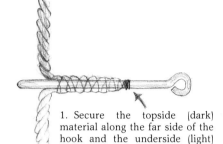

40

1. Secure the topside (dark) material along the far side of the hook and the underside (light) material along the near side. Half hitch and cut the thread.

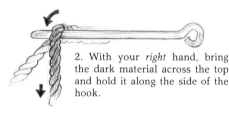

2. With your *right* hand, bring the dark material across the top and hold it along the side of the hook.

3. With your *left* hand, bring the light material across the dark material and under the hook, holding it in position along the far side of the hook.

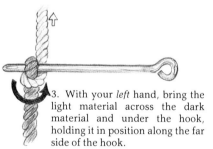

4. Constant tension must be kept on each material and hands are not changed (right hand constantly holds the dark material on top). Bring the dark material back across the top.

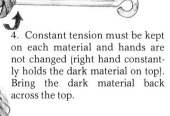

Rubber Legs Brown Stone

Rubber Legs Brown Stone (George Anderson)

George's Brown Stone was originated in the late '60s by George Anderson, Montana angler-guide and shop proprietor. George relates that the current rubber leg version was developed in the early '70s during a trip to the Colorado River in Colorado for big rainbows. A stonefly nymph was needed that looked and acted like a real insect. The flattened woven body, buggy thorax, and rubber legs produced well, and although George has experimented with other colors of rubber legs, white has proved the best. George likes to dead drift the fly a few feet and then twitch it to get the legs moving.

Woven body and rubber leg flies are not new to Montana anglers. As a youngster I remember seeing the beautiful Pott's woven hair flies, the Hank Roberts' series, and Bitch Creek's in just about every fishing establishment. Franz B. Pott was the originator of weaving hair hackles and George Grant, the dean of woven body flies and longtime Montana angler and conservationist, authored *The Master Fly Weaver* in 1980. Tyers interested in the art of weaving (and there are many techniques) should obtain a copy.

HOOK:	Tiemco 5263, 8-12, weighted and flattened
THREAD:	Brown
TAIL:	White rubber strips tied in "V"
ANTENNAE:	Same as tail, tie back after fly is complete
BODY:	Woven body with chocolate brown yarn on top and tan yarn (burlap works best) underneath
LEGS:	One pair of white rubber strips protruding from body immediately behind thorax
THORAX:	Hare's ear

5. Wrap the light material around the dark and underneath the hook, repeating step three. The light, or bottom material, always stays along the bottom of the fly, wrapping around the dark material and moving underneath the hook to the opposite side of the fly.

6. Bring the top (dark) material across the top as in step four. The top material merely moves back and forth across the top of the fly. The light material loops around the dark material and moves across the bottom of the fly. When the body is formed, reattach the thread and continue.

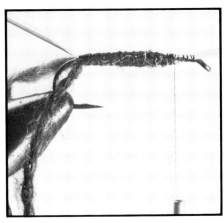

1. Secure legs, antennae and build up under-body as shown.

2. Secure the tan burlap along the far side of the hook and the dark brown yarn along the near side of the hook. Remember to keep the taper even throughout the entire length of the body. Throw a couple of half hitches and trim off the thread.

3. Upon completion of the woven body, grasp the two ends tightly and hold them in place.

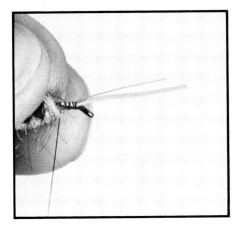

4. Secure the thread onto the hook by holding the woven body ends in place *and* the end of the thread. Once thread is secured, tie down the woven body ends. Several turns of thread back over the body will be required, but the thorax will cover these up.

5. Body secured by thread. Loose ends should be trimmed off.

6. Two rubber strips are now tied in place on top of the body at the rear of the thorax area. Notice the position of the thread and leg tie down position.

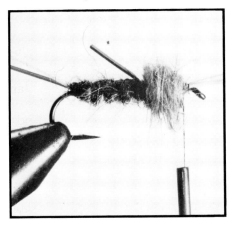

7. Dub and wrap the fur thorax, being certain it is of large diameter. Do not crowd the thread head area. Next, pull back one of the antennae (rubber strip) along one side of the hook and secure. Repeat with the other rubber strip on the opposite side of the hook.

8. Finished Rubber Legs Brown Stone.

41

Casual Dress

Casual Dress (E.H. "Polly" Rosborough)

The Casual Dress is only one of many innovative nymphs from the bench of Polly Rosborough, legendary Oregon angler and early nymph pioneer. Polly's book, *Tying and Fishing the Fuzzy Nymph*, was originally published in 1965 and opened a new frontier to anglers craving information about nymphs. Over the years Polly has greatly influenced anglers and tyers and his original tying style is readily seen in many of today's patterns. Polly has a flair for enthusiastically sharing his hard found knowledge and has always welcomed visitors. He is easily located in Chiloquin, Oregon, near the famed Williamson River.

Polly originated the Casual Dress to "simulate nothing more than just food," and it is easy to visualize fish accepting it for a host of underwater organisms. The Casual Dress has, however, become somewhat of a favorite drowned mouse imitation! Tie up a few in various sizes and fish them accordingly.

The major tying technique to be gleaned from the Casual Dress is the spun noodle, which Polly uses for most of his fuzzy nymphs, and a collar.

HOOK:	Tiemco 300, 4-10
THREAD:	Black
TAIL:	A short thick bunch of muskrat hair with all guard hairs left in
BODY:	Muskrat tied noodle style
COLLAR:	Muskrat extending back 1/3 of body length
HEAD:	Wide black ostrich

1. Cut a clump of muskrat fur with guard hairs from the skin. Guard hairs are those actual hairs that extend up through and beyond the length of fur. Secure the muskrat clump as a standard tail. Notice the level tie-in along the hook shank.

2. If the muskrat clump is not long enough to tie down along the entire hook shank, dub and wrap a little fur in front of the tail tie-down, thus creating a level underbody along the entire hook shank.

3. Shown is some muskrat fur that has been slightly blended. It will be prepared for forming a "noodle," which is an effective method of installing a very durable, buggy, segmented fur body, characteristic of most Polly Rosborough patterns.

4. Spread the fur into a rough line. It is best not to break apart the fur but to reshape it into a line.

5. When the fur is spread to the desired length (about 4-inches) and quantity, gently roll it between your fingers much like you would when dubbing fur onto thread but not nearly as tight. You will be surprised at how much fur is required for this process.

6. Form a loop of thread at the rear of the body and wrap the thread forward to the location you will tie-off the noodle. It is necessary to keep the thread loop spread apart with one hand or the two strands of thread will roll around each other, creating a mess.

7. Place the prepared fur into the loop and, aligning the fur best as possible, close the thread loop around the fur.

8. Hold the lower end of the loop and spin until it is to the point of kinking. Do not let off on the tension.

9. Begin wrapping the body, each turn immediately in front of the last, forming a nice segmented body. It is easy to understand how important a level underbody is when you reach this point of construction.

10. Finished body. If there is leftover fur, simply tie off the noodle as you would any other body material and trim the excess. If the noodle is too short, form another one and continue. You will soon be able to judge how much you need.

11. Cut a clump of muskrat a little heavier than the tail. The fur and guard hairs are easily seen in this photo. This muskrat clump will form the collar.

12. Holding the muskrat in your right hand, bring the clump over the top and down along the sides in such a manner that it completely encompasses the body. The actual fur should extend back along the body to about the half-way mark. The guard hairs will be longer.

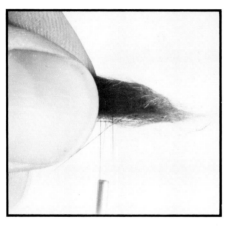

13. Grasp the positioned muskrat collar with your left hand, being certain not to change its position. It is important that the thread be positioned properly for the collar tie-down.

14. Collar secured in place. A loose turn of thread might help keep the collar from rolling to one side at the onset, but be certain the fur is securely in place.

15. Select and tie-in 2-4 ostrich herls by the tips. Carefully notice the head area. This fly will have a very small thread head, and because of the fur collar, it is difficult to avoid a little bulk. Also, the ostrich herl requires a level underbody or it will "fall off" the front.

16. Position the thread where you intend to secure, or tie-off the ostrich head. Twist the ostrich herls together and begin wrapping the head, back to front. A few turns will be plenty.

17. The ostrich herl head is in place and the excess ends have been trimmed. While the ostrich herl head is very close to the eye, it will not be in the way. Stroke the herl fibers back away from the eye and finish off the thread head.

18. Finished Casual Dress.

42

Waterboatmen

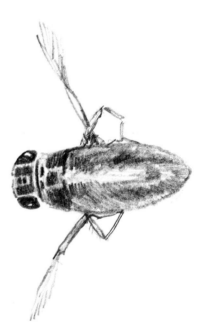

Waterboatmen

To some observers, waterboatmen look like a flattened football, or, as their name implies, a small boat complete with oars. To other observers, waterboatmen are beetle-like in appearance with somewhat large eyes and a hard shiny back. The back of a mature waterboatman is actually its folded wings. Adults can take flight at any time but only seem to utilize their flying capabilities during times of mating or migration. Waterboatmen lack tracheal gills; therefore, they must make frequent trips to the surface to obtain oxygen, which is in the form of an air bubble which they trap between their hind legs. A silvery stream of rising air bubbles trail behind as they make their way toward the bottom. This trait is probably a strong "key" that attracts trout.

Waterboatmen are not the most important food source of trout but, during times when they are a preferred meal, you will want a few imitations tucked into the corner of your fly box. Panfish, however, consume fair quantities of waterboatmen. Some new techniques are encountered in constructing this unique imitation, including a triple back and a double-back thorax.

HOOK:	Tiemco 5262, 10-16, weighted and smashed flat
THREAD:	Olive
TAIL:	Clear (white) Antron fibers
BACK:	Triple back. Plastic strip over pearl Flashabou, over ring-neck pheasant tail fibers
RIB:	Fine oval silver tinsel
BODY:	Olive marabou fibers
LEGS:	Olive stripped goose, tied back along each side of the body
HEAD:	Peacock, with plastic strip reversed back over the head and tied off at back of the head

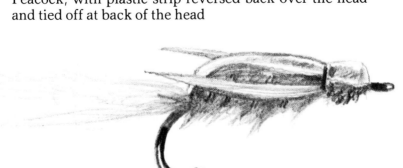

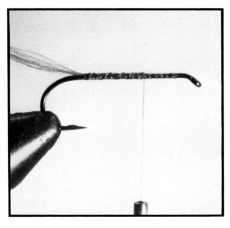

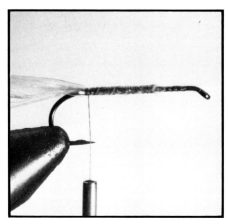

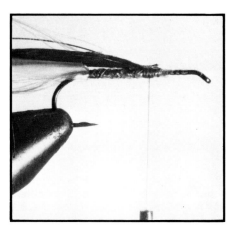

1. Secure the Antron tail, shagging it to about 1/2 the body length. Keep the body area level. The Antron tail helps represent trailing air bubbles.

2. Cut a 2-inch piece of plastic about 1/4-inch wide. Double it over and secure in place, tying it down to the extreme back of the body.

3. At the front of the body, tie in the pheasant tail fibers, Flashabou strips, and the rib, in that order. The pheasant tail fibers should be tied in by the tips. Wrap the thread to the back, keeping these newly tied-in-place materials along the top of the body area.

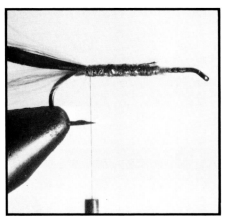

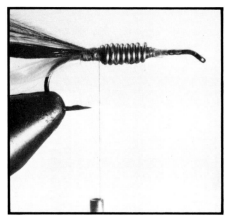

4. Properly constructed underbody.

5. Tie in a few long marabou fibers by the tips. Next, the lead, positioning it as shown. There must be space at the rear to begin a slight taper and ample room in front. Lead positioned at this time allows for a heavy and wider body, and the materials are easily secured.

6. Secure the lead with thread, smash it flat and dub and wrap some fur in front and behind the lead. Note the taper in front of the lead. Position the thread at the front of the body area.

7. Wrap the marabou around the hook, forming the body and tie off.

8. Wrap the rib over the body, tie off and trim the excess.

9. First, pull the pheasant tail over the top of the body and tie off. Next, pull the Flashabou strips forward over the pheasant and tie off. Finally, bring the plastic strip over the top of the body and tie it off right at the hook eye. Notice the position of the tie-off.

10. Trim off the excess Flashabou and pheasant, but not the plastic. Select a strip goose fiber and secure along each side of the body with the tips curving toward the inside, and extending to the end of the body.

11. Tie in place one or two peacock herls.

12. Wrap the peacock herls, forming the head. Tie the herls off at the front of the head, then wrap the thread back to the rear of the head, reinforcing the peacock and positioning the thread to secure the plastic over the top of the peacock head.

13. Pull the plastic back over the peacock head and tie down. Trim off the excess, half hitch and lacquer.

14. Finished Waterboatman.

43

Crayfish

Crayfish (Dave Whitlock)

Very few anglers are tuned into the fishing possibilities crayfish offer. They inhabit all types of trout water and when available in good numbers produce very large trout. Bass and steelhead also prize crayfish for their high calorie count and surely they must love their flavor just as we do.

Dave Whitlock, master of many angling arts, has a unique signature associated with his nymphs, which incorporate Swiss Straw (substitute raffia), antennae and eyes. Those interested in more of Dave's patterns should read his book, *Guide to Aquatic Trout Foods*.

HOOK:	Tiemco 300, 4-10, weight heavy
THREAD:	Color to match body
EYES:	Burned monofilament or black nylon beads. See Floating Dragon, page 160 for instructions
ANTENNAE:	Two strands of dark moose
NOSE (TAIL):	Dyed deer hair to match body
PINCHERS:	Speckled hen hackle feather on top and cream hen feather underneath glued together with Flexament. Top feather is Pantone colored to match body
RIB:	Copper wire
LEGS:	Grizzly hackle dyed to match body color (Pantone)
BODY:	Antron blend, color to suit, picked out along sides
TAIL AND BACK:	Raffia to match body
HIGHLIGHTS:	Black Pantone pen

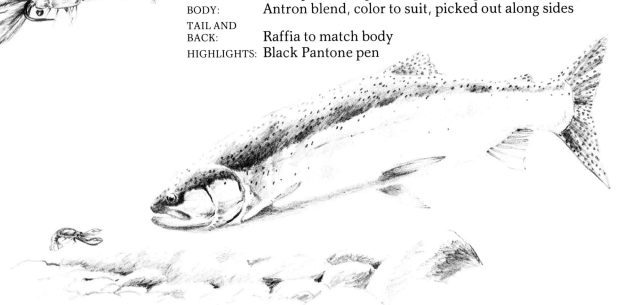

1. Secure hook in vise upside down. Secure burned monofilament eyes slightly forward of the hook point. Next, tie in two dark moose fibers about half the body length, followed by a bunch of deer hair, which forms the tail (nose). Hook point will split the tail.

2. Select a brownish speckled and white hen neck, or saddle feathers. Match the two feathers and glue together with Flexament. Prepare another set and let dry. Strip off the ends slightly and secure in place, flaring outwards, light side down, forming the pinchers.

3. Dub and wrap the body material up to the eyes. Now, tie in the rib material and then dub and wrap a little more fur between and *slightly* in front of the eyes. Prepare and tie in place tip first style hackle. Weight to suit.

4. Dub and wrap the body over the lead wire.

5. Wrap the hackle through the body palmer style and tie off at about the 75% mark. Notice that the hackle is only wrapped through the middle 50% of the hook shank. Dub and wrap some more fur toward the eye of the hook.

6. Select and flatten a piece of raffia (Swiss Straw is nice but is currently unavailable) and tie in place at the head area. Raffia should be flat over the top of the body and some excess should protrude out the front of the fly.

7. Maneuver the legs down along the sides of the hook and tie the raffia down behind the eyes with the rib material. Wrap the rib through the body, being careful to keep the legs (hackle) neatly in position. Tie off the rib.

8. Trim off the excess raffia behind the eyes. Trim the rib off in front and trim the excess raffia at the front to shape, leaving some excess protruding out the front. Finish off a thread head, lacquer and highlight Crayfish with Pantone pen.

9. Finished Crayfish.

44

Floating Dragon

Floating Dragon (Randall Kaufmann)

It is only recently that dragonfly nymphs have begun to receive the attention they deserve. With the strong advent of lake fishing in America, anglers are discovering how important they are and beginning to recognize the differences between dragonfly, hellgrammite, stonefly and damselfly nymphs, or larvae. Dragonflies offer trout a tasty morsel and a great number of calories (energy).

The majority of hatching activity takes place in spring and early summer, but several species also hatch during mid and late summer. Nymphs inhabit shallow bottom strata and aquatic vegetation, and can be casually recognized by their somewhat robust size. Nymphs crawl out of the water to hatch or transform into adults and if any migration of lake dwelling insects can excite a feeding frenzy, dragonflies can. A general guideline is to fish brownish colors over bottom rubble, mud, etc., and olive colors around vegetation. There are three dragonfly patterns detailed here, each requiring different tying techniques and each offering various angling applications. Experiment on your own and observe the shape and animation of naturals, for this will dictate the final imitation and presentation technique you should employ.

This dragonfly nymph has emerged from the water and is ready to begin the transformation into a winged adult. Notice the stonefly passenger.

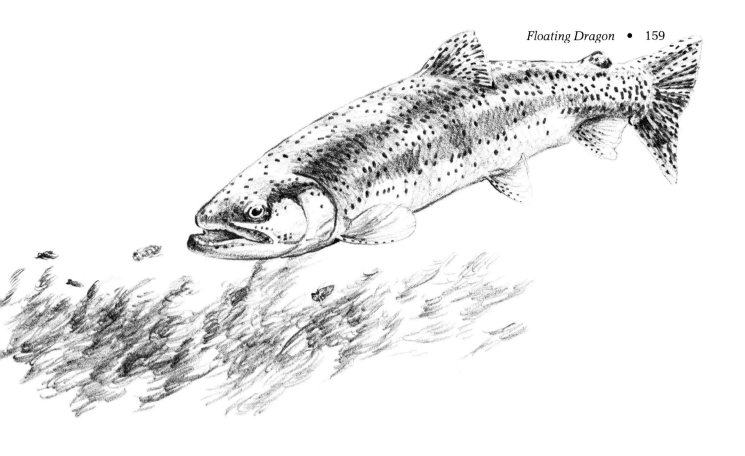

This is a comparatively recent innovation designed to be fished with a floating line over shallow submerged weed beds and in very shallow shoreline areas. The Floating Dragon also has great value to anglers fishing a sinking line when you want your fly to float up off the bottom or stay above floating bottom weeds. It is also of value when dragonfly nymphs are actively swimming, crawling, and otherwise active either while foraging for food or during emergent migrations. Its value as a probe and attractor pattern should not be overlooked either, as its broad silhouette attracts fish from a long distance. During windy conditions the Floating Dragon can be left to ride the riffles. Attacks are aggressive and firm.

This is the only pattern we will tie that incorporates a clipped hair body. The technique for installing burned monofilament eyes is also described.

HOOK:	Tiemco 300, 4-10
THREAD:	Olive
EYES:	Burned monofilament (50 lb.)
TAIL:	Grizzly marabou dyed olive, tied *heavy*, but short
BODY:	Olive deer hair, clipped to shape, flat on bottom so hook gape is not impeded. Color back with Pantone pen 119, brown-olive
LEGS:	Grizzly marabou dyed olive tied *heavy* along sides of body, extending 3/4 length of body
WINGCASE:	Light mottled turkey or goose lacquered and pre-clipped to "V" and tied extended style. Wingcase should extend slightly down along side of body and encompass legs. Color with Pantone pen same as body
HEAD:	Dark olive Hairtron

1. To prepare the burned monofilament eyes, cut a short section of large diameter monofilament (about 50 pound test for larger dragon imitations) and hold with a smooth nose pliers.

2. Hold one end over a burning candle, melting the monofilament nearly to the pliers edge. Blow out the burning monofilament, holding the pliers in a horizontal position as shown, so the melted monofilament sags slightly downward.

3. Repeat the above process with the other side of the monofilament, being certain to allow the soft monofilament to sag in the same direction. Holding the monofilament in the heat of the flame away from the outer edges helps keep it clear.

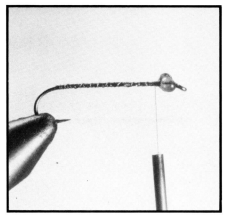

4. Secure eyes at the front of the hook, being certain they are positioned at a right angle to the shank.

5. Select a thick clump of grizzly dyed marabou and tie onto the hook. The tail shown could be shorter.

6. Select a bunch of dyed olive deer hair that is soft and pliable and hold in your right hand.

7. Trim the tips even. This will allow for easy handling of the deer. Your thread should be positioned at the extreme rear of the body.

8. Change the deer hair to your left hand and place on top of the hook at the rear of the body. Bring the thread up between your fingers and tie down slowly, allowing the fibers to flare. A half dozen tight turns of thread is sufficient.

9. As the deer is being secured and flaring out in all directions, it may have a tendency to roll slightly clockwise until the thread is firmly tightened. During this process, do not let the tail roll off to one side of the hook.

10. Stroke the deer back and wrap a few turns of thread immediately in front of the deer hair bunch nearly at the original tie-down.

11. Prepare another bunch of deer and secure in place immediately in front of the last clump. Be careful not to tie down any of the existing fibers.

12. It may look like there is no room left on the hook, but there is plenty. As you spin, or flare the second bunch of deer, hold onto the first bunch so it does not roll around the hook.

13. This fly required three bunches of deer to properly fill the hook shank. Deer must be packed tightly together. Notice the space at the front of the hook. This will be plenty. If you have slightly less space, there will be no problem.

14. Tie off the thread and remove the fly from the vise. Dragonfly nymphs have a wide abdomen. I like to trim the body mostly flat on the underside, being certain the hook gape is not impeded, slightly rounded on top, and with a fast triangle taper along the sides.

15. Finished body trimmed to shape. Tie the thread back onto the hook in front of the body.

16. Select a thick bunch of marabou fibers and secure in place along one side of the body, no longer than the body. Next, secure a bunch along the opposite side of the hook. The legs are now in place.

17. Prepare a section of lacquered turkey or goose wing quill, clip to "V" and secure in place (see Kaufmann Stone). The wingcase section should be wide enough so that it slightly encompasses the legs. Dub and wrap fur behind, between (figure 8), and in front of the eyes.

18. Finished Floating Dragon.

45

Assam Dragon

Assam Dragon (Charles E. Brooks)

Charles Brooks is the highly respected author of several books pertaining to western nymph fishing. *All* of his books are on the "must read" list, especially *Nymph Fishing for Larger Trout.* The Assam Dragon is unique, yet the most simple of all his fly patterns. It, along with the Brooks' Montana Stone, is also the most popular. Charlie relates that the name came from Assam Province, India. Years ago a man-eating tiger was eating women and children. The men, "great hunters," could not admit this and invented the legend of the Assam Dragon. Charlie chose the name because it is catchy and the fly is intended to represent a dragonfly nymph.

It is fished mostly in lakes with silt, mud, or sand bottoms, with a slow hand twist retrieve in conjunction with 6-inch jerks every 10-15 seconds. It is the jerk that usually entices the grab. Best results are obtained when the fly is on the *bottom*, but it should be retrieved right up until it comes out of the water. In moving water it can be dead drifted or crawled over bottom strata, possibly representing stonefly and dragonfly larva, leech, and perhaps a drowned mouse, bird or who knows what.

The strip fur body and reverse hackle are the new techniques described.

HOOK:	Tiemco 300, 4-10, weight to suit
THREAD:	Brown
BODY:	Natural brown seal, rabbit, or other short, dark fur on the skin. Cut a narrow strip 1/8 to 1/16 inch wide and about 4 inches long. Tie in at bend of hook and wrap to front
LEGS:	Long and soft grizzly dyed brown hackle or pheasant body, tied curving forward

1. To prepare the fur strip, an X-Acto blade or very sharp, fine-point scissors is needed. Trim a 3-inch long piece of fur strip as narrow as possible. Be careful not to cut the actual fur. Trim off the fur and narrow-up the hide area that will actually be secured onto the hook.

2. The fur strip should be tied onto the hook *very* securely as pictured, with the hide side facing you. Begin wrapping the fur strip around the hook, cinching tightly on each wrap.

3. Stroke the fur back after each wrap.

4. Finished body just before fur strip tie-down.

5. Tie off the fur strip as usual, then take a few extra turns of thread in front of the tie-down *before* you trim the excess. After trimming excess, wrap more thread slightly back over the last wrap of fur strip.

6. The tie-down will be a little bulky. If the body is positioned too close to the eye, push, or pack the body wraps closer together. Select and tie in a hackle on *top* of the bulk, reverse style so fibers curve forward.

7. The wraps, or turns of hackle, should be spaced out through the remaining area, with the first wrap *over* the top of the bulk and the next two wraps in *front* of the bulk.

8. Proper positioning of legs. Tie off legs and finish the thread head.

9. Finished Assam Dragon.

46

Lake Dragon

Lake Dragon (Randall Kaufmann)

Anglers usually arrive at the water's edge ready to fish, instantly. I suppose this habit is not a bad idea, especially if the act of fishing is what is important to you. I usually like to clean the fly line, taper out a leader, select a fly, sharpen the hook, smash the barb, and attend to the many other little preparations one should do prior to fishing along the water's edge. These waterside preparations slow me down and keep me from barging into the water without some prefishing observation. While I prepare my tackle I am consciously aware of my surroundings, observing the presence or absence, and locations and habits, of both insects and fish, and the many other subtleties that will dictate where, when, and how I will fish.

Dragonfly lifecycle

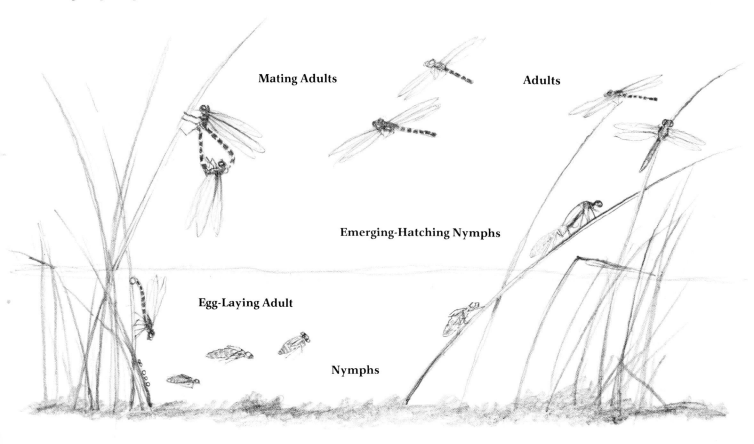

Mating Adults

Adults

Emerging-Hatching Nymphs

Egg-Laying Adult

Nymphs

A "hatching dragonfly" that has crawled from the water, split its case at the thorax area and is in the process of transforming into a winged adult. This amazing phenomenon was witnessed along the Williamson River in Oregon and required about thirty minutes.

I often wonder how many anglers notice empty or spent nymph cases, or how many have observed the amazing dragonfly transformation from nymph to adult. Probably very few, and yet the dragonfly is one of the easier aquatic insects to observe during this stage of its life. It is too easy for anglers to miss many of the enjoyable and enlightening aspects angling offers. S-l-o-w d-o-w-n — look, watch, listen, and think. After all, fly fishing is an intellectual pursuit. The main characters are trout and insects. They play a serious game of survival while interacting with nature. Man is the player, and while nature is constantly changing the rules, she is always offering new clues.

The Lake Dragon is a very effective imitation to fish over bottom strata and near vegetation. A succession of short, quick pulls on the fly line will bring it to life, hopefully teasing any nearby trout into attacking. This useful pattern will depict how to tie on glass eyes and how to form a wide, flattened, lead underbody.

HOOK: Tiemco 300, 4-8, weighted and flattened *rear* half of hook only

THREAD: Color to match body

EYES: 3mm bronze glass eyes or burned monofilament

TAIL: Marabou fluff color to match body tied short and full

RIB: Copper wire

BODY: Olive or brown Hairtron blended with the following colors of goat for highlights: blue, purple, green, amber, olive, brown, rust. Body to be wider than thorax and flattened in appearance

LEGS: Pheasant rump or body to match body color, tied half circle and not to extend beyond the body

WINGCASE: Mottled light or white tip turkey colored with Pantone pen to match body, lacquered and clipped in "V," tied short

HEAD: This is also the thorax area, same as body only of much smaller diameter

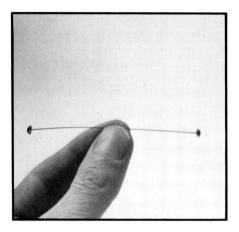

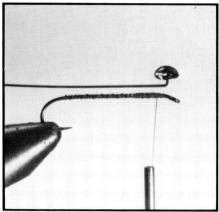

1. Glass eyes come attached to a 3-inch length of wire. They are available in clear and amber but are easily customized with a touch of paint on the back side.

2. With a fine point pliers, bend the wire at a right angle close as possible to the eye. Position the eye and thread at the front of the hook.

3. Trim the wire and secure in place, being careful not to break the thread on the trimmed end of the wire, which will be very sharp.

4. Secure another eye on the opposite side of the hook. Notice the eye position in relation to the hook eye.

5. Select a very thick bunch of marabaou fluff (fibers), secure in place and even up to the proper length with your fingers. Tie in the rib. Notice the tapered underbody.

6. By placing lead onto the hook at this point of construction, more weight is added and the body will be wider. Notice that lead is tied on the back half of the hook, deviating from the norm because a wide body and narrower thorax is desired.

7. The large diameter lead creates a considerable "drop-off" at each end. To facilitate body construction, a slight amount of dubbing has been added at each end, tapering out the abrupt edge, or drop-off.

8. Smash the lead flat. The foundation is properly prepared and the body will easily wrap in place.

9. The dubbed body is finished. Notice the space in front where the legs, wingcase and head will be placed.

10. Wrap the rib and tie it off.

11. Select a pheasant body feather and trim out the center stem. Individual fibers are attached to the center stem, which inhibits fiber action. Center stems are seldom desired and should be trimmed prior to installation or pulled off afterward.

12. Hold the feather in your right hand over the top of the body. Change hands and secure in place as shown. Fibers should not extend beyond the length of the body and should be tied half circle.

13. Prepare a lacquered turkey tail segment (see Kaufmann Stone) and place in position with your right hand. The wingcase should slightly encompass the legs.

14. Change hands, holding the wingcase in place while it is secured. Notice that the finger tips and thread meet at the exact tie-in position, and that the wingcase folds slightly down over the sides of the hook.

15. The wingcase is properly secured. Notice again how the wingcase folds slightly down along the side of the body and the length of the legs. Dub and wrap the thorax. There is no thread head to speak of, just place a few turns of thread and a half hitch in front of the eyes.

16. Finished Lake Dragon.

A stonefly adult, *Pteronacys californica*, and empty nymph case decorate streamside vegetation along an Oregon stream.

Part Three

Pattern Directory

Part III is the pattern directory. If you have mastered all thirty demonstration patterns you will be able to construct all two hundred patterns listed here.

Pattern Directory

Whenever possible, I have attempted to give the original dressing. Many patterns were developed before the advent of today's highly effective synthetics. Had such materials been available in the past, most patterns would have been tied differently. Patterns that originally called for materials that are no longer available have been changed, incorporating today's most applicable material.

Dressings are given in the order in which they are *tied* onto the hook. This is not necessarily the order in which they are *wrapped* onto the hook. By now you should be able to "read" any nymph dressing and not only understand the tying sequence and associated tying technique, but also visualize the finished fly. If you have any trouble remembering how to handle a particular technique, refer back to the instruction section.

ALL PURPOSE, Dark
HOOK:	Tiemco 5263, 8-16, weight to suit
THREAD:	Black
TAIL:	Ringneck pheasant tail fibers
RIB:	Gold wire
BODY:	Dark brown beaver
WINGCASE:	Brown white tip turkey quill segment
THORAX:	Dark brown beaver
LEGS:	Black hen hackle tied divided style
COMMENTS:	The all purpose series were designed to represent the familiar silhouette of many nymphal forms. Vary the sizes and colors and you can suggest many food types in a variety of water

ALL PURPOSE, Light
HOOK:	Tiemco 5263, 8-16, weight to suit
THREAD:	Brown
TAIL:	Mallard dyed woodduck
RIB:	Brown floss or silk thread
BODY:	Cream or buff fox
WINGCASE:	Ringneck pheasant tail fibers
THORAX:	Cream or buff fox
LEGS:	Cream or light ginger hen hackle tied divided style

All Purpose

ALL PURPOSE, Medium
HOOK:	Tiemco 5263, 8-16, weight to suit
THREAD:	Brown
TAIL:	Ringneck pheasant tail fibers
RIB:	Gold wire
BODY:	Grayish brown red fox
WINGCASE:	White tip turkey quill segment
THORAX:	Grayish brown red fox
LEGS:	Brown hen hackle tied divided style

ALPHA-BEATA (John Orrelle)
HOOK:	Tiemco 5262, 14-18, weight to suit
THREAD:	Olive
TAIL:	3-4 moose hairs tied short
BODY:	Stripped peacock herl
THORAX:	Olive fur, shade to suit
COMMENTS:	Imitation developed for *Callibaetis*

A.P. BLACK (Andy Puyans)
HOOK:	Tiemco 200 or 5262, 12-18, weight to suit
THREAD:	Black
TAIL:	Dark moose
RIB:	Copper wire
BODY:	Black beaver or substitute Hairtron
WINGCASE:	Dark moose
THORAX:	Same as body
LEGS:	Dark moose, leftover tips from wingcase tied divided style
COMMENTS:	There is an entire series of A.P. nymphs. Other body colors are easily substituted. Ringneck tail fibers can also be substituted in place of the moose. A peacock thorax is also a possibility. Popular throughout Western America

ASSAM DRAGON (Charles E. Brooks) See Page 162
HOOK:	Tiemco 300, 4-10, weight to suit
THREAD:	Brown
BODY:	Natural brown seal, rabbit, or other short, dark fur on the skin. Cut a narrow strip 1/8 to 1/16 inch wide and about 4 inches long. Tie in at bend of hook and wrap to front
LEGS:	Long and soft dyed brown grizzly hackle, ringneck pheasant body, or hen saddle hackle tied curving forward

ATHERTON, Medium (John Atherton)
HOOK:	Tiemco 5262, 12-18, weight to suit
THREAD:	Brown
TAIL:	Brown partridge
RIB:	Fine oval gold tinsel
BODY:	Blended hare's ear
WINGCASE:	Bright blue goose or duck wing quill segment
THORAX:	Same as body
LEGS:	Brown partridge tied half circle
COMMENTS:	Longtime favorite, described in John Atherton's book, *The Fly and the Fish*

BAETIS (Doug Swisher and Carl Richards)
HOOK:	Tiemco 200 or 101, 14-22
THREAD:	Olive
TAIL:	Dyed olive mallard or light partridge
BODY:	Blend of medium olive and medium brown fur
WING:	Black ostrich clump, represents wing pads
LEGS:	Dyed olive mallard or light partridge, tied beard or divided style
COMMENTS:	Widespread hatch of immense value to many anglers

BAETIS SOFT HACKLE (Rick Hafele)

HOOK: Tiemco 101 or 200, 14-20
THREAD: Gray
TAIL: Soft blue dun hackle fibers
BODY: Gray angora goat
LEGS: Blue dun hen hackle tied full

BEAVER

HOOK: Tiemco 5262, 10-16, weighted
THREAD: Brown
TAIL: Gray partridge
RIB: Gold wire
BODY: Beaver
LEGS: Gray partridge tied beard style

BEAVERPELT

HOOK: Tiemco 300, 6-12, weighted
THREAD: Brown
BODY: Beaver fur, tied fat
LEGS: Natural black hen hackle, long and soft
COMMENTS: Impressionistic, dragonfly nymphs

BIRD'S STONEFLY (Cal Bird)

HOOK: Tiemco 300, 4-8, weighted
THREAD: Orange
TAIL: Brown strip goose tied in "V"
RIB: Orange floss
BODY: Beaver or brown yarn
WINGCASE: White tip turkey quill segment
LEGS: Palmered brown saddle hackle through thorax
THORAX: Peacock

BITCH CREEK

HOOK: Tiemco 300, 2-8, weighted
THREAD: Black
TAIL: Two strands white rubber strips, small-medium diameter
ANTENNAE: Same as tail
BODY: Black chenille with piece of yellow chenille pulled underneath and secured by crisscrossing thread through body, or weave chenille
LEGS: Brown saddle hackle palmered through thorax
THORAX: Black chenille

BLACK DRAKE (E.H. "Polly" Rosborough)

HOOK: Tiemco 5263, 10-14
THREAD: Gray
TAIL: Guinea, 1/2 inch long
BODY: Blend two parts muskrat, two parts beaver and one part jackrabbit without guard hairs (substitute hare's ear) and form a noodle (see specific tying instructions for Casual Dress) and smash flat
LEGS: Guinea tied alongside of body, extending slightly over half the body length
WING: Grayish black ostrich clipped square 1/4 to 1/3 body length

BLACK HELLGRAMMITE (Doug Prince)

HOOK: Tiemco 300, 4-10, weighted
THREAD: Black
TAIL: Black strip goose
RIB: Black ostrich
BODY: Black yarn or Hairtron
WINGCASE: Dark gray or black goose quill segment
LEGS: Black saddle hackle palmered through thorax
THORAX: Black fur with strip of red yarn along underside
LEGS: Black strip goose tied back alongside of thorax and extending to half body length
COMMENTS: Developed by noted California tyer Doug Prince, recipient of Buz Buszek award

BLACK MARTINEZ (Don Martinez)

HOOK: Tiemco 5262, 8-14, weight to suit
THREAD: Black
TAIL: Guinea
RIB: Fine oval gold tinsel
BODY: Black angora goat
WINGCASE: Green goose quill segment or raffia
THORAX: Black chenille
LEGS: Mallard flank or gray partridge, tied full
COMMENTS: Longtime favorite, originated in Yellowstone area and now fished throughout America

BLACK QUILL

HOOK: Tiemco 5262, 12-18
THREAD: Black
TAIL: Medium color blue dun hackle fibers
BODY: Stripped peacock quill
WINGCASE: Gray mallard wing quill segment
THORAX: Muskrat
LEGS: Medium color dun hen hackle fibers tied divided style

BLOND BURLAP (E.H. "Polly" Rosborough)

HOOK: Tiemco 5263, 10-12
THREAD: Tan
TAIL: Soft honey dun or light ginger hackle
BODY: Burlap, three strands in a spinning loop (noodle). Taper body and score
LEGS: Soft honey dun or light neck or saddle hackle extending to bend of hook

Black Drake

BLOOD WORM

HOOK: Tiemco 101 or 200, 12-22
THREAD: Red
TAIL: Red marabou
ANTENNAE: Whitish gray marabou or clear Antron fibers tied sparse and short, not to extend beyond hook eye
BODY: Red marabou
COMMENTS: Designed to imitate the chironomid specie *Tendipes* which is one of the few insects to contain hemoglobin. Colors range from reddish brown to red and purplish

BLUE QUILL

HOOK: Tiemco 5262, 14-18
THREAD: Tan
TAIL: Ringneck pheasant tail fibers
BODY: Amber (yellow-brown) fur
WINGCASE: Black duck quill segment
THORAX: Same as body
LEGS: Ginger hen hackle fibers tied divided style

BLUE WING OLIVE

HOOK: Tiemco 5262, 14-18
THREAD: Olive
TAIL: Mallard dyed woodduck
RIB: Brown floss or silk thread
BODY: Medium olive fur
WINGCASE: Dark gray goose wing quill segment
THORAX: Medium olive fur
LEGS: Brown partridge tied divided style

BOATMEN-BACKSWIMMER (Al Troth)

HOOK: Tiemco 5262, 10-18, weighted and flattened. Lead may be tied alongside of hook to give flat appearance
THREAD: Olive
BACK: Double back. Tie in heavy mill plastic first, which will become the top of body. Next tie in mallard dyed woodduck or light mottled turkey wing quill
RIB: Fine oval silver tinsel
BODY: Hare's ear dyed olive
LEGS: Olive duck or goose quill fibers taken from short side of quill and tied in at back of thorax alongside of hook
THORAX: Same as body with shellback tied reverse back from hook eye and tied off at back of thorax at legs

BOX CANYON STONE (Mims Barker)

HOOK: Tiemco 300, 4-10, weighted
THREAD: Black
TAIL: Black stripped goose
BODY: Black yarn "twisted" to give segmented effect
WINGCASE: White tip turkey quill segment
LEGS: Furnace saddle hackle palmered through thorax
THORAX: Black fur

BRASSIE (Gene Lynch)

HOOK: Tiemco 5262, 10-18
THREAD: Black
BODY: Copper wire. A fur underbody may be constructed to form a tapered base on larger sizes
HEAD: Gray muskrat with guard hairs
COMMENTS: Gary LaFontaine believes this pattern might realistically represent the cases of caddisfly species which are constructed in part with reddish yellow or metallic minerals. One specie which builds such cases is *Oligophleboides* or Little Western Dark Sedge. Smaller sizes could perhaps imitate the *Hydroptila* cases

BREADCRUST

HOOK: Tiemco 5262, 10-16
THREAD: Black
RIB: Stripped ruffed grouse tail quill or strip peacock eye quill double ribbed with gold wire
BODY: Burnt orange fur
LEGS: Grizzly hen hackle tied full

BROOKS STONE-Montana Stone (Charles E. Brooks)

HOOK: Tiemco 300, 4-8, weighted
THREAD: Black
TAIL: Black strip goose fibers tied in a "V"
RIB: Heavy copper wire
BODY: Black fuzzy yarn
THORAX: Light gray ostrich herl, ribbed through body at thorax area to represent gills
LEGS: One natural grizzly and one dyed dark brown grizzly saddle hackle. Hackle is tied in at butt end and wound to front and tied off. Ostrich is now wound to the hook eye and tied off
COMMENTS: Designed to imitate the stonefly genus *Pteronarcys*, especially *P. californica*

BROWN BOMBER

HOOK: Tiemco 200 or 5262, 12-16
THREAD: Black
RIB: Flat gold tinsel
BODY: Muskrat or beaver
LEGS: Brown partridge tied full

BROWN DRAKE (Mike Lawson)

HOOK: Tiemco 5263, 10, weight to suit
THREAD: Brown
TAIL: Dark mottled brown hen saddle fibers or partridge
RIB: Fine gold wire
GILLS: Grayish-brown ostrich
BODY: Medium tannish-brown fur mixed with clear Antron blend
WINGCASE: Mottled turkey, creased at back
LEGS: Brown partridge palmered through thorax
THORAX: Same as body

CADDIS LARVA

HOOK:	Tiemco 200, 10-20, weighted
THREAD:	Black or brown
BODY:	Hairtron, color to suit
LEGS:	Brown partridge tied beard style
HEAD:	Dark brown or black Hairtron
COMMENTS:	Standard caddis larva imitation in wide use today

CADDIS LARVA (Gary LaFontaine)

HOOK:	Tiemco 200, 10-20, weight to suit
THREAD:	Brown
RIB:	Optional brown rooster hackle stem stripped of fibers
BODY:	Hairtron, color of your choice
THORAX:	Hairtron, dark brown or two shades darker than body
LEGS:	Mallard dyed woodduck or brown partridge tied beard style

CADDIS PUPA

Caddis Pupa

HOOK:	Tiemco 200, 12-10
THREAD:	Brown
RIB:	Thread or floss, slightly darker than body
BODY:	Fur, color to suit. Body can begin slightly beyond bend of hook. The noodle technique can be employed if a more segmented effect is desired. Omit rib if noodle is used
LEGS:	Brown partridge fibers tied beard style
WING:	Gray mallard quill tied along each side of body curving down and extending *slightly* past hook point. Mallard dyed woodduck over top of body
COLLAR:	Woodchuck, Australian opossum or dark muskrat with guard hair left in, trimmed on top and slightly on upper sides
COMMENTS:	A composite pattern good for imitating caddis pupa. Vary colors to suit your need. To simplify confusion from other books and articles, caddisflies are often referred to as Grannon or Sedge, especially throughout the British Empire

CAENIS FUR

HOOK:	Mustad 94859, 18-26
THREAD:	Brown
TAIL:	Three dark pheasant fibers splayed out
RIB:	Tan thread
BODY:	Grayish tan fur
WING:	Black rabbit or ostrich

CAREY SPECIAL (Lloyd A Day and Tom Carey)

HOOK:	Tiemco 300, 6-12
THREAD:	Black
TAIL:	Ringneck pheasant tail fibers
RIB:	Copper wire
BODY:	Ringneck pheasant tail fibers or red, green, olive, or black yarn, fur, or peacock herl
LEGS:	Ringneck pheasant tail or ringneck body feathers tied full and extending to bend of hook
COMMENTS:	Popular west coast and Canadian pattern, especially with lake anglers

CARROT (Ed Schroeder)

HOOK:	Tiemco 200, 12-20
THREAD:	Orange
TAIL:	Furnace or brown hackle fibers
BACK:	Peacock herl
RIB:	Gold wire
BODY:	Orange thread
WINGCASE:	Pearl flashabou strips
LEGS:	Furnace or brown neck hackle palmered through thorax
THORAX:	Peacock herl

CARROT (Rube Cross)

HOOK:	Tiemco 5262, 12-18
THREAD:	Orange
TAIL:	Black hackle fibers
BODY:	Orange thread or fur
THORAX:	Black fur
LEGS:	2-4 turns of soft black hackle tied back

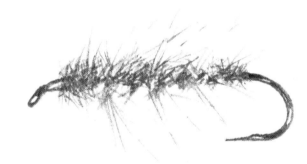

CASED CADDIS (Gary LaFontaine)

Cased Caddis

HOOK:	Tiemco 400 or 101, 8-16, bend front 1/3 of 101 hook shank up at a 45 degree angle. Weight straight portion of hook shank as explained in tying directions for Emergent Sparkle Pupa
THREAD:	Brown
BODY:	Actually represents the caddis case, two soft hackle feathers wrapped one at a time not so close that lead and thread is obscured. Trim to desired shape of insect you intend to imitate
THORAX:	Represents insect body protruding from case, fur dubbing to suit
LEGS:	Hackle fibers tied beard style, color to suit

CASED CADDIS (Randall Kaufmann)
HOOK: Tiemco 200, 10-18, weighted
THREAD: Black
BODY: One undersized hackle tied in tip first, two peacock herls and 2-3 ostrich herls, all materials color of your choice and a piece of copper or gold wire. Twist all materials together until tight and wrap around hook to form body (caddis case)
HEAD: Optional, color to match natural. Fur, marabou, ostrich, or filoplume. The head represents the caddis body extended from its case. This is a natural position when crawling or drifting, attempting to secure a hold

CASUAL DRESS (E.H. "Polly" Rosborough) See Page 150
HOOK: Tiemco 300, 4-10
THREAD: Black
TAIL: A short thick bunch of muskrat hair with all guard hairs left in
BODY: Muskrat tied noodle style
COLLAR: Muskrat extending back 1/3 of body length
HEAD: Wide black ostrich

CATE'S TURKEY (Jerry Cate)
HOOK: Tiemco 200, 14-18
THREAD: Black
TAIL: Mallard dyed woodduck
RIB: Gold wire wound through body and head
BODY: Turkey tail
HEAD: Peacock
LEGS: Mallard dyed woodduck beard style
COMMENTS: Developed at Davis Lake, Oregon, in the late '60s

CATSKILL CANADENSIS
HOOK: Tiemco 5263, 14
THREAD: Orange
TAIL: Ringneck tail fibers
RIB: Brown floss or silk thread
BODY: Amber colored fur
WINGCASE: Ringneck tail fibers
THORAX: Same as body
LEGS: Brown partridge tied half circle

CATSKILL HENDRICKSON
HOOK: Tiemco 5263, 12-14
THREAD: Olive
TAIL: Mallard dyed woodduck
RIB: Gold wire
BODY: Grayish brown fur
WINGCASE: Gray goose or duck quill segment
THORAX: Grayish brown fur
LEGS: Brown partridge tied beard style

Catskill March Brown

CATSKILL MARCH BROWN
HOOK: Tiemco 5263, 12
THREAD: Orange
TAIL: Ringneck tail fibers
RIB: Brown floss or silk thread
BODY: Amber goat
WINGCASE: Ringneck tail fibers
THORAX: Amber goat
LEGS: Brown partridge tied full

CHIRONOMID LARVA (Randall Kaufmann)
HOOK: Tiemco 101 or 200, 10-24, weighted
THREAD: Black
TAIL: Antron fibers tied *sparse* and *short*, not extending beyond bend of hook
ANTENNAE: Same as tail, *not to extend beyond* eye of hook
RIB: White silk thread or copper wire
BODY: Black, olive, yellow, gray, or brown Hairtron tied *sparse* and *slender*. Marabou is also good
THORAX: Body color blended with dark brown or black Hairtron
COMMENTS: A simple fly but one which entices many, many selective trout

CHIRONOMID PUPA (Randall Kaufmann) See Page 114
HOOK: Tiemco 101 or 200, 12-24
THREAD: Black
TAIL: Clear Antron fibers tied short, not to extend beyond bend of hook
ANTENNAE: Same as tail, not to extend beyond eye of hook
RIB: White silk thread
BODY: Hairtron, black, olive, browns, etc. Bodies must be *slender*
THORAX: Black Hairtron
WING: Wide grizzly hen hackle tips tied 1/3 body length
COMMENTS: Represents what is thought to be the most widespread and important food source of trout. Fish these imitations just subsurface. Dead drift or retrieve in still water *very slowly*, just keeping the line tight

CRAYFISH (Dave Whitlock) See Page 156
HOOK: Tiemco 300, 4-10, weighted heavy
THREAD: Color to match body
EYES: Burned monofilament or nylon beads
ANTENNAE: Two strands of dark moose
NOSE (TAIL): Dyed deer to match body color
PINCHERS: Speckled hen hackle feather on top and cream hen hackle feather underneath, glued together with Flexament. Top feather is colored with Pantone pen to match body color
RIB: Copper wire
LEGS: Grizzly hackle dyed to match body color (Pantone)
BODY: Antron blend, color to suit, picked out along sides
TAIL: Raffia to match body
BACK: Same as tail
HIGHLIGHTS: Black Pantone pen

CREAM CADDIS

HOOK: Tiemco 5262, 10-18, weighted
THREAD: Black
TAIL: None
RIB: Copper wire or brown or olive buttonhole twist thread (buttonhole available at sewing counter)
BODY: Creamy tan fur
THORAX: Black or gray ostrich
LEGS: Soft, short black neck or hen hackle tied full

CREAM VARIANT

HOOK: Tiemco 5263, 12-14
THREAD: Tan
TAIL: Mallard dyed woodduck
RIB: Tan floss or silk thread
BODY: Blend of yellow, tan and amber fur
WINGCASE: Light gray goose quill segment
THORAX: Same as body
LEGS: Golden ginger hen hackle tied full

CREAM WIGGLER (Charles E. Brooks)

HOOK: Mustad 94843 (x-fine, x-short up eye) size 14
THREAD: Brown
BODY: A narrow piece of cream chamois or elastic 3/4" long is tied in at the head area and it is ribbed backward with tying thread. When properly secured it will look like a tail extending 2-3 times longer than the hook shank
LEGS: Light partridge tied full
COMMENTS: Pattern was designed to represent midge larva and is said to best be fished around weed beds

DAMSEL (E.H. "Polly" Rosborough)

HOOK: Tiemco 300, 10-12
THREAD: Olive
TAIL: Light golden olive marabou
RIB: Olive thread
BODY: Yarn, fuzzy and medium golden olive, slender at back, fatter at front
LEGS: Medium olive hackle or teal slightly darker than tail, extending to hook point
WING: Marabou, slightly darker than body

DAMSEL (Hal Janssen)

HOOK: Tiemco 300, 10-12, weight to suit
THREAD: Olive
TAIL: Pale golden olive marabou
RIB: Olive thread, 6/0
BACK: Mottled brown turkey
BODY: Medium olive dubbing (beaver preferred)
WINGCASE: Mottled brown turkey with drop of epoxy placed on top
LEGS: Cree hackle palmered and clipped short
THORAX: Same as body

DARK CADDIS EMERGENT (E.H. "Polly" Rosborough)

HOOK: Tiemco 5262, 10
THREAD: Black
RIB: Burnt orange monocord thread
BODY: Burnt orange yarn
LEGS: Soft furnace neck hackle extending to the bend of hook. Trim off all fibers on top and bottom
HEAD: Four twisted flues (herl) of black ostrich
COMMENTS: Tied to represent the caddisfly genus *Discosmoecus* which hatches in Oregon about late August

DARK HENDRICKSON

HOOK: Tiemco 5262, 12-16, weight to suit
THREAD: Olive
TAIL: Mallard dyed woodduck
RIB: Brown floss or silk thread
BODY: Gray brown red fox
WINGCASE: White tip turkey tail segment
THORAX: Same as body
LEGS: Brown partridge, tied full or divided style

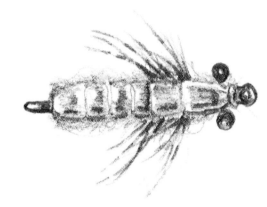

DAVE'S DRAGON (Dave Whitlock)

Dave's Dragon

HOOK: Tiemco 300, 4-10, weight rear portion of hook and smash flat
THREAD: Color to match body
EYES: Burned monofilament, .011 or larger
BACK, WINGCASE: Raffia to match body. Wingcase is doubled back twice.
RIB: Gold or copper wire
BODY, THORAX: Dubbing, color to suit, browns, olive, and black are best

DAVE'S RED SQUIRREL (Dave Whitlock)

HOOK: Tiemco 5263, 8-16, weighted
THREAD: Black
RIB: Fine oval gold tinsel, take a couple of turns behind body before beginning rib
BODY: Red fox squirrel body blended with like color of Antron blend
THORAX: Red fox squirrel body blended with charcoal and brown Antron blend
LEGS: One turn of mottled black or brown hen hackle

DAVE'S STONEFLY (Dave Whitlock)

HOOK:	Tiemco 300, 4-10, weighted
THREAD:	Color to match body
TAIL:	Dyed black monofilament, .009-.011 diameter tied "V" style
ANTENNAE:	Same as tail
BACK:	Raffia, color to complement body
WINGCASE:	Wingcase and back are the same piece so allow extra length including coverage of the head
RIB:	Gold or copper wire
BODY:	Antron dubbing, common colors include black, brown, gold, tan
LEGS:	Speckled hen pulled over thorax
THORAX:	Same as body or slight contrast
WINGCASE:	There are two folded back wingcases whereby the raffia is doubled back over itself and brought forward again. Do not trim when finished as the head is also covered
HEAD:	Same as body or slight contrast

DAVE'S SHRIMP (Dave Whitlock)

HOOK:	Tiemco 200, 10-18, weight to suit
THREAD:	Color to match body
ANTENNAE:	Stripped hackle stem or fine monofilament 1-2 times length of body. Note that imitation is tied backwards on hook but tying begins at back of hook
TAIL:	Short and soft grizzly hackle fibers
BACK:	Heavy mil plastic
LEGS:	Grizzly hackle, 1-2 turns in front of eyes, optional
EYES:	Burned monofilament .009-.010 diameter
RIB:	Gold wire
BODY:	Dubbing, picked out along underside, color to suit, brown, olive, gray best
COMMENTS:	Tying sequence is similar to Crayfish, see instructions

Dave's Shrimp

DEEP SPARKLE PUPA, Brown and Yellow
(Gary LaFontaine)

HOOK:	Tiemco 200, 10-20
THREAD:	Brown
UNDERBODY:	Blend 1/2 rust or gold Antron yarn and 1/2 brown fur
OVERBODY:	Strands of rust or gold Antron yarn tied in at end of body pulled forward around body and tied off at head
LEGS:	Mallard dyed woodduck fibers tied divided style and extending to bend of hook
HEAD:	Brown marabou or brown fur
COMMENTS:	Other color variations to suit

DIVING CADDIS, Brown and Yellow
(Gary LaFontaine)

HOOK:	Tiemco 200 or 5262, 12-18, weight to suit
THREAD:	Yellow
BODY:	Blended rusty yellow antron yarn
UNDERWING:	Brown partridge fibers extending to bend of hook
OVERWING:	Clear (white) Antron filaments extending to bend of hook
LEGS:	Ginger neck hackle tied full
COMMENTS:	Developed to represent female caddisflies that swim below the water's surface to deposit eggs. The silvery Antron strip helps represent the silvery air bubble the insect is encased in, which is an important "trigger." See Gary's book *Caddisflies*. Other colors to suit

Dave's Stonefly

DOC SPRATLEY (Dick Prankard)

HOOK:	Tiemco 5263, 8-12
THREAD:	Black
TAIL:	Grizzly hackle fibers
RIB:	Flat silver tinsel
BODY:	Black wool
LEGS:	Grizzly neck or saddle hackle tied back along sides and bottom of fly
WING:	Ringneck pheasant tail
HEAD:	Peacock
COMMENTS:	Pattern probably originated for caddis hatches in British Columbia lakes and is still popular

DUN VARIANT

HOOK:	Tiemco 5263, 12
THREAD:	Olive
TAIL:	Peacock
BODY:	Blend claret and black angora goat
LEGS:	Brown partridge tied full

EARLY BLACK

HOOK:	Tiemco 5263, 10-16, weighted
THREAD:	Brown or black
TAIL:	Gray strip goose "V"
BODY:	Dark brownish black fur
WINGCASE:	Dark gray or black goose quill segment tied double at rear and front of thorax. Treat with Flexament and allow to dry before using
LEGS:	Dark blue dun hen hackle tied half circle
COMMENTS:	Other colors to suit

EMERGENT SPARKLE PUPA, Brown and Yellow
(Gary LaFontaine) See Page 81

HOOK:	Tiemco 200, 12-20
THREAD:	Brown
OVERBODY:	Strands of rust or gold Antron yarn tied in at end of body and pulled forward somewhat loosely around body and tied off at head
BODY:	Blend 1/2 rust or gold Antron yarn and 1/2 brown fur
WING:	Light deer hair tied sparse and extending to bend of hook
HEAD:	Brown marabou or brown fur

EMERGER (Doug Swisher and Carl Richards)

HOOK:	Tiemco 5262, 12-18
THREAD:	Color to match body
TAIL:	Brown partridge
RIB:	Thread or floss to match body
BODY:	Olive, gray, tan, or brown fur
LEGS:	Brown partridge tied beard style
WINGS:	Blue dun hen hackle tips tied short

EMERGING *CALLIBAETIS* (Hal Janssen)

HOOK:	Tiemco 5263, 14-16, weight to suit
THREAD:	Olive
TAIL:	Golden pheasant tippets dyed olive
BODY:	Build underbody with olive thread and overwrap with narrow plastic strip
WINGCASE:	White tip turkey tail segment with a drop of epoxy on top to represent an expanding damp wing
THORAX:	Same as body
LEGS:	Mallard dyed woodduck tied divided style
COMMENTS:	*Callibaetis* are very prevalent in lakes. More information is available in *Lake Fishing with a Fly*.

EPHEMERELLA (Mike Lawson)

HOOK:	Tiemco 5262 or 200, 12-18, weight to suit
THREAD:	Brown
TAIL:	Mallard dyed woodduck
BODY:	Blend orange, yellow, amber angora goat, and brown fur
WINGCASE:	Gray duck or goose wing quill
THORAX:	Same as body, picked out slightly

FAIR DAMSEL (Charles E. Brooks)

HOOK:	Tiemco 300, 10-12, weight to suit
THREAD:	Brown or black
TAIL:	Two dyed brown grizzly hackle tips spread on edge about half as long as the body
RIB:	Small oval gold tinsel
BODY:	Blend dark brown and lesser amounts of olive, orange, and black fur
LEGS:	Grizzly saddle hackle dyed dark brown, palmer three turns through thorax
THORAX:	A continuation of the body slightly tapered
COMMENTS:	Represents *Argia* genus of damselflies

FILOPLUME DAMSELFLY (E.H. "Gene" Armstrong)

HOOK:	Tiemco 200, 8-10 See Page 142
THREAD:	Olive, or color to suit
TAIL:	Olive marabou strands or other color to suit
RIB:	Silver wire, reverse wrapped through body, thorax, and head
BODY:	Same as tail
LEGS:	Silver or silver badger saddle hackle palmered through thorax
THORAX:	Filoplume, color to match body
HEAD:	Peacock herl

FILOPLUME DRAGONFLY (E.H. "Gene" Armstrong)

HOOK:	Tiemco 300, 4-10, weight to suit
THREAD:	To match body
TAIL:	Mallard flank (6 or 8 wisps) and a small wisp of ringneck pheasant rump marabou
RIB:	Fine copper wire
BODY:	Filoplume, brown or olive, tied dense
WINGCASE:	Ringneck back feather, blue-green phase
THORAX:	Spun noodle of blended angora goat, rabbit and Antron yarn to obtain desired color. Pick out underside
LEGS:	Leftover tips from wingcase tied beard style
COMMENTS:	Body should be considerably larger diameter than thorax

FILOPLUME LEECH (E.H. "Gene" Armstrong)

HOOK:	Tiemco 200 or 300, 6-10
THREAD:	Black
TAIL:	Black marabou
RIB:	Copper wire
BODY:	Black filoplume tied dense. It will be necessary to wrap 4-6 filoplumes (one at a time)
LEGS:	Ringneck rump or back feather, tied full. Tie in tip first and take 1-2 wraps

FILOPLUME MAYFLY (Randall Kaufmann) See Page 66

HOOK:	Tiemco 200, 12-20, weight to suit
THREAD:	Color to match body
TAIL:	Marabou color to match body tied short and full
RIB:	Copper wire
BODY:	Marabou of desired color, olive, brown, black, and gray
WINGCASE:	Peacock sword fibers
THORAX:	Filoplume, color to match body

Fledermouse

See Page 106

FLEDERMOUSE (E.H. "Polly" Rosborough)

HOOK:	Tiemco 300, 8-12
THREAD:	Brown
BODY:	Blend two parts muskrat, two parts medium brown mink and one part jackrabbit (substitute hare's ear) with guard hairs removed. Use noodle technique and taper body
COLLAR:	Australian opossum
UNDERWING:	Teal or mallard extending halfway back over top of body
OVERWING:	Bronze mallard fibers

GAMMARUS-HYALELLA SCUD (Randall Kaufmann)

HOOK:	Tiemco 200 or 5262, 10-18, weighted
THREAD:	Color to match body
TAIL:	Hackle fibers tied short, color to match body
ANTENNAE:	Same as tail
BACK:	Heavy mill plastic strip
RIB:	Clear monofilament .006-.007 diameter
BODY:	Blend of angora goat and Hairtron. Best color combinations are olive-gray, tannish-gray, yellowish-olive, brown-olive, and gray-gray

FLOATING CADDIS PUPA   **Floating Caddis Pupa**

HOOK:	Tiemco 5263, 12-18
THREAD:	Black
BODY:	Sparsely spun deer hair clipped to shape
LEGS:	Brown partridge tied beard style
HEAD:	Fluorescent lime ostrich

FLOATING DRAGON (Randall Kaufmann) See Page 158

HOOK:	Tiemco 300, 4-10
THREAD:	Olive
EYES:	Burned monofilament (50 lb.) or plastic eyes
TAIL:	Grizzly marabou dyed olive, tied *heavy*, but short
BODY:	Olive deer hair, clipped to shape, flat on bottom so hook gape is not impeded. Color back with brown olive Pantone pen #119
LEGS:	Grizzly marabou dyed olive tied *heavy* along sides of body, extending 3/4 length of body
WINGCASE:	Light mottled turkey or goose lacquered and pre-clipped to "V." Wingcase should extend slightly down along side of body and encompass legs. Color with Pantone same as body
HEAD:	Dark olive Hairtron
COMMENT:	Other colors to suit

FLOATING MAYFLY   See Page 128

HOOK:	Tiemco 101, 12-20
THREAD:	To match body
TAIL:	Split dark dun (or color to match body) hackle fibers
RIB:	Silk thread or floss to match or slightly contrast with body
BODY:	Antron, your choice of color
WINGCASE:	Dark dun poly dubbing shaped into "ball" and secured on top of body at thorax area
LEGS:	Same as tail, tied divided style

GENIE MAY (Charles E. Brooks)   **Genie May**

HOOK:	Tiemco 300, 10-14
THREAD:	Brown
TAIL:	Grizzly hackle fibers dyed dark orange
RIB:	One thin strand of purple yarn and one gray ostrich herl wound together
LEGS:	Grizzly hackle fibers dyed dark orange wound two turns through thorax area
BODY:	Mottled brown dubbing
COMMENTS:	Intended to represent *Hexagenia* genus of mayflies

GEORGE'S BROWN STONE (George Anderson)

HOOK:	Tiemco 300, 8-12, weight to suit
THREAD:	Brown
TAIL:	Brown or dun brown hackle fibers
BODY:	Woven yarn with chocolate brown on top and tan or burlap underneath, tapered slightly
LEGS:	Brown or dun brown hackle

GIRDLE BUG

HOOK:	Tiemco 300, 2-10, weighted
THREAD:	Black
TAIL:	Black rubber strips
ANTENNAE:	Black rubber strips
LEGS:	Black rubber strips, three legs spaced out along each side of the hook. Tie all legs before wrapping body
BODY:	Black chenille
COMMENTS:	Many anglers prefer this dark version of the Rubber Legs pattern during hours of dim light. It is commonly referred to as "the bug" and is employed by some steelhead anglers. Bounce it along the bottom

GOLDEN QUILL
HOOK: Tiemco 5262, 10-16
THREAD: Yellow
TAIL: Gray stripped goose tied "V" fashion
RIB: Strip mallard quill (face) and over-rib with gold wire
BODY: Yellow floss
LEGS: Brown partridge tied full

GOLDEN STONE (Al Troth)
HOOK: Tiemco 5263, 8-10, weighted
THREAD: Yellow
TAIL: Golden strip goose "V" about 3/4 length of hook shank
BODY: Blend of amber, yellow and gold angora goat, and a little tan fox fur
RIB: Stripes painted across top of body with black Pantone pen
LEGS: Golden partridge, tied half circle or beard style
WING: Golden teal or mallard extending 1/3 length of hook shank
HEAD: Same as body
COMMENTS: Fished extensively by Al Troth in western Montana rivers during early summer

GOLDEN STONE (E.H. "Polly" Rosborough)
HOOK: Tiemco 300, 6-10
THREAD: Antique gold silk size A, #3715 Belding
TAIL: Teal dyed gold or use Pantone pen color #136
RIB: Buttonhole twist #3715 Belding
BACK: Teal dyed gold
BODY: Antique gold yarn. Lacquer hook generously before tying and smash body flat with smooth nose pliers before it completely dries
WING: Teal dyed gold
LEGS: Teal dyed gold tied divided style and extending about 1/2 way back along body
COMMENTS: Smash body and head again after tying

Gold Rib Hare's Ear

GOLD RIB HARE'S EAR See Page 70
HOOK: Tiemco 5262, 8-18, weighted
THREAD: Brown
TAIL: Hare's ear fur
RIB: Oval or flat gold tinsel
BODY: Blended hare's ear
WINGCASE: White tip turkey tail segment
THORAX: Blended hare's ear, picked out

GRAY
HOOK: Tiemco 5263, 10-16, weighted
THREAD: Gray
TAIL: Grizzly hackle fibers
BODY: Muskrat, leave all guard hairs in
LEGS: 2-3 turns of soft grizzly neck or hen hackle

GRAY DRAKE (Mike Lawson)
HOOK: Tiemco 5263, 12-16, weight to suit
THREAD: Gray
TAIL: Three gray ostrich flues
RIB: Gray thread
GILLS: Gray ostrich
BODY: Light gray fur
WINGCASE: Mallard dyed woodduck
THORAX: Same as body
LEGS: Gray partridge tied half circle

GRAY DRAKE WIGGLE (Fred Arbona) See Page 90
HOOK: Tiemco 5262, 12
THREAD: Gray
PLANER: Clear plastic trimmed from a coffee can lid
TAIL: Three dark moose fibers 1½ length of hook shank
EXTENDED BODY: Gray dun ostrich herl
WINGCASE: Gray goose wing quill section
BODY: Gray dun ostrich herl

Great Leadwing Drake

GREAT LEADWING DRAKE (E.H. "Polly" Rosborough)
HOOK: Tiemco 300, 10
THREAD: Reddish or dark brown
TAIL: Three reddish brown ringneck pheasant church window (shoulder feathers) fibers
RIB: Gold wire
BODY: Medium dark fiery brown yarn
LEGS: Same as tail, tied divided style
UNDERWING: Marabou the same color as the body, extending almost to end of body. This is to represent gills
OVERWING: Reddish fiery brown duck shoulder feather. Can be dyed or colored with Pantone pen

GREAT LEADWING OLIVE DRAKE
(Ernest Schwiebert)

HOOK:	Tiemco 5262, 10-12, weight to suit
THREAD:	Olive
TAIL:	Mallard dyed dark woodduck
RIB:	Fine gold wire
GILLS:	Olive gray marabou
BODY:	Brownish mottled dubbing with light olive sternites (segments)
THORAX:	Same as body with light olive highlight
LEGS:	Dark olive partridge tied half circle
WING:	Mottled olive brown turkey extending 1/3-1/2 body length
COMMENTS:	Represents *Ephemerella grandis grandis*. Note that Pantone pens can be used to color turkey, mark body segments, and other color highlights

GREEN DAMSEL (Al Troth)

HOOK:	Tiemco 300, 8-10, weight to suit
THREAD:	Olive
TAIL:	Olive marabou
BODY:	Mottled olive yarn
WINGCASE:	Dyed olive white tip turkey quill segment (color with Pantone pen)
THORAX:	Peacock
LEGS:	Dyed olive partridge tied half circle back along sides and bottom of hook
COMMENTS:	A brown version is also effective

GREEN DAMSEL (E.H. "Polly" Rosborough)

HOOK:	Tiemco 300, 8-12
THREAD:	Olive to match body. Polly likes limerick green silk by Belding
TAIL:	Light golden olive marabou
RIB:	Same as tying thread
BODY:	Medium golden olive synthetic yarn
WING:	Golden olive marabou, darker than body extending 1/2 over top of body
LEGS:	Medium olive teal, hackle, or mallard tied beard style and extending to hook point
COMMENTS:	Patterned after the damselfly family *Calopteryx yakima*

GREEN DRAKE (Mike Lawson)   See Page 84

HOOK:	Tiemco 5262, 10-12, weighted
THREAD:	Olive
TAIL:	Mallard dyed woodduck
RIB:	Copper wire
BODY:	Blended hare's ear with slight amounts of dyed gold and olive hare's ear
WINGCASE:	White tip turkey tail segment
THORAX:	Same as body
LEGS:	Brown partridge, tied half circle or beard style

GREEN DRAKE EMERGER (Mike Lawson)

HOOK:	Tiemco 5262, 10-12
THREAD:	Olive or brown
TAIL:	Mallard dyed woodduck
RIB:	Yellow floss
BODY:	Dark olive fur
LEGS:	Dyed yellow-olive grizzly neck hackle

GREEN ROCKWORM (E.H. "Polly" Rosborough)

HOOK:	Tiemco 300, 10-12
THREAD:	Black
RIB:	Blue green thread darker than body
BODY:	Green spray mohlon or other yarn
LEGS:	Dyed green teal or mallard tied beard style along the underside of the fly and extending to hook point
HEAD:	About three turns of four black ostrich flues (herls) twisted together

HAIRY BROWN LEECH (Al Troth)

HOOK:	Tiemco 300, 6-10, weight to suit
THREAD:	Color to match body
TAIL:	Marabou, color to suit, length of body
BODY:	Leech yarn, color to match tail, scoured to portray buggy appearance

HALFBACK

HOOK:	Tiemco 5263, 8-14, weight to suit
THREAD:	Olive
TAIL:	Brown hackle fibers
RIB:	Gold wire
BODY:	Peacock
WING:	Brown partridge
LEGS:	Brown neck or saddle hackle fibers tied beard style

HARE AND COPPER

HOOK:	Tiemco 5262, 10-18, weighted
THREAD:	Brown
TAIL:	Ringneck pheasant tail fibers
RIB:	Heavy copper wire
BODY:	Blend equal parts of cream angora goat and otter or brown mink tail. Tie heavy and pick out body in thorax area
COMMENTS:	New Zealand pattern of merit. The fur mix is the same for Trueblood Otter and Matt's Fur

HELLGRAMMITE (Randall Kaufmann)

HOOK:	Tiemco 300, 2-8, weighted, flattened, or tie strip of lead along each side and along underside of hook
THREAD:	Color to match body
ANTENNAE:	Strip goose to match body tied short, "V" style
BACK:	Ringneck pheasant tail fibers tied in tip first
TAIL:	Strip goose tied "V" style, color to match body
RIB:	Gold or copper wire all the way to head
BODY:	Antron blend picked out heavy along sides, best colors are black, browns
WINGCASE:	Same as back
LEGS:	Speckled hen saddle pulled over thorax
THORAX:	Same as body
HEAD:	Same as body

HENDRICKSON

HOOK:	Tiemco 5262, 12-14
THREAD:	Olive or brown
TAIL:	Mallard dyed woodduck
RIB:	Gold wire or orange thread
BODY:	Blend 2/3 muskrat and 1/3 brown angora goat
WINGCASE:	Natural gray duck quill segment
THORAX:	Same as body
LEGS:	Brown partridge tied full
COMMENTS:	Designed to imitate the mayfly *Ephemerella subvaria*

HENDRICKSON (Art Flick)

HOOK:	Tiemco 5262, 12-14, weight to suit
THREAD:	Olive
TAIL:	Mallard dyed woodduck
RIB:	Gold wire
BODY:	Blend gray fox, beaver, and claret angora goat until mixture is grayish brown
LEGS:	Brown partridge tied full

HENDRICKSON EMERGER (Mike Lawson)

HOOK:	Tiemco 5262, 14-18
THREAD:	Brown
TAIL:	Blue dun hackle fibers
RIB:	Brown floss
BODY:	Dyed brown hare's ear
LEGS:	Dark blue dun neck hackle, three turns

HENDRICKSON WIGGLE

Hendrickson Wiggle

HOOK:	Two hooks are required, a ring eye Tiemco 101 and Tiemco 5262, 10-16, weight to suit
THREAD:	Olive
TAIL:	Mallard dyed woodduck
RIB:	Gold wire or olive thread
BODY:	Blend 2/3 beaver and 1/3 claret angora goat
WINGCASE:	Light gray goose quill segment
THORAX:	Same as body
LEGS:	Mottled brown hen fibers tied divided style
COMMENTS:	Other patterns also lend themselves to this style tying

HENRY'S LAKE LEECH

HOOK:	Tiemco 300, 6-12, weight to suit
THREAD:	Brown
TAIL:	Rusty brown marabou tied length of hook
LEGS:	Palmered brown saddle hackle clipped short
BODY:	Rusty brown chenille
COMMENTS:	Vary other colors to suit, rib optional

IDA MAY (Charles E. Brooks)

HOOK:	Tiemco 5263, 10-12
THREAD:	Brown or black
TAIL:	Grizzly hackle fibers dyed dark green
RIB:	Peacock herl and gold wire. Wrap peacock herl first then reverse wrap gold wire
BODY:	Black fuzzy wool
LEGS:	Grizzly neck or saddle hackle dyed dark green, 1-2 turns tied slanted back. Hackle should be soft
COMMENTS:	Tied to represent larger *Ephemerella* nymphs that swim with their legs tucked back along the side of their body

IMMATURE NAIAD (Hal Janssen)

HOOK:	Tiemco 5263, 12
THREAD:	Olive
TAIL:	Fluorescent green hackle fibers
RIB:	Olive thread
BODY:	Fluorescent green rabbit fur tied thin
WINGCASE:	Pale olive duck quill segment topped with drop of epoxy
THORAX:	Same as body
LEGS:	Fluorescent green neck hackle, two turns tied back

INVISIBLE (Charles E. Brooks)

HOOK:	Tiemco 101, 18-22
THREAD:	Black
BODY:	Black fur tapered thin to eye
WING:	Mallard dyed woodduck, sparse and extending to bend of hook
COMMENTS:	An emergent designed to be fished just subsurface

ISONYCHIA bICOLOR (E.H. "Polly" Rosborough)

HOOK:	Tiemco 300, 8-10
THREAD:	Brown
RIB:	Heavy yellow thread or floss
BODY:	Fiery brown yarn
LEGS:	Dyed dark brown ringneck pheasant tail fibers tied beard style
UNDERWING:	Tuft of marabou one shade lighter than body and extending 2/3 body length (represents gills)
OVERWING:	Dyed dark brown hen hackle tip, 1/3 body length (represents wingcase)
COMMENTS:	"Polly" designed this pattern to represent *Isonychia bicolor*, a prevalent hatch in central Oregon. Rick Hafele and Dave Hughes, writing in *Western Hatches*, mention this is a good representation of the mostly overlooked and confusing mayfly genus *Ameletus*

JENNINGS

HOOK:	Tiemco 5262, 10-16, weight to suit
THREAD:	Black
TAIL:	Ringneck pheasant tail fibers
RIB:	Fine oval gold tinsel
BODY:	Blend 1/3 claret and 2/3 black angora goat
THORAX:	Peacock
LEGS:	Speckled hen hackle tied full and back

KAUFMANN HARE'S EAR (Randall Kaufmann)

HOOK: Tiemco 5262 or 200, 10-20, weighted
THREAD: To match body
TAIL: Dyed hare's ear clump to match body (select well barred fur from center of mask)
RIB: Medium to heavy copper wire or flat copper tinsel
BODY: Blended hare's ear, black, rust, brown, golden-olive, olive, or gray are best colors
WINGCASE: White tip turkey tail segment (peacock is also good)
THORAX: Same as body, pick out
COMMENTS: A takeoff on the standard Gold Rib Hare's Ear with a few subtle changes. Useful for many mayfly nymphs and a very consistent producer

KAUFMANN STONE (Randall Kaufmann) See Page 144

HOOK: Tiemco 300, 2-10, weighted and flattened
THREAD: To match body
TAIL: Strip goose to match body
ANTENNAE: Strip goose to match body
RIB: Swannundaze to match body
BODY: Mixture of several colors of angora goat (50%) and predominant color of Hairtron (50%). Black, brown, tan and golden-brown are most popular
WINGCASE: Three separate sections of lacquered turkey clipped to shape before tying in. The wingcase should occupy 1/2 of hook shank. Each thorax is tied in separately alternated with thorax fur
THORAX: Same as body
HEAD: Same as body

Latex Caddis Pupa

KEMP BUG

HOOK: Tiemco 5262, 8-16, weight to suit
THREAD: Olive
TAIL: Peacock herl fibers clipped short
RIB: Gold wire
BODY: Peacock herl over tapered underbody
LEGS: Furnace hackle 2-3 turns tied full and back
WING: Grizzly hackle tips tied short
COMMENTS: This pattern was the forerunner to the Zug Bug and many anglers feel it is more effective. Perhaps the grizzly hackle tip wings have something to do with its effectiveness

LAKE DRAGON (Randall Kaufmann) See Page 164

HOOK: Tiemco 300, 4-8, weighted and flattened *rear* half of hook only
THREAD: Color to match body
EYES: 3mm bronze glass eyes (burned monofilament eyes may be substituted)
TAIL: Marabou fluff, color to match body, tied short and full
RIB: Copper wire
BODY: Olive or brown Hairtron with the following colors of goat for highlights: blue, purple, green, amber, olive, brown, rust. Body to be wider than thorax and flattened in appearance
LEGS: Pheasant rump or body to match body color, tied half circle and not to extend beyond the body
WINGCASE: Mottled light or white tip turkey colored with Pantone pen to match body, lacquered and clipped in "V," tied short
HEAD: This is also the thorax area, same as body only of much smaller diameter

LATEX CADDIS PUPA (Raleigh Boaze, Jr.)

HOOK: Tiemco 200, 10-20, weight to suit
THREAD: Black
BODY: 1/8-inch strip of "heavy" latex (color natural cream latex with Pantone pen. A bright-colored underbody will also show through)
LEGS: Grayish-brown fur with guard hairs left in or brown partridge tied beard style
WINGS: Gray mallard wing quill segment tied short along each side of the body
HEAD: Peacock or brownish-black dubbing
COMMENTS: Do not stretch latex too tightly or it will not feel soft and segmentation will be lost

LEADWING COACHMAN

HOOK: Tiemco 5263, 10-14
THREAD: Black
TAIL: Brown hackle tip
RIB: Gold wire
BODY: Peacock
LEGS: Brown hackle fibers tied beard style
WING: Mallard wing shoulder feather tied flat, clipped, and extending about 1/2 back over body

LEIB'S BUG (Don Leib)

HOOK: Tiemco 5263, 8-14, weighted
THREAD: Black
TAIL: Brown strip goose tied in "V"
RIB: Fine gold wire
LEGS: Furnace saddle hackle palmered through body
BODY: Peacock
LEGS: Brown strip goose extending back along sides to end of body, fibers curving toward inside

LIGHT CADDIS EMERGENT (E.H. "Polly" Rosborough)

HOOK:	Tiemco 5262, 10
THREAD:	Black
RIB:	Medium yellow
BODY:	Light yellow Antron yarn
LEGS:	Light ginger neck hackle soft and extending to bend of hook. Trim top and bottom
HEAD:	Four twisted flues (herl) of black ostrich
COMMENTS:	Designed to represent various *Limnephilid* caddis. Rich Hafele and Dave Hughes in their excellent book *Western Hatches,* tell of a good hatch of *Limnephilid* which drive Atlantic salmon crazy in Oregon's Hosmer Lake

LIGHT CAHILL

HOOK:	Tiemco 5262, 12-18
THREAD:	Cream
TAIL:	Mallard dyed woodduck
BODY:	Creamy tan fox or suitable substitute
WINGCASE:	Mallard dyed woodduck
THORAX:	Same as body
LEGS:	Mallard dyed woodduck tied beard style

LINGREN'S OLIVE (Ira Lingren)

HOOK:	Tiemco 5262, 14-18
THREAD:	Black
TAIL:	Black hackle fibers
RIB:	Gold wire
BODY:	Olive marabou
THORAX:	Peacock herl
LEGS:	2-3 turns black neck hackle clipped top and bottom
COMMENTS:	This style of fly produces well, especially when fish are feeding on mayflies, and other color combinations should not be overlooked

LITTLE BROWN STONE (E.H. "Polly" Rosborough)

HOOK:	Tiemco 5263, 12-16
THREAD:	Brown
TAIL:	Brown ringneck pheasant body feathers
RIB:	Brown thread
BODY:	Dark brown fuzzy yarn, flattened
WING:	Same as tail, clipped and extending 1/3 length of body
LEGS:	Same as tail tied divided style extending 3/4 length of body
COMMENTS:	Designed to be fished dead drift just subsurface

LITTLE GRAY CADDIS LARVA (Charles E. Brooks)

HOOK:	Tiemco 5263, 12-18
THREAD:	Black
RIB:	Stripped peacock quill and gold wire, reverse wind. Space peacock quill so body and peacock are about the same width
BODY:	Gray wool or fur
LEGS:	Black hackle, soft and short, tied full
COMMENTS:	Represents cased form of *brachycentrus* and is to be fished with a slow crawl along the bottom at the edge of current

LITTLE GREEN CADDIS (Charles E. Brooks)

HOOK:	Tiemco 5262, 12-18, weighted
THREAD:	Olive
EGG SACK:	Tuft of fluorescent green yarn tied like a short tail
RIB:	Gold wire
BODY:	Dark green yarn or fur
THORAX:	Two strands of tan or gray ostrich herl
WINGS:	Ends of above tied back length of hook shank
LEGS:	Brown partridge, tied full
COMMENTS:	Designed to imitate *Rhyacophila*

LITTLE GREEN CADDIS LARVA (Charles E. Brooks)

HOOK:	Tiemco 5263, 12-18
THREAD:	Black
RIB:	Gold wire
BODY:	Bright green wool or fur
THORAX:	Dark brown fur
LEGS:	Soft black hackle, one turn very short, tied full

LITTLE YELLOW STONE (E.H. "Polly" Rosborough)

HOOK:	Tiemco 5263, 10-14
THREAD:	Yellow
TAIL:	Mallard dyed yellow chartreuse
BACK:	Mallard dyed yellow chartreuse, tips can be tied back for legs if proper length
RIB:	Yellow thread
BODY:	Yellow chartreuse yarn, flattened
WING:	Same as back, tips can be tied back over top of hook to form wing, clip 1/3 body length
LEGS:	Same as tail tied divided style extending 3/4 body length
COMMENTS:	This pattern represents an emergent nymph with fully developed wingcases and is intended to be fished in the top film. the thread head should be a bit oversized and well flattened. This is a characteristic trait of many of Polly's patterns

MARABOU

HOOK:	Tiemco 5262, 12-18, weight to suit
THREAD:	To match body
RIB:	Gold wire
BODY:	Marabou dubbed on thread
TAIL, BACK, WINGCASE, LEGS:	Moose body hair tied in at bend of hook with gold wire and ribbed forward through body securing moose back. Butt ends form wingcase and legs
THORAX:	Same as body
HEAD:	Same as body

MARABOU DAMSEL (Randall Kaufmann) See Page 110

HOOK:	Tiemco 200, 8-10, weight to suit
THREAD:	Olive
TAIL:	Olive marabou
RIB:	Copper wire or olive silk thread
BODY:	Olive marabou tied in by the tips. Left over ends can form the wing. Pull off ends to 1/3 body length with fingers
WING:	Olive marabou (actually represents advanced wingcase)

MARABOU LEECH (Hal Janssen)

HOOK: Tiemco 300, 4-10, weight to suit
THREAD: To match wing and tail color
TAIL: Can be olive, black, brown, gray, or tan marabou tied length of hook shank
WING: Two separate "wings" are tied in along the top of the body spaced out between the tail and head. Middle wing is slightly shorter than hook shank. Front wing is length of hook shank
HEAD: Marabou or filoplume to match wing color
COMMENTS: Hal Janssen, noted California angler and writer, has designed many nymphs, of which the Marabou Leech is the most popular.

MARCH BROWN (Al Troth)

HOOK: Tiemco 200, 10-16
THREAD: Yellow
TAIL: Three ringneck pheasant tail fibers
RIB: Dark brown silk or floss twisted tight
BODY: Blended tan fur and lesser parts of amber and yellow angora goat
WINGCASE: Mottled turkey
THORAX: Same as body
LEGS: Brown partridge tied half circle back along sides and bottom of hook
HEAD: Same as body

MARCH BROWN, American

HOOK: Tiemco 200, 12-18
THREAD: Brown
TAIL: Dark moose
RIB: Strip peacock herl or copper wire
BODY: Tobacco brown floss or rusty fur
WINGCASE: Brown turkey tail
LEGS: Palmered brown neck or saddle hackle through thorax
THORAX: Peacock

MARCH BROWN (Art Flick)

HOOK: Tiemco 200, 12-18
THREAD: Brown
TAIL: Ringneck pheasant tail fibers
RIB: Dark brown silk
BODY: Blend red fox fur and amber goat, two to one
WINGCASE: Ringneck pheasant tail fibers
THORAX: Same as body
LEGS: Brown partridge, tied half circle

MARCH BROWN (Bob Jacklin)

HOOK: Tiemco 5263, 10-14, weight to suit
THREAD: Brown
TAIL: Two ringneck tail fibers
RIB: Dark brown floss
BODY: Medium brown dubbing, somewhat robust
WINGCASE: Dark brown turkey
LEGS: Dark mottled brown hen saddle pulled over thorax
THORAX: Same as body

MARCH BROWN, Soft Hackle

HOOK: Tiemco 5262, 12-18
THREAD: Orange
RIB: Fine oval gold tinsel
BODY: Blended hare's ear
LEGS: Brown partridge, tied full

MATT'S FUR (Matt Lavell) See Page 74

HOOK: Tiemco 300, 6-12, weighted
THREAD: Brown
TAIL: Mallard dyed woodduck
RIB: Oval or flat gold tinsel
BODY: Blend even parts of cream angora goat and otter or brown mink tail
WINGCASE, LEGS: Mallard dyed woodduck. Leftover tips of wingcase are pulled back and tied divided style along side of body or beard style underneath body. Legs should extend to hook point
THORAX: Same as body

MEDIUM CASE CADDIS

HOOK: Tiemco 5263, 12-16, weighted
THREAD: Black
UNDERBODY: Silver tinsel chenille
OVERBODY: Gray muskrat wound so some of the tinsel chenille shows in between muskrat
HEAD: Black ostrich herl

MEDIUM SPECKLED WING QUILL
(Ernest Schwiebert)

HOOK: Tiemco 5262 or 200, 14-18, weight to suit
THREAD: Brown
TAIL: Ringneck pheasant tail fibers
RIB: Pale yellowish brown goose quill or fine ostrich
BODY: Light brown fur with guard hairs
WINGCASE: Light brown turkey wing quill segment
THORAX: Same as body
LEGS: Light brown partridge tied half circle
COMMENTS: Represents *Callibaetis pacificus*, a widespread western specie

MICRO CADDIS (Randall Kaufmann)

HOOK: Tiemco 101, 18-22
THREAD: Black
RIB: Copper wire
BODY: Black, browns, olives, or yellow Hairtron or Antron dubbing. Peacock is also good
LEGS: Brown or gray partridge, tied beard style
THORAX: A shade or two darker than body or blend black fur with body fur

MOHAIR LEECH

HOOK: Tiemco 300, 6-10, weight to suit
THREAD: Red or color to match body
TAIL: Marabou, color to match body
BODY: Mohair or leech yarn. Rusty gray, olive brown, rust, gray, and black are best colors. Body should be shaggy
COMMENTS: The mohair body can either be tied by wrapping the mohair around the hook shank and picking it out, or it can be shredded and placed onto the hook strategically so it forms a flattened profile

MONTANA STONE

HOOK:	Tiemco 300, 6-10, weighted
THREAD:	Black
TAIL:	Black hackle fibers
BODY:	Black chenille
WINGCASE:	Two pieces of black chenille
LEGS:	Black saddle hackle palmered through thorax
THORAX:	Yellow chenille
COMMENTS:	Longtime favorite in Madison and other Montana rivers. Thorax and wingcase chenille should be smaller diameter than body chenille

MOSQUITO LARVA

HOOK:	Tiemco 101 or 200, 14-20
THREAD:	Black
TAIL:	Grizzly hen hackle fibers tied *short*
ANTENNAE:	Grizzly hen hackle fibers tied *short*
BODY:	Stripped peacock quill wrapped over tapered fur underbody. Wire rib optional
THORAX:	Peacock herl, continuation of body piece only herl is not stripped off

MOSQUITO PUPA (Randall Kaufmann) See Page 118

HOOK:	Tiemco 101 or 200, 14-20
THREAD:	Olive
TAIL:	Grizzly marabou, tied *short*
RIB:	Gold or copper wire over body and thorax
BODY:	Stripped peacock quill
THORAX:	Peacock herl. If judged properly the thorax can be the same quill as the body. Strip off just enough herl to form the body and continue wrapping herl to form the thorax
WINGS:	Wide grizzly hen hackle tips tied short, 1/2 length of body
COMMENTS:	Excellent surface film pattern during mosquito, midge and some mayfly hatches

MUSKRAT (E.H. "Polly" Rosborough)

HOOK:	Tiemco 5263, 10-16
THREAD:	Black
BODY:	Blend two parts muskrat belly, two parts beaver belly, and one part jackrabbit, with the guard hairs removed from the jackrabbit. Secure with noodle method. See specific tying instructions for Casual Dress pattern. After complete, score body
LEGS:	Guinea tied underneath body beard style and extending not quite to the hook point
HEAD:	Three or four twisted flues of black ostrich
COMMENTS:	Designed to simulate the larvae stage of both the gray cranefly and the black midge

NATANT NYLON (Charles E. Brooks)

HOOK:	Tiemco 101, 12-16
THREAD:	Black
RIB:	Gold wire
BODY:	Tan, gray, olive, or black
LEGS:	Grizzly neck hackle dyed brown, or brown partridge, tied beard style
THORAX:	Cut a small square of nylon stocking mesh, make a pouch and stuff with polyurethane foam or other floatable material. Tie onto hook in an upright position. This should be secured into place before you construct the body
COMMENTS:	Fish in the surface film

NEAR ENOUGH (E.H. "Polly" Rosborough)

HOOK:	Tiemco 5263, 8-18
THREAD:	Gray or tan
TAIL:	Mallard dyed gray-tan
BODY:	Gray fox underfur, remove all guard hairs, tied noodle style, slender with good taper
WING:	Same as tail, clipped 1/3 length of body
LEGS:	Same as tail, tied divided style extending 3/4 body length
COMMENTS:	In his book, *Tying and Fishing the Fuzzy Nymphs*, Polly mentions that the sides of the body can be roughed up a bit to simulate gills but this does not seem to enhance its fish taking abilities . . . it's a killer any way you look at it!

NONDESCRIPT (E.H. "Polly" Rosborough)

HOOK:	Tiemco 300, 10-12
THREAD:	Brown
TAIL:	Fiery brown marabou
RIB:	Bright yellow nylon or floss
HACKLE:	Furnace saddle hackle palmered tip first with three extra turns in front. When complete trim in a cone shape 1/4" long in front to zero at tail
BODY:	Fiery brown shaggy yarn flattened so body looks like a piece of pie
COMMENTS:	Represents the mayfly genus *Stenonema*

NYERGES (Gil Nyerges)

HOOK:	Tiemco 5263, 10-12, weighted
THREAD:	Olive
TAIL:	Brown hackle fibers
LEGS:	Palmered brown saddle hackle clipped off on top
BODY:	Dark olive chenille
COMMENTS:	Popular in Washington lakes

OLIVE DRAKE (George Anderson)

HOOK:	Tiemco 5263, 14-18
THREAD:	Olive
TAIL:	Brown partridge
RIB:	Olive thread
BODY:	Olive brown dubbing
WING:	Brown ostrich clipped short, 1/3 body length
LEGS:	Brown partridge, tied divided style extending 3/4 body length

OLIVE DUN

HOOK: Tiemco 5262, 12-18, weight to suit
THREAD: Brown
TAIL: Ringneck pheasant tail fibers
RIB: Brown floss or silk thread
BODY: Olive gray fur
WINGCASE: Light gray goose quill segment
LEGS: Brown hen hackle palmered through thorax
THORAX: Olive gray fur

OSTRICH (Fred Arbona)

Ostrich

HOOK: Tiemco 5262 or 5263, 12-18
THREAD: Color to match body
TAIL: Ringneck pheasant tail fibers
RIB: Thread color to match
BODY: Ostrich, color to suit
WINGCASE: Dark gray goose wing
THORAX: Same as body
COMMENTS: Useful in imitating a variety of mayfly nymphs

PALE EVENING DUN

HOOK: Tiemco 5262, 16-18
THREAD: Olive
TAIL: Mallard dyed woodduck
RIB: Gold wire
BODY: Grayish brown fox
WINGCASE: Light gray goose quill
THORAX: Grayish brown fox
LEGS: Brown partridge tied divided or beard style

PALE GRAY WING OLIVE (Ernest Schwiebert)

HOOK: Tiemco 101 or 200, 16-22
THREAD: Tan
TAIL: Light partridge or mallard dyed light olive
RIB: Pale olive gray goose quill to represent gills
BODY: Light brownish olive fur
WINGCASE: Same as rib
THORAX: Light brownish olive fur
LEGS: Same as tail, tied half circle
COMMENTS: It is advisable to remember that there are several species of *Baetis* and they can vary from water to water. Colors commonly range from light olive to brownish olive

PALE MORNING DUN
(Doug Swisher and Carl Richards)

HOOK: Tiemco 101 or 200, 16-20, weighted
THREAD: Brown or olive
TAIL: Dark brown partridge
BODY: Mixture of dark brown and medium olive fur
LEGS: Dark brown partridge tied divided style
WING: Olive brown duck quill segment
COMMENTS: This imitation should be fished dead drift near the bottom

PALE MORNING DUN (Ernest Schwiebert) See Page 87

HOOK: Tiemco 5262, 12-14, weight to suit
THREAD: Brown
TAIL: Mallard dyed woodduck
RIB: Gold wire
GILLS: Brownish amber marabou (color with Pantone pen)
BODY: Amber-brown fur
WINGCASE: Brown turkey tail
LEGS: Pale brown partridge, pulled over thorax
THORAX: Amber-brown fur
COMMENTS: Designed to imitate the mayfly *Ephemerella infrequens*, a very prolific and widespread hatch in the western states

PALE MORNING DUN EMERGER (Mike Lawson)

HOOK: Tiemco 101 or 200, 14-18
THREAD: Yellow
TAIL: Mallard dyed woodduck
RIB: Olive floss or silk thread
BODY: Yellow fur
LEGS: Light blue dun neck hackle, three turns tied full

PALE OLIVE DRAKE (George Anderson)

HOOK: Tiemco 5263, 14-18
THREAD: Pale yellow
TAIL: Mallard dyed woodduck
RIB: Optional, pale yellow, or pale olive
BODY: Pale olive dubbing
WING: Pale olive ostrich clipped short, 1/4 body length
LEGS: Mallard dyed woodduck tied divided style 3/4 length of body

PARTRIDGE AND PEACOCK (Al Troth)

HOOK: Tiemco 5262, 12-18, weighted
THREAD: Black
TAIL: Red wool, tied short, single strand
RIB: Gold wire
BODY: Peacock
LEGS: Gray partridge tied full
COMMENTS: A simple fly but one which Al Troth fishes consistently on the Beaverhead River in Montana

PEACOCK MATT'S FUR (Ed Schroeder)

HOOK:	Tiemco 5263, 8-18, weight to suit
THREAD:	Tan or cream
TAIL:	Mallard dyed woodduck
RIB:	Fine flat gold tinsel or gold wire
BODY:	Blend of cream goat and otter
WINGCASE:	Peacock fibers
THORAX:	Same as body
COMMENTS:	California angler-tyer Ed Schroeder specializes in fishing lakes and spring creeks in California, Oregon, Idaho and Montana.

PEEKING CADDIS (George Anderson)

HOOK:	Tiemco 200, 12-18, weighted
THREAD:	Black
RIB:	Fine gold wire
BODY:	Blended hare's ear-mask
THORAX:	Pale yellow or olive fur
LEGS:	Brown partridge tied full
HEAD:	Black ostrich
COMMENTS:	Tied to represent a caddis larva extending out of its case as larva do when crawling, swimming, or drifting

PHEASANT TAIL (Al Troth) See Page 78

HOOK:	Tiemco 5262 or 200, 10-18, weight to suit
THREAD:	Brown
TAIL:	Ringneck pheasant tail fibers
RIB:	Gold wire
BODY:	Same as tail
WINGCASE, LEGS:	Same as tail. Leftover wingcase tips are tied divided style
THORAX:	Peacock
COMMENTS:	This and an olive version are Al Troth's best selling nymph imitations

PHEASANT TAIL (Frank Sawyer)

HOOK:	Tiemco 200 or 5262, 12-18, weight to suit
THREAD:	Brown·
TAIL:	Ringneck pheasant tail fibers
RIB:	Copper wire (8-10 inches), reverse wrap. Thorax is covered with this same piece of wire just prior to pulling wingcase over thorax
BODY:	Ringneck pheasant tail fibers
WINGCASE:	Ringneck pheasant tail fibers
THORAX:	Copper wire
HEAD:	Copper wire
COMMENTS:	First, build up thorax with smooth fur and cover tightly with thread. Thread can be used to secure wire at back of head. This is the original Pheasant Tail pattern developed by English angler Frank Sawyer. Those interested in more Frank Sawyer patterns and nymphing technique should read his book, *Nymphs and the Trout*.

PRE-EMERGER (Hal Janssen)

HOOK:	Tiemco 5263, 16
THREAD:	Olive
TAIL:	Golden pheasant tippets dyed olive (or color with Pantone pen)
RIB:	Olive thread
BODY:	Olive-gray-brown fur
WINGCASE:	Mottled turkey, drop of epoxy on top
THORAX:	Same as body
LEGS:	Mallard dyed woodduck tied divided style
COMMENTS:	Generally imitative of *Callibaetis*

Peeking Caddis

PRINCE NYMPH (Doug Prince)

HOOK:	Tiemco 300, 4-10, weighted
THREAD:	Black
TAIL:	Brown strip goose "V"
RIB:	Flat gold tinsel
BODY:	Peacock
LEGS:	Brown neck hackle, 2-4 turns tied full and back
WING:	White strip goose tied flat over body in "V" with tips curving up

QUILL GORDON

HOOK:	Tiemco 5262, 12-16
THREAD:	Olive
TAIL:	Ringneck pheasant tail fibers
RIB:	Brown floss or silk thread
BODY:	Light beaver
WINGCASE:	White tip turkey tail segment
THORAX:	Light beaver
LEGS:	Brown partridge, tied half full or divided style

QUILL GORDON

HOOK:	Tiemco 5262, 14-18
THREAD:	Gray or olive
BODY:	Tannish gray fur
WING:	Bronze mallard flank
LEGS:	Ginger hackle soft and sparse tied full
COMMENTS:	Designed to imitate the mayfly *Epeorus fraudator*

RABBIT LEECH

HOOK:	Tiemco 300, 6-8, weight to suit
THREAD:	To match body
BODY:	Thin strip of rabbit, color to suit wrapped around body just like the Assam Dragon
COMMENTS:	Popular in Northwest lakes and in Alaska. Retrieve with short jerks, quick pulls or hand twist with occasional rod tip twitches

RANDALL'S CADDIS (Randall Kaufmann)

HOOK:	Tiemco 200, 10-18, weight to suit
THREAD:	Black
RIB:	Copper wire
BODY:	Twisted yarn, color to suit
THORAX:	Black fur
COMMENTS:	The twisted yarn body makes for a nicely segmented and durable body. Twist yarn until tight and wrap around hook without letting yarn unspin. Material should be twisted about four inches down the strand so it does not become soiled from your fingers. This pattern first appeared in the *American Nymph Fly Tying Manual* in 1975. Today many caddis larva imitations are tied with Antron or dubbed bodies, but this one is still good

RANDALL'S CADDIS PUPA (Randall Kaufmann)

HOOK:	Tiemco 200, 10-18, weight to suit
THREAD:	Black or brown
RIB:	Copper wire
BODY:	Hairtron, tan, brown, olive, yellow, or bright green (peacock herl is also good)
ANTENNAE:	Mallard dyed woodduck extending slightly beyond body
LEGS:	Brown partridge tied beard style. Clear (white) Antron fibers tied short alongside of body
WINGCASE:	Clear plastic trimmed to shape and tied along side of body enclosing or bunching together legs. Wingcase should extend half way back along the body
THORAX:	Body color blended with slight amount of dark brown or black Hairtron
COMMENTS:	Excellent light reflector and effective producer

RANDALL'S DRAGON (Randall Kaufmann)

HOOK:	Tiemco 300, 4-10, weight back center of hook shank and flatten
THREAD:	Brown or olive
TAIL:	Brown or olive strip goose "V"
RIB:	Brown or olive Swannundaze
BODY:	Blend several shades of browns or olives of angora goat with like color of rabbit or Hairtron
LEGS:	Brown or olive strip goose, tied along side of body curving inward and extending to end of body
THORAX:	Same as body
WINGCASE:	Brown or olive duck or goose quill pre-lacquered with Flexament, tied in at back of thorax *and* after thorax is complete, pull over and tied at front of thorax. Wingcase should be preclipped to "V" at rear, extending slightly over top of body
LEGS:	Brown or olive strip goose tied in front of thorax and extending along sides of body to midway point of body. Tips of goose should curve inward
HEAD:	Same as body

RED BROWN (Gary Borger)

HOOK:	Tiemco 101 or 200, 8-18, weight to suit
THREAD:	Brown
TAIL:	Ringneck pheasant tail fibers
BODY:	Rusty brown dubbing
WINGCASE:	Peacock herl, 3-8 strands
THORAX:	Same as body
LEGS:	Rabbit or hare's ear guard hairs, tied sparse along the thorax area, trimmed off along the bottom
COMMENTS:	A favorite of Gary Borger, author of *Naturals* and *Nymphing* and flyfishing video personality

RHYACOPHILA (Randall Kaufmann) See Page 54

HOOK:	Tiemco 200, 12-20, weight to suit
THREAD:	Black
RIB:	Fine green wire, thread, or floss twisted tight
BODY:	Antron caddis blend #5 (cream green)
HEAD:	Slight amount of black Hairtron blended with body material

RIFFLE DEVIL (Charles E. Brooks)

HOOK:	Tiemco 300, 4, weighted heavily
THREAD:	Olive or black
LEGS:	Palmered ginger saddle hackle. Hackle can be trimmed short over body area but not thorax or head area
BODY:	Olive green chenille, large
COMMENTS:	Represents the larva of the riffle beetle *Dysticus*. According to Charles Brooks it is best fished quartered downstream and crawled over bottom rubble

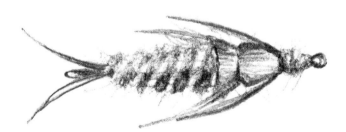

Randall's Dragon

RUBBER LEGS See Page 52

HOOK:	Tiemco 300, 2-10, weighted
THREAD:	Black
TAIL:	Two medium diameter white rubber strips tied "V"
LEGS:	Three pair of medium white rubber strips spaced evenly along the body extending at right angles and clipped to desired length
BODY:	Black, yellow, olive, or brown chenille

See Page 148
RUBBER LEGS BROWN STONE (George Anderson)

HOOK: Tiemco 5263, 8-12, weighted and flattened
THREAD: Brown
TAIL: White rubber strips tied in a "V"
ANTENNAE: Same as tail, tie back after fly is finished
BODY: Woven body with chocolate brown yarn on top and tan yarn (burlap works best) underneath
LEGS: One pair of white rubber strips, protruding from body immediately behind thorax
THORAX: Hare's ear

RUEL'S DUCK WING (Ruel Staynor)

HOOK: Tiemco 5263, 8-14, weighted
THREAD: Olive
TAIL: Orange hackle fibers
RIB: Flat gold tinsel
BODY: Olive chenille
WING: Mallard fibers or complete feather tied flat extending to end of tail or bend of hook
LEGS: Orange hackle fibers

SCUD (Fred Arbona)   **Scud**

HOOK: Tiemco 200, 12-20, weight to suit
THREAD: Color to match body
BACK: Heavy mill clear plastic strip
RIB: Clear monofilament about .006 diameter
BODY: Ostrich, color to suit, slight taper
COMMENTS: Simple yet effective imitation. Fred prefers to tie this series with a pronounced curve to the body

SIMULATOR (Randall Kaufmann) See Page 139

HOOK: Tiemco 300, 4-10, weight to suit
THREAD: To match body
TAIL: Strip goose "V" or marabou to match body
RIB: Copper wire
LEGS: Saddle hackle palmered standard style through body, clipped to shape if desired, or palmered through thorax only
BODY: Blend of several colors of Angora goat and predominant Hairtron color. Pick out fur at thorax area
COMMENTS: One of the most useful nymphs of the day. Vary the color, size, shape to suit a wide variety of underwater organisms

SIPHLONURUS (Hal Janssen)

HOOK: Tiemco 5263, 12-14, weight to suit
THREAD: Olive
TAIL: Golden pheasant tippet dyed olive
RIB: Olive thread
BODY: Brown-olive ostrich overwound with thin piece of mottled turkey
WINGCASE: White tip turkey tail segment with drop of epoxy placed on top
THORAX: Hare's ear
LEGS: Mallard dyed woodduck tied divided style

SIX PACK (Karl Haufler)

HOOK: Tiemco 5263 or 200, 8-12
THREAD: Black
BODY: Dyed yellow, golden olive, or brown ringneck pheasant tail fibers
RIB: Black thread "X." Rib backwards from head area to tail and back to head
LEGS: Ringneck pheasant rump or body feather tied in at the tip, 1-2 turns, tied full. Fibers should extend slightly beyond bend of hook
COMMENTS: Popular Northwest pattern

Skunk Hair Caddis

SKUNK HAIR CADDIS (Charles E. Brooks)

HOOK: Tiemco 5263, 8-12, weighted
TAIL: None
BODY: Blackish skunk hair from tail at least 4" long
RIB: Copper wire
LEGS: Black hackle, short and soft, tied full
COMMENTS: Stack skunk hair, tie in match size clump by tips at head area, lash down to bend of hook. Twist hair counter clockwise and wrap very tightly to form body. Tie off securely. Tie in rib, wrap to back of body and back to head area (9x rib). Tie in hackle. Represents cased caddis

SLATE WING OLIVE

HOOK: Tiemco 5262, 14-18
THREAD: Olive
TAIL: Three gray goose quill fibers
RIB: Gray floss or silk thread
BODY: Gray-brown red fox fur
WINGCASE: Gray goose quill segment
THORAX: Same as body
LEGS: Medium blue dun neck hackle tied back along sides and bottom of fly (half circle)

SMALL DUN VARIANT

HOOK: Tiemco 5262, 16-18
THREAD: Brown
TAIL: Mallard dyed woodduck
RIB: Copper wire
BODY: Dark brown beaver
WINGCASE: Dark gray goose quill segment
THORAX: Dark brown beaver
LEGS: Mallard dyed woodduck tied divided, beard, or half circle

SOFT HACKLE See Page 62

HOOK: Tiemco 5262 or 200, 10-18
THREAD: Color to match body
BODY: Floss or fur. Olive, green, black, orange, yellow, and brown are most useful. Fine wire or thread rib is optional, and usually omitted
THORAX: Blended hare's ear
LEGS: Gray or brown partridge, tied full. Soft hen hackle can also be used, color to suit

SOWBUG

HOOK: Tiemco 5262, 14-18, weighted and flattened
THREAD: To match body
TAIL: Strip goose or soft, short side of goose wing quill, tied "V" fashion, color to match body
BACK: Section of duck or goose quill, color to match body
RIB: Buttonhole twist thread to match body color, copper, or gold wire, or clear monofilament
BODY: Olive, brown, gray, or tan fur
HEAD: Same as body
COMMENTS: Body should be somewhat flattened. Dubbing may be picked out slightly along sides. When beginning construction back may be tied in before tail and a couple turns of body fur applied so the tail extends from the side of the actual body. Monofilament or plastic eyes are optional. Represents the water sowbug, *Asellus*. Writing in the book *Trout Streams*, Paul R. Needham claims these are rare in western states but common elsewhere.

STONEFLY CREEPER (Art Flick)

HOOK: Tiemco 5263, 12
THREAD: Yellow
TAIL: Ringneck pheasant tail fibers
BACK: Mallard dyed woodduck
BODY: Stripped ginger hackle stem over wrapped (ribbed) with light amber angora goat dubbing, heavier at thorax
LEGS: Brown partridge along sides and bottom (half circle)

STRAWMAN (Paul Young)

HOOK: Tiemco 5263, 8-12, weight to suit
THREAD: Yellow
RIBBING: Pale yellow floss worked through hair ribers
BODY: Sparsely spun deer hair clipped in a taper from tail to head
COMMENTS: One of the earliest cased caddisfly larva imitations

SURFACE EMERGER (René Harrop)   Surface Emerger

HOOK: Tiemco 101, 14-20
THREAD: Olive
TAIL: Mallard dyed woodduck
RIB: Silk thread or floss a shade darker than body
BODY: Fly Rite or Antron dubbing, color to suit
WING: Gray duck wing quill segment, two pieces back to back, shiny side out, extending flat about 1/2 way over top of body and trimmed square
LEGS: Brown partridge fibers tied divided style
THORAX: Same as body

SWANNUNDAZE STONE

HOOK: Tiemco 300, 4-10, weighted
THREAD: Brown
TAIL: Stripped goose "V" or ringneck pheasant tail fibers
ANTENNAE: Same as tail
RIB: Natural gray ostrich
BODY: Dark transparent amber Swannundaze. Wrap the body so that there is a slight space between each wrap of Swannundaze. The rib will be placed in this space
LEGS: Speckled hen fibers tied divided style after each wingcase
THORAX: Amber angora goat
WINGCASE: Speckled hen body feather (saddles okay) or ringneck body feather. Burn feathers to shape with wingcase burner and apply Flexament. Let dry before securing in place
HEAD: Same as thorax
COMMENTS: The tying sequence after the body is complete is wingcase, legs, thorax, legs, wingcase, wingcase, head, legs, pull wingcase over head

TDC (Richard B. Thompson)
HOOK:	Tiemco 5262, 12-16
THREAD:	Black
RIB:	Fine oval or flat silver tinsel
BODY:	Black wool or fur
THORAX:	White ostrich

TED'S STONE (Ted Trueblood)
HOOK:	Tiemco 5263, 8-10, weighted
THREAD:	Black
TAIL:	Brown strip goose "V"
BODY:	Tobacco brown chenille
WINGCASE:	Two pieces of brown chenille
LEGS:	Palmered black saddle hackle through thorax
THORAX:	True orange chenille

TEENY (Jim Teeny)
HOOK:	Tiemco 300, 6-10 or Tiemco 5263, 8-10, weighted
THREAD:	Black
BODY:	Ringneck pheasant tail fibers
LEGS:	Ringneck pheasant tail fibers tied beard style in front of body
THORAX:	Ringneck pheasant tail fibers slightly larger diameter than body
LEGS:	Ringneck pheasant tail fibers tied beard style
COMMENTS:	Designed by noted Northwest angler, Jim Teeny, to imitate a varietyof underwater life forms and is usually fished deep. Other colors are also popular, especially black, olive, and burgundv

TELLICO
HOOK:	Tiemco 5262, 12-16, weighted
THREAD:	Black
TAIL:	Guinea
BACK:	Ringneck pheasant fibers
RIB:	Peacock
BODY:	Yellow floss or fur
LEGS:	Furnace neck hackle tied full

TERRIBLE TROTH (Al Troth)
HOOK:	Tiemco 300, 2-6, weighted and flattened
THREAD:	Black
TAIL:	Black stripped goose tied "V" style
ANTENNAE:	Same as tail
LEGS:	Three sets extending from side of thorax area. Dyed dark brown neck hackle clipped close to stem. Tie legs in before body. Kink after fly is complete and coat joints with Pliobond
BODY:	Black or brown chenille doubled in thorax area over wound with blended black and brown angora goat. Clip top and bottom to give oval or flattened effect
COMMENTS:	Designed to imitate the larger stonefly species. Colors and size can be varied

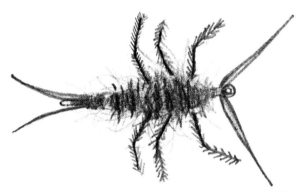

Terrible Troth

TIMBERLINE (Randall Kaufmann)
HOOK:	Tiemco 5262, 12-18, weighted
THREAD:	Color to match body
TAIL:	Ringneck pheasant tail fibers
RIB:	Copper wire
BODY:	Blend of fur and like color of angora goat. An example would be muskrat and gray angora goat. Best colors are olive, tan, brown, black, and gray
WINGCASE:	Ringneck pheasant tail fibers, tips form the legs
THORAX:	Same as body
LEGS:	Ringneck pheasant tail fibers tied divided style
COMMENTS:	Generally representative of mayfly nymphs

See Page 124

TIMBERLINE EMERGER (Randall Kaufmann)
HOOK:	Tiemco 5262 or 200, 12-16, weight to suit
THREAD:	To match body
TAIL:	Dark moose, sparse, or marabou, short and heavy
RIB:	Copper wire
BODY:	Blend of angora goat and like color of Hairtron. Best colors are olive, tan, brown, and gray
LEGS:	Brown neck hackle or color to match body
WINGS:	Grizzly hen hackle tips natural color or dyed to match body. Wings should be tied short, about 1/2 length of body

Swannundaze Stone

TRICORYTHODES

HOOK:	Mustad 94859, 20-26
THREAD:	Brown
TAIL:	Brown partridge or mottled hen hackle
BODY:	Brown fur, exact color to match naturals. Pick out dubbing at thorax
LEGS:	Bronze mallard, brown partridge, or mottled hen hackle tied divided or beard style

TRUEBLOOD OTTER (Ted Trueblood) See Page 58

HOOK:	Tiemco 5262, 10-16, weighted
THREAD:	Brown
TAIL:	Brown partridge
BODY:	Blend even parts of cream angora goat and otter or brown mink
LEGS:	Brown partridge tied beard style with fibers extending to bend of hook

TUPS INDISPENSABLE

HOOK:	Tiemco 200, 12-18
THREAD:	Primrose
TAIL:	Four or five whisks of blue dun hen hackle fibers
BODY:	Primrose (light yellow) floss
THORAX:	Light pink fur
LEGS:	Blue dun hen hackle tied full, 1-2 turns
COMMENTS:	This is the only Soft Hackle pattern calling for poultry hackle. Light partridge hackle dyed blue dun would certainly look nice. A "Tups" pattern is described by James E. Leiserneing and Vernon S. Hidy in their book, *The Art of Tying the Wet Fly and Fishing the Flymph.* Those interested in surface film imitations, nymphs, and flymphs should obtain a copy, though the book is out of print

VELMA MAY (Charles E. Brooks)

HOOK:	Tiemco 5263, 10, weighted
THREAD:	Olive
TAIL:	Grizzly hackle fibers dyed dark green
OVERRIB:	Gold wire
RIB:	One strand purple wool and gray ostrich herl
BODY:	Mottled brown wool
LEGS:	Soft dyed green grizzly neck or saddle hackle

WATERBOATMEN See Page 153

HOOK:	Tiemco 5262, 10-16, weighted, smashed flat
THREAD:	Olive
TAIL:	Clear (white) Antron fibers
BACK:	Triple back. Plastic strip over pearl Flashabou over ringneck pheasant tail fibers
RIB:	Fine oval silver tinsel
BODY:	Olive marabou fibers
LEGS:	Olive strip goose tied back along each side of the body
HEAD:	Peacock with plastic strip reversed back over head and tied off at back of head

WESTERN BLACK QUILL (Ernest Schwiebert)

HOOK:	Tiemco 5263, 12-14
THREAD:	Tan
TAIL:	Mallard dyed light woodduck
RIB:	Fine gold wire
GILLS:	Grayish-olive marabou
BODY:	Medium grayish hare's ear blended with guard hairs and sparsely dubbed over light olive thread
WINGCASE:	Grayish brown turkey or white tip turkey tail segment
LEGS:	Grayish-olive hackle fibers tied beard style

WESTERN BLUE QUILL (Ernest Schwiebert)

HOOK:	Tiemco 5262, 14-16, weight to suit
THREAD:	Tan
TAIL:	Mallard dyed dark woodduck
RIB:	Fine gold wire
GILLS:	Pale grayish marabou
BODY:	Grayish brown dubbing
WINGCASE:	Grayish brown turkey
THORAX:	Grayish brown dubbing
LEGS:	Grayish brown hackle tied half circle (underneath and along sides of body)
COMMENTS:	Represents the mayfly species *Paraleptophlebia californica* and *Paraleptophlebia gregalis,* a prolific Northwest species. Imitations should be slender and slightly tapered

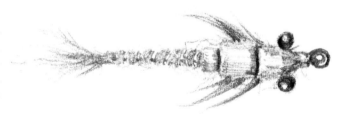

Whitlock Damsel

WHITLOCK DAMSEL (Dave Whitlock)

HOOK:	Tiemco 300, 8-10, slightly weighted
THREAD:	Olive
EYES:	Plastic beads painted flat olive or brown. Dave uses Hyplar paint
TAIL:	Grizzly marabou dyed olive
BACK, WINGCASE, HEAD:	Olive raffia
RIB:	Gold wire
BODY:	Olive fur
THORAX:	Olive fur
LEGS:	Ringneck pheasant back feather dyed olive, tied half circle

WIGGLE DAMSEL (Dave Whitlock and others)

HOOKS:	Two hooks required, a ring eye Tiemco 101 and Tiemco 5262, 10-16, weight to suit
THREAD:	Olive
HINGE:	.010 to .012" piano wire
TAIL, GILLS:	Grizzly or turkey marabou dyed olive or golden brown
RIB:	Size 18 (fine) oval gold tinsel
EYES:	Plastic beads painted flat olive or brown. Dave uses Hyplar paint
RIB:	Size 18 (fine) oval gold
BODY:	Light olive or golden brown fur
WINGCASE:	Swiss straw, olive or brown
THORAX:	Light olive or golden brown fur
LEGS:	Ringneck pheasant or partridge dyed light olive or golden olive brown, tied half circle. Pantone pens will also color the legs

WOOLLY BUGGER See Page 136

HOOK:	Tiemco 300, 2-10, weighted
THREAD:	To match body color
TAIL:	Black marabou or color to match body (black, olive, and brown are most common colors)
LEGS:	Saddle hackle palmered, black or color to match body. Take 1-2 extra turns at front of body
BODY:	Black, olive, or brown chenille, fur mixes are also good

WOOLLY WORM   **Woolly Worm**

HOOK:	Tiemco 300, 2-12, weight to suit
THREAD:	To match body
TAIL:	Red hackle fibers or wool
LEGS:	Hackle tied palmered style to match or contrast with body. Black hackle – black body, grizzly hackle – black body, etc. Hackle can also be back wrapped as demonstrated on the Woolly Bugger
RIB:	Flat, narrow gold or silver tinsel, wire, or no rib at all
BODY:	Chenille in various colors, the most popular of which are black, brown, olive, yellow, or peacock herl

YELLOW DRAKE (E.H. "Polly" Rosborough)

HOOK:	Tiemco 5263, 10-12
THREAD:	Pale yellow
TAIL:	Mallard dyed pale woodduck
BACK:	Optional, same as tail
RIB:	Same as thread
BODY:	Pale cream yarn, slender, well tapered, and flattened
WING:	Same as tail tied low over body and clipped 1/3 length of body
LEGS:	Same as tail tied divide style extending 3/4 body length
COMMENTS:	Thread head is flattened and slightly oversize

YELLOW STONE (Charles E. Brooks)

HOOK:	Tiemco 300, 6-12, weighted
THREAD:	Tan
TAIL:	Turkey quill fibers or brown stripped goose tied "V" fashion
RIB:	Gold yarn and gold wire
BODY:	Brownish yellow yarn or fur
GILLS:	Light gray or white ostrich herl
THORAX:	Light gray ostrich herl ribbed through body at thorax area to represent gills
LEGS:	One natural grizzly and one dyed dark brown grizzly saddle hackle. See Brooks' Stone pattern for tying instructions
COMMENTS:	Designed to imitate the stonefly genera, *Acroneuria* and *Perla*

YUK BUG (Al Troth)

HOOK:	Tiemco 300, 2-8, weighted
THREAD:	Black
TAIL:	Gray squirrel
BODY:	Black chenille
LEGS:	Palmered grizzly saddle hackle, take one or two extra turns in front. Palmered hackle begins 1/4" forward of tail
UNDERBODY:	Fluorescent orange chenille. Tied in two separate locations along underbody so that underbody is black, orange, black, orange, black, all colors evenly spaced. Secure with thread in "X" pattern, wrapping front to back to front
LEGS:	White rubber strips threaded with a needle through body, 8 legs total, 4 on each side, or tie rubber legs in *first* and work chenille through them

ZUG BUG (Cliff Zug) See Page 94

HOOK:	Tiemco 5262, 10-14, weighted
THREAD:	Black
TAIL:	Peacock sword, 3-6 fibers
RIB:	Silver tinsel
BODY:	Peacock herl (form underbody if desired)
LEGS:	Brown or furnace hackle tied beard style or half circle
WING:	Mallard dyed woodduck, extending 1/3 length of body, trimmed to shape (represents wingcase)

No Kill

No Kill And You

An angler was walking back to his car after spending a very productive day fishing a famous lake. The lake is not very large as lakes go and while it is reasonably isolated, a great many anglers take advantage of the fine fishing it offers. Its waters are not stocked and its wild fish are protected with a no-kill, barbless hook regulation.

As the angler walked through the check gate he asked why he could not keep just *one* fish to eat. The gate attendant related some facts most anglers fail to consider. The lake supports about 4,000 fish, which seems to be a healthy number, as the fish are in excellent condition and food sources do not seem to be declining. This season over 2,000 angler days will be tallied. If each angler kept just one fish, what would the fishing be like next year or the year after?

Lack of fishing pressure in conjunction with suitable habitat is what allows any water to provide outstanding angling. In waters where a "kill" is allowed, wild fish cannot populate to their maximum density and size. You cannot eat them today and expect to catch them tomorrow — certainly not the larger, more exciting and challenging fish.

There are many waters throughout the country which could provide unbelievable angling if they had less *harvest management* and more *protection*. Nearly every water in the country is open to the catch and kill, factory fish philosophy. Perhaps a few more waters which are able to sustain populations of fish without the hatchery truck should be protected. Many such waters come to mind where, instead of catching hatchery fish, we could be releasing three- to six-pound trout on a consistent basis. Why plant expensive and inferior hatchery trout when nature will provide healthy, naturally propagated fish at no cost?

Wild trout provide such immeasurable pleasure, thrills and enjoyment that it is impossible to equate them with dollars or to be so selfish as to justify eating one. It simply does not make sense to kill wild trout, or *any* big fish.

There are no disadvantages to protecting self-sustaining fisheries. Catch and release fisheries ultimately provide what all anglers desire — large numbers of healthy trout of all age groups. Such waters provide the utmost enjoyment for the maximum number of anglers.

With the expertise of today's huge population of fishermen and diminishing habitat, the future is bleak for wild fish and quality angling unless there is a turnaround in state management policy toward those waters capable of natural reproduction. If you enjoy fishing over maximum numbers of big trout without spending thousands of dollars and traveling thousands of miles, there is only one solution: *no kill and you.*

State fish and game departments need to hear your views on a consistent basis. Write, call and drop into their offices from time to time and support organizations which actively support such views. While some of these organizations are not directly related to fisheries, they are greatly concerned with protecting the environment, or habitat — and without habitat there are no fish.

Trout Unlimited, Box 1944, Washington, D.C. 20013. 202-281-1100.

Federation of Fly Fishermen, Box 1088, West Yellowstone, MT 59758. 406-646-9541.

Cal-Trout, Box 2046, San Francisco, CA 94126. 415-392-8887.

Oregon Trout, Box 19540, Portland, OR 97219. 503-246-5890.

Sierra Club, 730 Polk St., San Francisco, CA 94109. 415-776-2211.

National Wildlife Federation, 8925 Leesburg Pike, Vienna, VA 22180. 703-790-4000.

Nature Conservancy, 1800 North Kent St., Arlington, VA 22209. 703-841-5300.

Land fish quickly and gently, keep them in the water, and do not release them until they have *completely* recovered. Pictured is the best photo pose, but have camera set *before* landing and lifting fish *slightly* out of the water.

Landing and Releasing Fish

Try to land fish in a reasonable amount of time. The longer some fish are played the more lactic acid builds up in the bloodstream and the more difficult it becomes to revive such fish. Most fatal damage occurs to fish through improper handling, not during the actual hooking and playing of fish.

It is best not to handle or remove fish from the water. When a fish is removed from the water it begins to suffocate immediately and the risk is great that the fish will flop about on the bank, slip from your grasp or that you may squeeze it to death. If you must handle fish be certain your hands are wet for wet hands will not destroy the protective mucous film on fish (especially trout).

To remove the hook, gently grip the fish by the tail or jaw with one hand, removing the hook with the other. If you are wading, both hands can be freed by slipping the rod into your waders. If a fish is hooked really deeply the hook can often be removed with the aid of a long-nose pliers or forceps. If the hook is barbless (it should be), push back and turn it sideways. If the hook cannot be removed, cut the leader leaving the fly in the fish. Nature supplies a built-in mechanism which will dissolve the hook in a matter of days. Often a friend can lend a hand in unhooking and reviving tired fish.

A barbless hook will help ensure safe handling and facilitate a quick release. You seldom have to touch the fish because barbless hooks can usually be backed out very quickly using only one hand.

I have mixed emotions about using a net. When fish become entangled in the mesh and struggle, there is a negative impact upon them. A net can alleviate fish flopping and thrashing over rocks in shallow water and can greatly aid you in landing a fish when you are waist deep in water or fishing from a float tube. Don't allow fish to become entangled in the mesh.

Do not release a tired fish until it has completely recovered. Hold a played fish firmly by the tail with one hand and gently support the fish from underneath just behind the head with your other hand. Face the fish upstream (when current is available) in an upright position in fairly calm water where there is enough oxygen to allow the fish to breathe easily. Move the fish back and forth in this position. The gills will begin pumping life-giving oxygen into its system, thus the fish is allowed to rest and regain strength lost during the battle. In lakes it will be mandatory to move fish back and forth to ensure the flow of oxygen-rich water through their gills.

The author carefully releasing an Alaskan rainbow.

Fish being revived will often attempt to escape before they are completely recovered. Do not let the fish swim away the *first* time it attempts to. When fish are released prematurely they will often swim out of sight, lose their equilibrium, turn onto their side and die. It doesn't hurt to revive fish a bit longer than you feel is necessary. This will ensure a complete recovery without complications. This process usually takes a minute or two but fish that are extremely tired can require several minutes. I have revived bleeding and exceptionally tired fish for 30 minutes or longer. Fish tire easily preceding, during and after spawning periods and should be left alone.

When you release a fish do so in calm water allowing the fish to swim away at its leisure. Never toss fish back into the water! After releasing a fish, move slowly, for sudden movement may spook the fish prematurely.

If you wish to take a photo, set up everything before you remove the fish from the water. Cradle the fish and lift it just inches above the water so that if it should happen to fall it will not crash onto the hard shoreline. Do not lay fish on their sides. Do not put undue strain on fish by lifting them by the tail or in an unnatural position. Never put your fingers in their gills for this is like puncturing a lung. Never squeeze fish; vital organs are easily damaged. Fish will seldom struggle when handled gently or turned upside down.

A quick, harmless way to measure fish is to tape off measurements on your rod or buy a tape which adheres to your rod. Simply slide the rod alongside the fish in the water and you get an accurate measurement. Spring scales are deadly for fish and should only be used for hoisting a net with the fish inside. It is easy to estimate the weight by the length and condition of the fish. The important consideration is to release fish quickly and unharmed. A fish which is bleeding slightly will probably survive. Even a fish that is bleeding profusely can usually be revived if *you* are patient enough.

Index

Bold face numbers indicate captions